Soviet Perceptions of
U.S. Foreign Policy

Soviet Perceptions of U.S. Foreign Policy

A Study of Ideology, Power, and Consensus

John Lenczowski

Cornell University Press ITHACA AND LONDON

First published 1982 by Cornell University Press.
Published in the United Kingdom by Cornell University Press Ltd.,
Ely House, 37 Dover Street, London W1X 4HQ.

International Standard Book Number 0-8014-1451-2
Library of Congress Catalog Card Number 81-70713
Printed in the United States of America
*Librarians: Library of Congress cataloging information
appears on the last page of the book.*

*The paper in this book is acid-free, and meets the
guidelines for permanence and durability of the
Committee on Production Guidelines for Book Longevity
of the Council on Library Resources.*

To my family

Contents

Preface   9
Introduction   15

1. The Struggle between the Two Social Systems   27
   The Basis of Marxist-Leninist Ideology   27
   Struggle between Two Social Systems   30
   The Forms and Theaters of Struggle   37
   The Measurement of the Struggle   51
   The Conclusion of the Struggle:
     The Question of Soviet Optimism   59

2. Domestic Determinants of U.S. Foreign Policy   61
   The Ruling Circles and Other Active Political Forces   62
   Internal Contradictions and the Crisis of Capitalism   75
   Coping with the Crisis of Capitalism   80

3. General Ends and Means of U.S. Foreign Policy   99
   The Ends of U.S. Foreign Policy and Their Determinants   99
   The Means of U.S. Foreign Policy   102
     Ideological Means   102
     Economic Means   138
     Scientific and Technical Means   143
     Military Means   151
     Diplomatic Means   177

4. U.S. Relations with Its Allies   194
   The Ends of American Alliance Policy   194
   The Means of American Alliance Policy   195
     Diplomatic Means   195

Contents

	Ideological Means	200
	Economic Means	200
	Scientific and Technical Means	204
	Military Means	206
	Conclusion	210
5.	U.S. Relations with the Third World	212
	The Ends of American Policy toward the Third World	212
	The Means of American Policy toward the Third World	212
	Ideological Means	212
	Economic Means	214
	Scientific and Technical Means	228
	Military Means	229
	Diplomatic Means	230
	Conclusion	231
6.	U.S. Relations with the Socialist Countries: Some Remaining Issues	232
7.	Traditionalists and Realists	239
	The Military and Detente	245
	The Dominance of the "Right" and Defense Budgets	248
	The "Left" and the Necessity of an Imperialist Enemy	251
	The "Left" as Optimists?	252
	Realists and Traditionalists: A Harmony of Interests	254
	Conclusion	261
	Notes	276
	Index	307

Preface

My primary motivations for writing this book stemmed from what I perceived to be a manifest disagreement among American scholars, journalists, and statesmen about the nature of Soviet politics and foreign policy in general, and the Soviet perception of U.S. foreign policy in particular. In recent years, even the most fundamental questions have been subject to acrimonious debate. Are the Soviets guided by the Marxist-Leninist ideology, or do they behave like the rulers of any other great power? Is the Soviet Union a totalitarian system or is it characterized by political competition among diverse interest groups? Are there "hawks" and "doves" within the Kremlin leadership?

Such questions are not new, and many were covered thoroughly in the classic works published during the 1950s and 1960s, the heyday of Western Sovietology. Despite their many enduring merits, these works are now dated in important particulars and it is the responsibility of contemporary scholarship and my intention to reexamine these fundamental questions in the light of more recent developments.

The challenge that such questions pose for the scholar is complicated by the fact that any conclusions about the nature of Soviet politics have immediate implications for the ongoing U.S. debate over relations with Moscow. It is difficult, therefore, to separate the consideration of these problems from the politics of that debate. Indeed, the scholarly debate all too often echoes the harsh dialogue that has emerged as a result of the breakdown in the foreign policy consensus that prevailed in the United States before the Vietnam War.

Nor can we ignore the complications arising from the efforts of nonscholarly parties to influence the debate for strictly political ends. According to a 1978 study conducted by the Central Intelligence Agency, the Soviets have used disinformation and propaganda to sway political and scholarly debates in both disguised and undisguised ways. For example, visiting Soviet scholars and diplomats have promoted the idea that there are "hawks" and "doves" in the Kremlin, and that Leonid Brezhnev is one of the "doves." The implication, of course, is that the United States should make a deal with Mr. Brezhnev rather than contend with the much less favorable negotiating terms that would result from the accession of the "hawks" should Brezhnev fall from power. Neither the interests of scholarship nor those of sound policy are well served when the empirical basis of honest debate is cluttered with influences of this sort.

It is my hope that two aspects of the present book will prove particularly useful in the formulation of contemporary U.S. foreign policy: (1) the examination of the Soviet view of the shifting world balance of power, and (2) the comprehensive consideration of official Soviet views on a broad range of domestic and foreign issues confronting U.S. policy makers. Since countless Soviet strategic decisions are made on the basis of balance-of-power assessments, it may be in the highest interest of America's national security to have a fuller understanding of the Soviet perception that this balance has recently shifted in their favor. A documented survey of Soviet writings on an array of domestic and international political questions may help us to hold Soviet analysts and officials more accountable for their published views.

This book is based entirely on primary documentation from the Soviet press. Most quotations are translated from the Russian-language originals, although I found that a number of books translated into English were useful. Occasionally, when using a translated source, I referred to the Russian original to check for any possible differences in the meanings of sensitive passages. I have used the Library of Congress system of transliteration throughout.

This undertaking owes much to a variety of intellectual influences. First among these is Herbert S. Dinerstein of the Johns Hopkins University School of Advanced International Studies, to whom I owe a great debt for his encouragement and his wise counsel; he has served and will continue to serve as an inspiration and a model for scholarship. I owe an intellectual debt of gratitude to Charles Burton Marshall, Thomas B. Larson, Robert E. Osgood, and Samuel L. Sharp. I must also thank Bruce Parrott for his helpful comments on the manuscript. I am especially grateful to Robert J. Pranger of the American Enterprise Institute, who originally encouraged me to pursue this line of research. Robert V. Gross and his staff at the Library of Congress provided me with tireless and invaluable assistance. Special thanks must go to Susan D. Koch for her encouragement, thoughtful editorial assistance on the text, and typing. I am also grateful to Iris Volkman of the American Enterprise Institute, who typed the manuscript so expertly and graciously under considerable pressure. And finally, I must thank Mine Sabuncuoglu for her expert assistance in preparing the index at the eleventh hour.

JOHN LENCZOWSKI

Washington, D.C.

Soviet Perceptions of
U.S. Foreign Policy

Introduction

Since the early 1970s, there have been two developments in international politics which deserve special scrutiny. One of these is the achievement of strategic parity between the Soviet Union and the United States; the other is the tremendous growth and intensification of Soviet analysis of American foreign policy and of world politics in general. The proliferation of such Soviet analysis in this international context raises a question crucial to the foreign policies of the superpowers and the prospects of world peace: How do the Soviets assess the world balance of power?

To answer this question, it is necessary to study the Soviet perceptions of American foreign policy revealed in the flood of recent Soviet analyses. By doing so, one may learn: (1) what the Soviets perceive as America's values and interests; (2) their assessment of the strength with which Americans hold these values; (3) their view of the areas in which American interests conflict with their own; (4) the terms in which they criticize and sometimes even commend American policy; (5) the Soviet values that determine these judgments; and (6) what situations the Soviets regard as threatening and why. Familiarity with these issues not only helps us to understand how the Soviets view the relative strengths and weaknesses of the United States and their own country, but also deepens our insight into the interests, priorities, and determinants of Soviet foreign policy. Moreover, the analysis of Soviet perceptions of American foreign policy raises other vital questions about the very nature of the Soviet system, its ruling circles, and their political functions.

These subjects have stimulated an intense debate among Western students of the USSR, a debate that has in many respects come to resemble an academic and political tug-of-war that holds little prospect of resolution. Though the specific topics debated are numerous and variegated and the crux of the dispute is thus often difficult to identify, the basic issue is the nature of the ideas and intentions of the ruling group in the USSR and of those who either influence or oppose its decisions. The primary indexes of these ideas and intentions are the statements and analyses that appear in the Soviet press. It is the problem of interpreting these statements and analyses which has spawned the controversy at hand.

Since the mid-1950s, Soviet analysts have become increasingly sophisticated in their study of international relations. As William Zimmerman pointed out in his pioneering work in 1969, it was during the Khrushchev years that Soviet specialists on international affairs ceased to function exclusively as ideologues and began to adopt both analytic and policy-prescriptive roles. The emergence of International Relations as a more legitimate academic discipline was accompanied by a variety of doctrinal innovations and fluctuations as Soviet analysts wrestled with such problems as the likelihood of general war in the atomic age.[1] The transfer of power to Brezhnev and his associates initiated another stage in the Soviet analysis of international relations: as some of the doctrinal and policy innovations of the Khrushchev era were abandoned, assessments of the potential for world revolutionary success began to conform more closely to reality—a contrast to many of the statements of the Khrushchev years, which appeared to represent wishful thinking rather than the real world situation.

At the root of these changing analyses was a shift in the Soviet estimation of the world balance of power. The Khrushchev period had witnessed an evolution in the terminology used to describe this balance. As Zimmerman has observed, before 1954 Soviet commentary described the balance of power with the neutral term "distribution of power," or "correlation of forces" (*sootnoshenie sil*). In 1959, the term "preponderance of power," or "favorable balance of power" (*pereves sil*), began to gain prominence, reflecting the increasing optimism of Soviet assessments of the international situation. By 1962, after the setback of the Cuban Missile Crisis, the expression "equilibrium" (*ravnovesie sil*) emerged—a term that clearly represented the Soviet leadership's diminished optimism concerning both the current balance and the prospects for world revolutionary success. Finally, by the time the Brezhnev regime had established itself, the original expression "correlation of forces" was reinstated. As Zimmerman explained, "It is evident that even *ravnovesie,* in the eyes of many among the Soviet ruling group, was an excessively bold formulation."[2]

So long as these changing assessments of the balance of power and the prospects of world revolution were accompanied by corresponding changes in terminology, the task of identifying and interpreting them was easier than it has been in more recent years. Since the mid-1960s the Brezhnev regime has consistently used the expression "correlation of forces," despite such real changes in the balance of power as the attainment of strategic parity between the United States and the USSR. This situation makes it much more difficult to ascertain just how the Soviets view the balance of power and the prospects for worldwide political changes that will serve their interests. In trying to resolve this difficulty, we can continue to take the Soviets at their word. We can, for example, believe Andrei Gromyko when he says that "the predominance of the forces of peace and progress—a predominance that has now grown considerably—gives them the opportunity to determine the channel followed by international politics."[3] We can also believe Georgi Arbatov when he speaks of "the change in the correlation of forces in favor of socialism,"[4] and we can accept Leonid Brezhnev's view that "the international position of the Soviet Union is stronger than ever."[5]

Indeed, in a 1977 book Stephen Gibert and others cited just such statements as evidence of the new Soviet assessment of the United States and the world balance of power.[6] On the basis of this evidence, they concluded that "the present Soviet perception is that America's will to resist what the Soviets see as an ongoing shift in power and influence in their favor is eroding."[7] Gibert and his associates came to this conclusion, moreover, in full cognizance of their statement that many Soviet statements are "intended to serve propagandistic or other purposes and . . . appear not to represent true perceptions."[8]

In his critique of their study, Morton Schwartz accuses Gibert and his associates of having been deceived by precisely such propaganda. For example, when Gibert cites Soviet descriptions of the "crumbling of the capitalist system" as evidence of a Soviet perception of increasing American weakness, Schwartz observes that "Soviet sources have been saying much the same thing since 1917."[9] According to Schwartz, Gibert and his associates would have been better served had they directed their attention to Soviet assessments contrary to those of the Kremlin's propaganda mills.

Indeed, in his study of Soviet perceptions of the United States, Schwartz pays close attention to just such statements. In addition to pointing out the propagandistic content of some Soviet assessments of America, he ascribes a dual significance to the other, conflicting statements, maintaining: (1) that they are a clear indication of the increased sophistication of creative Soviet analysts, who have managed to extricate themselves from the rigid ideological fetters that used to confine them to dogmatic assessments of the international situation; and (2) that these sophisticated statements reflect the existence of a "moderate" faction within the Soviet leadership which is opposed to a "neo-Stalinist," "orthodox" faction—a faction whose more "dogmatic" analyses are primitive in comparison.[10] Schwartz argues that whereas most Western analysts agree that Soviet analyses have become more sophisticated, there is little agreement as to the implications of this change. It is on this issue, then, that the debate over how the Soviets view the balance of power acquires a new, more complex dimension. Whereas Gibert and his associates are inclined to see this contemporary, more sophisticated analysis as leading to a perception that the United States is weak and vulnerable—a conclusion with ominous implications for the world balance of power and American security— Schwartz believes that the new sophistication both reveals and reinforces the elements of "moderation" in the Soviet Union. He concludes that in recent years Soviet foreign policy has been formulated largely by this "moderate" faction, whose view of the world balance of power differs sharply from the view that Gibert describes. These moderates, according to Schwartz, see the United States as a strong, resilient power with a flexible political system— a power that will not easily fade, a power to be reckoned with on the international stage.[11] Clearly, then, if Schwartz is correct, these Soviet perceptions have implications much less threatening to American security and the power balance between the superpowers.[12]

The Gibert-Schwartz debate thus makes some important controversies explicit while implying others—all of which can be summarized as follows:

1. The controversy over how the Soviets view the correlation of forces in the world. Is the United States getting stronger or weaker in relation to the Soviet Union? Is the capitalist West getting stronger or weaker in relation to the communist East?

2. The controversy over whether the Soviet political system is strictly totalitarian or whether it is characterized by conflicting individuals or factions whose differing views can translate into significantly different policies.

3. The controversy over whether apparent differences of opinion may be definitively associated with distinct factions or groups; and to the extent that this is the case, whether such differing views are a function of group interests or of bureaucratic responsibilities.

4. The controversy over the impact of ideology on Soviet policy. Is Soviet policy ideologically or pragmatically inspired? To what extent are ideology and pragmatism mutually exclusive? Is it possible to identify some groups that are more ideological and others that are more pragmatic? And if so, can we determine their comparative impact on policy?

This book addresses each of these controversies. Throughout my investigation, however, the reader will note that I have already, and perhaps prematurely, arrived at one working assumption: that certain differences of opinion can be explained by the existence of different Soviet "schools of thought." Some introductory explanation, therefore, is in order.

The standard practice in almost all of the relevant Western literature has been immediately to identify the differences in Soviet opinion with different factions or "interest groups": hence, the tendency to distinguish between the Soviet "Right and Left," "hawks and doves," "radicals and moderates," or "opponents and advocates of detente." Signs of disagreement among Soviet commentators are also often taken as *prima facie* evidence in support of the "interest group" interpretation of Soviet politics. This book detects and documents many such differences in Soviet opinion—perhaps as many as have been documented in any other study—and, for purposes of distinction and clarity, it groups these differences into two broader classifications: the "traditionalist" and the "realist." This classification does not, however, mark the author's a priori adherence to an "interest group" approach (nor does the present disclaimer signal a commitment to the strict totalitarian model). Rather, these classifications serve merely to assist in categorizing observable differences in the views of Soviet analysts and in identifying certain patterns of thought. "Traditionalist" and "realist" are ascriptions, therefore, that signify schools of thought which are not so much "schools" in the literal sense as "tendencies of thought." The problem of whether such "tendencies" can in fact be connected to identifiable groups, political interests, or bureaucratic functions will be addressed once the specific data on Soviet perceptions and their patterns have been examined thoroughly.

The analysis of these data raises significant methodological problems: How can we tell which Soviet statements represent genuine perceptions? How can we tell whether or not a given statement expresses the view of some faction in the Kremlin? How can we identify such factions if they exist, and then distinguish their true motives and intentions? And further, what sources must we use to resolve these issues? To answer these questions properly, it is necessary to consider the nature of both the Soviet system and communist ideology.

In the Soviet system political power is the monopoly of the Communist party and its leadership. For all practical purposes, it is their perceptions alone which "count"—for it is on the basis of their perceptions that the domestic and foreign policies of the Soviet Union are formulated. Some might argue that in the final analysis everything depends on the perceptions of the entire Soviet people, but this view ignores the fact that the Soviet state has a system of coercion which enforces political uniformity and makes individual dissent, much less concerted revolutionary activity, virtually impossible. The only perceptions that can find political expression are thus those of the Party leadership.

Since the leadership exercises monopoly control over all legal news and information media, we are limited to the following indexes of Soviet perceptions: the various daily and weekly newspapers and newsmagazines; the journals of the Communist party, the Soviet military, and the institutes of the Soviet Academy of Sciences; the books of Soviet academicians and journalists; the speeches and articles of Party leaders; and domestic and international broadcasts. Because the Soviet media are closely censored, the views that appear therein reflect the general framework of discussion which the Soviet leadership will tolerate on any given issue. Thus, the opinions appearing in the media articulate the frame of reference through which the Soviet leaders view the world. The media are not only an instrument by which the Kremlin leadership feeds its people what it wants them to hear, but also, to some extent, a reflection of the real issues that it is deliberating. Thus, what appears in the media is a universe all its own: certain kinds of facts and arguments just do not appear—for they do not conform with certain values that are deemed by the leadership to be proper.

There has been considerable debate as to why the Soviet media are subject to such strict control. Some allege that it is maintained for purposes of political self-interest and self-preservation, while others argue that it is an expression of communist idealism. We shall examine the merits of these alternative suggestions later; for now, it is sufficient to note that this control has one undeniable effect: it restricts all concerned to a single method of perception.

In a free society one generally does not think of perception as being limited to a certain method.* In the United States we are accustomed to having the freedom to perceive as we please—through our senses, through "common sense," through scientific laws, through dreams, through imagination, and through faith. We do not *necessarily* perceive with any practical objective in mind, nor are we restricted to any discipline, systematic procedure, technique, or plan for our perceptions. Referring to the Soviet Union, however, it may not be inappropriate to say that such freedom to perceive, *on a collective basis,* has been denied; and that indeed there exists only one legitimate "method" of perception. This method consists of perceiving and thinking about the world through the scope of Marxist-Leninist ideology in its subtly different varieties. The restriction to this method of perception is all-

*A "method," according to the Merriam-Webster dictionary is: "a procedure or process for attaining an object: as a (1): a discipline that deals with the principles and techniques of scientific inquiry (2) a systematic procedure, technique or mode of inquiry employed by or proper to a particular discipline or art (3) a systematic plan followed in presenting material for instructions b (1): a way, technique or process of or for doing something" (*Webster's Seventh New Collegiate Dictionary* [Springfield, Mass.: Merriam, 1963]).

pervasive and constitutes the essence of Soviet totalitarianism. The society is force-fed a "discipline," a "systematic procedure," a "technique," and a "plan"—all parading under the guise of a "scientific" method that possesses a clear "objective." It is the *only* eyeglass through which the Soviet community is allowed to see the world, and its lens is a prism. As a result, the Soviet people, including intelligentsia and leadership, are bound to a common world view that is modified only by their national characters, their geopolitical perspectives on the world, and the meek impression of private perception. This is not to say that there are no disagreements in the Soviet Union—for most assuredly, as we shall see, there are—but it is crucial to note that the political elite insists that these disagreements be contained within certain bounds: one cannot argue in terms other than those which can be plausibly described as Marxist-Leninist.

Critical to the enforcement of this method is the dissemination of propaganda by the Soviet information media—a phenomenon that poses difficulties for anyone attempting to ascertain the true perceptions of the Soviet leadership. Some propaganda consists not only of what the leadership would like the Soviet people to hear, but also of what it would like to broadcast to the outside world. Furthermore, it often constitutes an expression of the desires of the leadership—desires for certain kinds of domestic or foreign behavior. Soviet propaganda may thus contain actual truths, statements that the leadership believes to be true, and outright lies. These varied contents constitute a continuum of information, from truth to falsehood, and only those who actually control the propaganda can make definitive delineations between what is believed to be true but may be false and what is really false. Indeed, even those in control may be unable to do much more than recognize outright distortions of very recent events. This situation is a consequence of the very pervasiveness of Soviet propaganda. It shapes the perceptions of the people from whom the Soviets recruit their political and cultural elite—people who cannot help but be affected by what they have spent their entire lives reading. Indeed, it is well-nigh impossible for an American historian to agree with his Soviet counterpart even on the chronology, much less the interpretation, of the origins of the cold war. The history of such controversial events has been sculpted by the Soviet propaganda apparatus—and so, needless to say, has the world view of anyone who has read that history.

Given that the Soviet press is riddled with propaganda and distortions, one must ask to what extent the Soviets mean what they say, to what extent they engage in "double-entry bookkeeping." In fact, with the exception of precisely those distortions of recent historical fact, certain cynical and propagandistic criticisms, and the occasional concealment or omission of political intent, the Soviets do mean what they say. The material that appears in their press is largely an index of real perceptions, real desires, or real policy priorities. Several factors support this assertion. First, there is historical evidence such as the Smolensk archive of Party documents captured during the Second World War, which shows the direct correspondence between internal Soviet political deliberations and the contemporaneous contents of the press.[13] Second, there is the implausibility of the existence in the press of a constant deception so divorced from reality that it hinders the coherent formulation of policy. Finally, one must remember that the communist world view is an entirely plausible one, even, one might say, a compelling one. After all, Marxism-Leninism has inspired several mass movements, and it has captured the imagination of many a Western intellectual who was free to choose from the open market of ideas. Communism has numerous appeals that give it intellectual and political strength, and it should not be surprising that such a mode of thought was adopted as the basis of a new political order. Marxism-Leninism's survival as the guiding (or constraining) ideology of this order should not evoke much surprise either. Indeed, in the context of totalitarian control over political discourse, one would expect some form of communist ideology to have survived, despite its inherent defects and the "adaptations" inflicted by some of its sponsors. This ideology supplies the Soviets with a comprehensive world view supple enough to account for almost any phenomenon that crosses their path. In the context of the Soviet system, which has itself been defined by this ideology, it is so basic to all perception that the Soviets must indeed mean what they say.

In light of this situation, how does one ultimately distinguish between what the Soviets actually believe, what constitutes propaganda, what constitutes lies, and what is being concealed or omitted? Such discriminations can be made only by analyzing a broad spectrum of the Soviets' publicly aired perceptions, defining the vocabulary with which these views are expressed, comparing these perceptions with reality as we perceive it, and finally, by examining the *patterns* of Soviet analysis and how they, in their totality, express broader Soviet concerns—ultimately forming complete images of the United States and the international situation. As the reader will see, part of this analysis involves generalizing about the "Soviet view" of a particular issue on the basis of an extract from a single article. Such a methodology, while unsuited to the analysis of a more pluralistic society's media, is perfectly appropriate for the study of official Soviet writings. Central control and the demand for effective propaganda subject the contents of the Soviet press to an extreme systematization, the result being the highly ritualized language and standardized formulas that are used to explain all issues. Thus, on the basis of a single document, it is possible to make very broad generalizations—if not about the "Soviet" view, then about the views of one or another of the Soviet schools of thought.

The "struggle between the two social systems" is the broader context within which these Soviet perceptions will be analyzed. For the Soviets this struggle is the fundamental contemporary international reality—a reality that cannot but affect U.S. foreign policy and condition all Soviet perceptions. An understanding of the Soviet view of this reality is thus essential to a true understanding of their perceptions of American foreign policy.

According to the Soviets, the United States is the main representative and bastion of capitalism, and as such it plays a primary role on the world stage. Conversely, they see their country with its own set of international responsibilities as the main representative and bastion of communism. In the Soviet view, however, this struggle between the two systems extends far beyond the scope of bilateral American-Soviet relations. It reaches to the farthest corners of the earth, affects the lives of virtually all of mankind, and reflects the primary philosophical question of the age: Which system, capitalism or communism, is "superior" and will therefore emerge victorious? Thus, the "struggle between the two social systems" epitomizes the Soviet world view and, as such, demands detailed consideration as a prelude to analysis of Soviet perceptions of American policy.

24

When analyzing American foreign policy, Soviet commentators consider many factors besides the actual implementation of policy decisions. These factors include: the world view of American policy makers; the ideas that are used as the basis for different policies and even ideas that are disseminated in the normal course of American academic life; the economic activities of both the public and private sectors; American activities within various international organizations; the development of science and technology; and the theory and practice of military affairs. As we shall see, Soviet analysts do not exclude the activities of private parties from their consideration of American foreign policy, for, in their view, unofficial activities may have as profound an effect as official ones.

The breadth of this subject demands that some restrictions, both thematic and chronological, be imposed. The specific objects of Soviet perceptions which I have chosen to analyze are the basic determinants, as well as the ends and means, of American foreign policy. Special attention is accorded the domestic determinants of American foreign policy, for, in the Soviet view, the American sociopolitical system provides the "springs and levers" of that policy. Its external determinants are treated in the general context of my analysis of the struggle between the two social systems, its evolution, and the changing degree to which it affects American policy. The ends and means of American policy will be discussed as they relate (1) to the world in general; (2) to U.S. relations with its allies; (3) to U.S. relations with the Third World; and (4) to U.S. relations with socialist countries. While Soviet analysts maintain that the ends of American policy are always a product of the imperatives of capitalism, they view its means as changeable, not always predictable, and most subject to external influence. The primary means of American policy to be discussed are the ideological, the economic, the scientific and technical, the military, and the diplomatic.

My approach to this analysis of Soviet perceptions is thematic and, as a result, I do not offer a systematic history of American foreign policy. Instead, historical examples, when relevant and illustrative, are applied to my analysis of the various themes. The book focuses, broadly speaking, on the Nixon-Ford era, a period that involved critical shifts in the nature of U.S.–Soviet relations and that is therefore a good laboratory for a study of this sort. During these years the Soviet Union achieved strategic parity with the United States while simultaneously demonstrating an intensified interest in the study of American foreign policy and world politics. It was during this time that the United States suffered defeat in Vietnam. This period was also the era of "detente," during which many U.S.–Soviet agreements were signed, and the immediate prelude to an intensification of global adventures by the Soviets and their proxies. Finally, the Nixon-Ford era has stimulated considerable scholarly controversy.

The Soviets' perceptions of U.S. foreign policy during this period can thus shed considerable light on how they have viewed the balance of power in the world and how this view relates to their more recent foreign policy actions. The juxtaposition of these Soviet perceptions and actions, in turn, can tell us a great deal about the character and intentions of the Kremlin leadership. Clearly, then, the conclusions to which a study of Soviet perceptions leads us are fraught with serious implications for the making of U.S. foreign policy.

In analyzing Soviet perceptions of this recent period in comparison with those of earlier times, this book discovers not only the changes that have taken place, but many important continuities as well. That such continuities of perception and ultimately of policy should exist in the wake of very major changes in the international balance of power suggests the possibility that these perceptions and policies may be more durable features of the Soviet political system than many have heretofore suspected. If one keeps these continuities in mind, one can see that most if not all of the generalizations made here about the Nixon-Ford period continue to apply today and probably will apply well into the future. In fact, one major reason the author chose not to update the documentation of this book is because of said continuities and of the extreme redundancies that more recent materials proved to contain.

Chapter 1

The Struggle between
the Two Social Systems

As was noted in the Introduction, the "struggle between the two social systems" represents for the Soviets the fundamental international reality of our era—a conclusion to which the Soviets are led by the Marxist-Leninist ideology, the only method by which they perceive the world. To understand how such an ideology can be a method of perception and why it should yield such a view of the world, we must first explore the essentials of this ideology.

The Basis of Marxist-Leninist Ideology

Dialectical materialism, the theoretical foundation of Marxist-Leninist ideology, is itself a method of perceiving the world.[1] The materialist component, which is the elemental premise of Marxism-Leninism, posits that all existence, all reality, is determined by the nature of the material "base," which is the foundation of all physical, biological, and social relations. Given this premise, the materialist holds that reality consists of matter, and is not in any way a product of the mind. Ideas and consciousness are thus only a reflection of a material world that exists independently of any perception of it.

Insofar as "perception" connotes "cognition," "comprehension," "understanding," and "mental image," it is an intrinsic part of knowledge. Those of us, on the one hand, who are free to perceive, do so and feel capable of doing so per se. Our perceptions lead to and/or constitute our knowledge. We may know the truth simply on the basis of our perceptions, however empirical or theoretical they may be. Marxist-Leninists, in contrast, base their

27

epistemology on Marx's famous point, elaborated in the "Theses on Feuerbach," that knowledge of the objective truth is a question not of theory but of practice.[2] A recent Soviet text explains that we do not attain complete knowledge of a phenomenon simply through "passive" or "theoretical" perception, but that we "can cognize the essential properties of a thing and the laws governing it only by dynamically interacting with the phenomenon under investigation."[3] Only through this emphasis on action as the prerequisite to the completion of a cognitive process can Marxist-Leninists explain *materialistically* why perceptions result in conscious activity, and only in this way can they distinguish revolutionary activity as a *conscious,* as opposed to a mechanical act. Ultimately, Marxist-Leninists maintain that "genuine scientific knowledge becomes available only in the course of remaking the world,"[4] that is, in the process of consciously imposing revolutionary action upon the perceived world. Marx thus criticized philosophy as simply an exercise in contemplation and not the "practical-critical" activity that it ought to be: "the philosophers have only *interpreted* the world in various ways; the point, however, is to *change* it."[5] As R. N. Carew Hunt observes, Marxists hold that

theory and action are one. A theory which does not lead to action is barren, and action without theory is purposeless. . . . It is practice alone which determines the truth of theory. . . . But on the other hand, theory equally determines practice, since, if the theory is wrong, its error will inevitably reveal itself in the sphere of action. This explains the jealous regard paid [in the Soviet Union] to ideological purity and the immense importance attached to theoretical indoctrination.[6]

Perception, therefore, in the Marxist ideology, has an objective. As a result, it can be properly said that Marxism-Leninism is a method of perception.

This method of perception is applied to physical and social phenomena through the theory of change known as the dialectic. The first law of the dialectic, the notion of the "transition of quantity into quality," holds that as a given phenomenon undergoes gradual "quantitative" changes, it keeps its same general appearance. As these changes accumulate, however, there arrives a point when the phenomenon must make a "qualitative" leap into another mode of existence. Whereas quantitative changes are indicated by such terms as "larger-smaller," "faster-slower," and "worse-better," qualitative changes are indicated when one can say, "something did not exist, but now does," or "something existed, but now does not."[7]

The second law of the dialectic is that of the "unity and conflict of opposites." According to this law, all material phenomena and all motion contain contradictory elements that are nevertheless interdependent. Common examples of this idea are the positive and negative poles of a magnet or an electrical dipole. In present-day society the basic contradiction, according to Marxists, is between labor and capital, although these two elements simultaneously depend on one another for survival.

The final law of the dialectic is the "negation of the negation," a law that describes the dynamics of change. Here, a given phenomenon, the "thesis," is negated by an "antithesis." This negation is in turn negated by the "synthesis," a phenomenon that retains some of the valid characteristics of both the thesis and its antithesis. The synthesis is a new thesis, ready to be dialectically negated anew. There is some ambiguity in this law of the dialectic. To begin with, it is often difficult to determine whether a given phenomenon is the first or second negation. At the same time, it is not clear to what degree the contradictory elements of the thesis constitute the source of a negation. Marxists reject the idea that a negation is an opposite to a given thesis, and at the same time reject the notion that external forces set change in motion. In sum, the Marxists say: "All movement takes its source from internal contradictions, so that the emergence of new contradictions gives rise to a new form of movement, while with their disappearance it gives place to another form of movement for which other contradictions are responsible."[8]

Thus the dialectic remains a flexible method, allowing Marxists to explain any phenomenon in terms that conform to and thereby confirm the stated objective of Marxist-Leninist theory. Since materialism holds that ideas are a direct reflection of material reality, and since only the objective factors of a given reality can be considered, it follows that the analysis of any issue in this "scientific," dialectical materialist fashion (e.g., in the Soviet press) is objective and therefore correct: it is a direct reflection of material reality properly perceived. Thus, Soviet ideology comes complete with its own justification, guaranteeing the correctness of its analyses and equipping it with great flexibility for rationalization.

The application of the dialectic to society and history—"historical materialism"—reveals that the world is and always has been divided into contradictory groups. This division is based on Marx's idea that the production of the essentials of life and the exchange of these products govern all social relations. As a result, society is divided between those who possess the means of production and those who do not—between the oppressors and the oppressed. With this explanation in mind, Marx described five historical types of society: primitive communal (means of production is socially owned), slave (means of production is owned by the slaveholder), feudal (means of production is owned by the feudal lord), capitalist (means of production is owned by the bourgeoisie), and socialist (first the workers and then the people as a whole own the means of production). History has thus been the history of class struggle whereby the oppressed classes rise as the antithesis to the existing social order and its ruling classes. In each historical stage, the increasingly bitter struggle culminates in a synthesis—the formation of a new social order. In the capitalist era, society is fundamentally divided between the oppressor bourgeoisie and the oppressed proletariat. The proletariat will rise, overthrow the ruling class, and exercise its own class dictatorship. As the world becomes subject to a universal dictatorship of the proletariat, the functions of the state—internal coercion and external defense—will gradually cease to be necessary. The state will "wither away" and true communism will emerge as the next social order, one that possesses no internal contradictions and is thus immortal.

Struggle between Two Social Systems

Historical materialism is thus the theoretical basis for the Soviet view that the struggle between two social systems is the basic international reality of our time. This notion of a dialectical struggle between two social systems is explained by the "law of uneven social development," a Soviet revision of Marx's original views which holds that revolution has not and will not occur simultaneously on the "world-historical" level.[9] As a result, some countries are under the dictatorship of the proletariat, while others are still ruled by the capitalist-imperialists, who not only oppress their own workers, but exploit Third World countries and attempt to effect counter-revolutionary change wherever they are not supreme. The resulting struggle between the two systems, which is a manifestation of the more basic class struggle, necessitates the continuing existence of the state as a base for the operations of the "vanguard" of the proletarian movement, the Communist party. The Soviet Union and the international community of socialist countries, which together constitute one of the two social systems, provide such a base.

The official postwar codification of this systemic dichotomy was made by Andrei Zhdanov, who enunciated the doctrine of the "Two Camps" at the opening session of the Cominform in 1947. Since then, Soviet scholars have developed an elaborate theoretical rationale for this notion of the struggle between two systems. The basic argument is that changes in international relations have affected the fundamental class struggle in a way that has transformed it into a systemic struggle. Broadly speaking, these changes include: (1) the rise of socialism as a world system, producing a community of socialist states; (2) the quickening of the scientific-technical revolution; (3) the increasing role of the masses in the making of foreign policy; and (4) the consequent rise in the role of ideology and ideological propaganda in foreign policy, leading to the struggle between two ideologies.

The Soviets interpret the rise of the world socialist system as a truly revolutionary development in international relations. Since, in their view, international relations are a form of "class relations," they argue that the history of international relations has been the history of interaction between ruling classes that were socially similar, for example, the bourgeoisie of one country versus that of another. There have, the Soviets admit, been exceptions to this general picture. After the French Revolution, for example, the victorious bourgeoisie conducted relations with the feudal lords of neighboring countries, men who now viewed France as a threat to the European status quo. In the Soviet view, however, this exception was simply part of the normal dialectical process: the neighboring countries eventually became bourgeois. The current state of affairs constitutes a "revolutionary" situation because there is no historical precedent for international relations conducted on the basis of a worldwide division of social systems, one pitted against the other. In the Soviet view, then, contemporary international relations consist primarily of relations between the ruling circles of the bourgeois nations and the "working class" of the whole socialist community.[10] This is not to say that today's international relations are restricted to this one "contradiction." Soviet analysts also point to the contradiction between the "imperialist" powers and the people struggling for "liberation" in colonies and "neo-colonies"; the tension between the big "imperialist" powers and the smaller capitalist states; and the struggles among the "imperialist vultures" themselves.[11] In addition, contemporary international relations are marked by the new cooperation among members of the socialist community and cooperation between that community and the nations that recently have won freedom from colonialism.

Soviet commentators have portrayed the so-called scientific-technical revolution as a decisive element in bringing the class struggle to world-systemic proportions. This revolution, which "powerfully influences economics, politics, people's minds and international relations,"[12] affects and is affected by the various radical social changes in today's world. One of the main aspects of this revolution, a factor of great concern to the Soviets, is its role in promoting the worldwide distribution of ideas. The development of different forms of mass communications—radios, films, television, as well as the use of telephones, teletypes, and satellites—is seen as indispensable to spreading socialist propaganda and expediting cooperation among those countries with congruent goals and strategies. Indeed, the Soviets see the monopoly of these means of communication as "just as important [in the worldwide struggle] as the monopoly over traditional instruments of power—the machinery of coercion."[13] These instruments of mass communication are doubly important to the Soviets in light of what they perceive as the increased roles of both the masses and ideology in international relations.

The Soviets regard the increased role of the masses in the formulation of foreign policy as the key factor in the growth of the world socialist system and the transformation of the class struggle into a struggle between two socioeconomic systems. The importance of mass communications grows in proportion to this increase in the influence of the masses. In the socialist countries, where the "masses" already hold power, mass communications enable them to broadcast their propaganda to their oppressed brethren abroad.

These two factors—the influence of the masses and their media—leapfrog in advancing the worldwide cause of socialism.[14] Regardless of ideological persuasion, most theoreticians agree that the masses have become a vital factor in contemporary politics. Indeed, Georgi Arbatov agrees with "bourgeois scholars" that it is impossible for governments to be successful unless they effectively communicate their policies and actions to all politically influential segments of foreign populations, as well as to the domestic population. Furthermore, he shares the view of bourgeois theorists that there now exists a "diplomacy of public opinion."[15]

The Soviets believe that the increased influence of the masses results from a complex of sociopolitical changes in the world, including the decline of capitalism, the rise of the proletariat, and the growth of socialism.[16] In an attack on some Western ideas on this subject, Arbatov clarifies the logic behind his thesis. First he points out that

> the growth of the people's role in politics is not preceded by democracy. On the contrary, the democratic rights and freedoms enjoyed by the masses sooner depend on this role. These rights and freedoms have never been presented to the working people. They have been won by them as a result of a persevering struggle. It was due to this struggle that some of the institutions and principles of the bourgeois state owe much of their vaunted "democracy."[17]

Arbatov then notes that bourgeois theorists "persist in their contention that the masses are not the makers of policy in history but the instruments of politics." An example of such thinking, according to Arbatov, is one "bourgeois" analysis of the changing political importance of the average peasant during different periods. As a medieval serf, the peasant was politically inert and therefore unimportant. But once educated and given a vote, his opinion became important: it was only natural that someone would attempt to manage his thinking. As Arbatov sees it, this very observation is bourgeois nonsense. As he explains: "It is utterly wrong to regard the masses as instruments of policy to be used at will by omnipotent manipulators in the same way as centuries ago with the sole difference that these manipulators now have to influence one more factor—namely public opinion." In the Soviet view, then, the "class interests" of the bourgeoisie dictate that the masses must be treated as an instrument of policy. But socialist propaganda, presumably, is disseminated according to the "class interests" of "masses" who are simultaneously rulers, and therefore the masses are not being manipulated; indeed, such a possibility cannot even arise. Arbatov concludes by noting that when the bourgeois theorists reduce this question of the will of the masses to the voting, civil rights, and other freedoms that are the foundations of bourgeois democracy, they are simply trying to belittle the significance of the "profound social and political changes" in the world—changes that favor socialism and the working class. "It is in these changes that one must look for the origin of the changes that have taken place in international relations, notably the increased influence of the masses, of public opinion, on foreign policy."[18]

Arbatov's argument, like much of Soviet thinking on this subject, describes a circular, yet mutually reinforcing relationship as difficult to untangle as that between the chicken and the egg. Thus, the rise of socialism (accompanied by the decline of capitalism and the upsurge of the proletariat) has led to the growth of the role of the masses in political affairs, and this role, in turn (the metaphysical mystery here is: which turn?), has led to the rise of socialism and the transformation of the class struggle into a worldwide struggle between the two social systems.

The facilities of mass communication and the increased influence of the masses in policy making have helped to spawn two new factors that, according to the Soviets, have changed the face of international relations and thereby broadened the class struggle to world-systemic dimensions. These factors are the increased roles of ideology and ideological propaganda in the making of foreign policy. Once again, the Soviet view is predicated upon the theme of a circular reciprocal relationship: the rise of the masses (and therefore of socialism) has increased the role of ideology in foreign policy, and this process in turn has advanced the cause of socialism.

Ideology and propaganda, of course, have long played a considerable role in foreign policy. Arbatov notes, for example, that ruling classes have always had recourse to "propaganda screens" in the pursuit of their international interests. In the case of the Western bourgeois ruling circles, these "screens" have included the invocation of the ideals of democracy and the values of Western civilization, and the proclamation of the struggle against communism—all of which "mask the utterly prosaic fear of the monopolies for their investments and their interests in sources of raw materials and markets."[19] Arbatov cites religion as a form of propaganda frequently used in the past, referring to the enslavement of colonial peoples by missionaries operating under the "direct guidance" of their respective governments.[20] In addition, the Soviets accuse the bourgeoisie of using moral justifications to conceal its true class aims thereby diverting attention from the real causes of a conflict: by referring to the "free struggle" for political power among individuals or groups, the bourgeoisie creates a false ideology, one that ignores the fact that every political struggle is, in essence, a class struggle. In times of conflict, such ideologies have regularly been used to propagandize ideas and thus influence men's minds and actions, even though the particular conflict had very little to do with ("rarely bore the nature of") the opposing ideologies. Propaganda was thus an auxiliary weapon of foreign policy, one that had no direct link with the real social and ideological conflicts that characterized the society.

Nevertheless, despite their philistine and squalid history of abuse by various ruling classes, ideology and propaganda have acquired new dimensions and significance within the framework of contemporary international relations and now employ tens of thousands of people worldwide. In the West, according to Arbatov, the apparatus for disseminating information and propaganda includes information agencies, radio broadcasting organizations such as Radio Liberty, and the use of the mass media by government officials through leaks, press conferences, and the creation of news-making events. In the Communist world all media are controlled by the government for propagation of the Party line, and everywhere the methods of foreign policies have been adapted to incorporate propaganda and ideological justification so as to achieve maximum success in foreign policy demarches. As Robert Strausz-Hupé put it:

> In diplomacy the task is no longer to anticipate a move by the opponent, but to anticipate its effect upon the psychology of the masses, one's own and the opponent's. This is the meaning of "direct" and "open" diplomacy, a contest for mass opinion in which the techniques of propaganda, commercial advertising and allied arts are more important than the techniques of diplomacy proper and the concrete diplomatic issue.[21]

In the United States, there have been mercurial changes in the attention accorded to this aspect of foreign policy, depending upon the policy-making style of different administrations and the international climate. During the height of the cold war, Americans were surely much more concerned about ideological propaganda than during the peak of "detente." Whereas some American circles regard the very idea of world opinion as ephemeral and think it has no significant potential in terms of *Realpolitik,* the Soviet leaders have consistently had a serious regard for the international impact of propaganda and the war of ideas. Their personal involvement in the Communist mass movement has enabled the Soviets to develop a deep respect for the power of ideology. They appreciate both the ease with which it can be propagated and the fervor with which it is espoused; they know well the propagandist's dictum that "if you label something well enough, you don't have to argue with it."[22] Manifestations of this extreme Soviet concern with propaganda are numerous, including not only the Soviet mass media, but also Soviet attempts to extract the maximum propaganda value from such highly visible international theaters as the United Nations, peace conferences, summit meetings, and the Olympic Games. The Moscow Olympics of 1980 were viewed as a tremendous opportunity to impose on the international media the usual Soviet prescription for propaganda: allow only one side of the story to be told (i.e., the "truth"), tell it repeatedly, and many people will believe some of it, often enough to make a difference in the outcome of a given situation. Further testimony to the great emphasis placed on ideological propaganda in the Soviet Union is the substantial literature that has appeared on the subject, not the least of which is the book by Georgi Arbatov, whose influential position as head of the USA Institute underscores the degree to which the Soviet leadership is conscious—or more properly, obsessed—with the political importance of the subject.

Even as ideological propaganda has reached new heights in terms of its contribution to the means and methods of foreign policy, the Soviets see ideology as a factor that increasingly influences policy per se. This view does not necessarily mean that the international "war of ideas" always manifests itself as an open clash between the two philosophies; instead, it often appears in terms of specific issues and in the context of specific crises. Thus, especially from the Soviet perspective, many current and seemingly unrelated international problems have an ideological core. Examples include such diverse problems as "European security" and the Helsinki agreements, arguments for and against military appropriations, the Sino-Soviet rift, and the foreign policies of the "non-aligned" countries of the Third World. Furthermore, the Soviets find that both the "subjects" and "objects" of foreign policy are now more apt to perceive foreign policy and international relations in terms of ideological concepts. Thus, Arbatov claims, actions that used to be the standard fare of imperialist foreign policy, such as the "aggression in Vietnam or the 'minor' police action of the USA in the Dominican Republic are today regarded by hundreds of millions of people as disgraceful not only for the United States but for capitalist foreign policy and the capitalist social system as such."[23] In light of these developments, international relations in general have become, in the Soviet view, an arena for the clash of the opposed ideologies of the two social systems.

The question of how much either side is truly motivated by its respective ideology is another question, however—one that forces us to ask how much each side really believes in its ideology and whether it represents a true guide to action for either of them. It is possible that one or the other side does not believe in its ideology much at all, but simply uses it as an instrument of power, for rationalization and proselytization. The Soviets constantly and vehemently deny that this is the case with them but one cannot be sure, for ideology is the major criterion determining the contents of their media and, as such, it is the object of direct state manipulation. It is hoped that the following discussion can shed some light on this subject.

The Forms and Theaters of Struggle

Since the Soviets believe the class-systemic struggle to be the main feature of international reality, they see this struggle as taking place in many forms and in different arenas, both violently and nonviolently. These forms can be classified into four broad categories: political, ideological, economic, and scientific-technical. The particular form that the struggle assumes depends, in Soviet eyes, on the course of relations between the Soviet Union and the United States, the leading representatives of the two social systems.[24] The form of the struggle determines whether there will be war or peace and, in general, has a tremendous bearing on the degree to which Soviet foreign policy can fulfill its ambitions.

The political struggle against capitalism has been described as "the struggle for the minds and hearts of people throughout the world"[25] (an American wartime expression, one might add, borrowed by the Soviets). Given this broad definition, the political struggle can take many forms, the ultimate of which is military conflict. The Soviets view the use of military force as "the continuation of the policy of the state and classes by violent means"[26] (this variation on Clausewitz's aphorism is occasionally attributed to Lenin). The arena of military struggle depends upon where the imperialists choose to "engender hotbeds of war," for Soviet theory holds that war is caused primarily by imperialist aggression in the following contexts: the struggle for international markets, the division of the world into spheres of influence among imperialist countries, the consequent oppression of third countries, and the unstable conditions of the changing relative strengths of capitalist countries resulting from greater or lesser profits extracted from unevenly developing oppressed countries.

Working from these assumptions, Marxist-Leninist theory is able to classify a war as either just or unjust. In the words of one Soviet military journal, "just wars include those waged by people, nations, and advanced classes for social progress and for liberation from exploitation and national oppression or in the defense of their state independence."[27] Thus, the argument continues, just wars consist of: (1) "wars in defense of the socialist Fatherland and the states of the socialist system against imperialist aggressors," (2) "wars of the working class against capitalists," (3) "national liberation wars of the peoples of colonial and dependent countries against imperialist oppression," and (4) "wars of the peoples of bourgeois states in defense of their national independence against imperialist predators." Therefore, when they are sufficiently provoked in a given situation and resort to a military rebuff against the imperialists, or give aid to "liberation" forces (as in Vietnam and Angola), the Soviets, the chief "strugglers for peace and the security of peoples,"[28] can be confident that they are acting for a "just cause."

Military struggle is of paramount importance in the Soviet world view, for only military strength or the threat (or prospect) of its employment can ultimately "restrain" the imperialists from continuing their violent adventures against worldwide Soviet interests (Soviet "interests" include the interests of all "progressive" movements around the world). As V. Matveyev points out, for example:

> After all, if the U.S. aggressive circles had succeeded to any extent in their plans of violence against the national liberation movement in Indochina, they would most certainly have undertaken new adventures in other parts of the globe. Consequently, in rendering aid to and supporting Vietnam's struggle for freedom and independence, the world's progressive forces are defending the cause of peace and security throughout the world.[29]

The Soviet prescription for peace here, of course, consists of supporting North Vietnamese military operations in order that, to put the matter crudely: "If we win, then you can no longer fight, and therefore, there will be peace." Any military campaign is thus a quest for peace so long as it is conducted by the "peaceloving forces." Now, one might observe that from all outward appearances, this formula is no different from American military doctrine, but such a view would ignore the crucial difference in the two definitions of "peace." The United States, as a power basically interested in preserving the international status quo, regards peace as the absence of war. The Soviets, however, as a power interested in changing the international status quo, believe that peace is impossible so long as there remain all those conditions of exploitation and oppression which produce class struggle. Peace can, therefore, exist only when the class struggle is over, that is, when people live under communist rule.

A corollary of this one-sided notion is the Soviet conviction that whereas even the most potent military strength "is powerless to reverse the course of historical development," the Soviet Union's military strength accelerates it.[30] It was Soviet strength which helped to defeat the imperialists in Vietnam, and which forced the United States to abandon a policy conceived of "from a position of strength" and begin to negotiate on questions of arms limitation. This same one-sided point of view also shapes Soviet attitudes toward the general issue of "militarism." They reason that militarism is today a uniquely capitalist-imperialist phenomenon that, "apparently having reached its apogee, has begun to display its growing political powerlessness."[31] Although the military forces of the Soviet Union and the other "peace-loving" countries are constantly lauded for their political efficacy by the communist press, one can infer that "militarism" does not exist in these countries. Similarly, the military-industrial complex of the United States is responsible for the arms race, whereas any Soviet acquisition of new weapons systems is simply a defensive measure with no propensity for fueling new rounds of the race. After all, "among the most important tasks in the political sphere is the struggle of all peace-loving peoples for the ending of the arms race . . . and in the long term—for total disarmament."[32] The fact that the Soviet deployment of powerful new weapons systems may tend to engender either fear or mistrust on the part of American policymakers is rarely mentioned in the Soviet press.*

The political struggle between the two social systems also encompasses the general struggle for the growth and exploitation of opportunities in the international arena. As part of the struggle for the "minds and hearts" of people, this "struggle for opportunities" is seen by the Soviets as a competition for the political allegiance and cooperation of third countries. Once political compatibility is achieved, economic and strategic benefits for the competing systems are expected as a consequence. Unflaggingly sanguine about their country's continuing success in this field, Soviet commentators constantly assert that "socialism's entry into the world arena dealt a blow to the positions of imperialism from which it is not destined to recover."[33] As L. A. Leont'ev goes on to explain:

> There originated immutable restraints that limit the range of possibilities that imperialism has at its disposal in the execution of its aggressive plans. With the growth of socialism's strength and with the changes in the balance of power between the two systems in favor of socialism, these restraints are having an increasingly fundamental impact and are narrowing the sphere in which the imperialist powers can hope to have a free hand.

The Soviets see political crises and international negotiations as forums for the political struggle, thus interpreting American partici-

---

*G. A. Trofimenko, in a rare example, notes that "colossal distrust built up on *both* sides during the cold war" (*SShA,* February 1974, p. 9, emphasis is mine).

pation in these situations as efforts to advance U.S. positions and concluding that they must struggle against such imperialist initiatives. Typically, with reference to SALT I, the Soviets argued that "the United States is not striving for a genuine reduction in armaments, but merely wishes to secure unilateral advantages in the talks with the Soviet Union."[34] This particular quotation is compellingly reminiscent of statements by many American commentators regarding Soviet purposes in negotiating forums. Despite this apparently mutual distrust, there is a fundamental difference between the two outlooks. On the one hand, in the United States such comments represent only a part of the composite American outlook, there being an equally strong contingent of analysts who believe that both protagonists, being rational about the nature of strategic weapons, are fundamentally motivated by goodwill in their efforts to negotiate arms control. Indeed, this group is apt to feel that its struggle is more with its "hard-line" fellow commentators than with the Soviets. On the other hand, Soviet analysts erect a solid front in presenting their outlook. Although divergent views may exist privately, the perception that negotiations with the West are a "struggle" is presented, like any vote in a Communist party central committee or congress, as unanimous.

The Soviets see "peaceful coexistence" as another form of political struggle, one "where the ideological dispute between the two systems and their competition in various fields are combined with many-sided cooperation, where inevitable differences are resolved through negotiations, and where the unbridled arms race is replaced with a course toward arms limitation and disarmament."[35] Soviet commentators repeatedly stress that under the conditions of "peaceful coexistence" the struggle against capitalism and imperialism continues unabated in every form save war and the arms race. As Leonid Brezhnev put it in his report "On the 50th Anniversary of the USSR":

> The class struggle between the two systems . . . will continue. It cannot be otherwise, for the world outlook and class aims of socialism and capitalism are opposite and irreconcilable. But we will strive to direct this historically inevitable struggle into a channel which poses no threat of wars, dangerous conflicts, and an uncontrolled arms race.[36]

The effort to determine which form the struggle takes is part of the struggle itself. In the context of the "detente" between the United States and the Soviet Union, the Soviets constantly spoke of the "positive changes" in these relations which tend toward a basis of peaceful coexistence. Referring to these changes, Arbatov noted that "the shifts of which we are talking, like everything new, are still very fragile. They were born as a result of a struggle and will remain an objective of struggle."[37]

The ideological struggle, like the political, comes in many forms, broadly classified by the Soviets as the acceptable and the unacceptable. In its acceptable forms, "the ideological struggle is the serious, consistent championing—based on the facts of life—of the objective truth and the scientifically true cognition and interpretation of reality and its natural laws."[38] The Soviet Union is, of course, the country which knows that it knows the truth and champions it. Thus, "between the USSR and the United States, as socialist and capitalist countries, even with the very best international relations, there will always be a fundamental, ideological struggle."[39] The acceptable forms of this struggle encompass ideological propaganda of many types, from radio broadcasts to cultural exchanges. Evidently, the unacceptable forms of the struggle (i.e., those forms which the Soviets do not like) constitute the propagation of anything that does not correspond to the objective truth as determined by Marxist-Leninist doctrine. As Mitin puts it:

> The representatives of the modern bourgeoisie identify the ideological struggle with the arbitrary manipulation of ideas and equate the ideological struggle with "psychological warfare" waged by imperialism, which is really an integral part of the cold war. Today it is well known that "psychological warfare" includes lies, misinformation, and slander about socialism and that it is waged by subversive methods with infringements of the generally accepted norms of interstate relations, including of the principles of sovereignty and noninterference in the internal affairs of states.[40]

Another analysis observes that the unacceptable forms of this struggle include "the preaching of hatred of the socialist countries, and various kinds of ideological sabotage for which special centers like Radio Free Europe and Radio Liberty were created."[41]

One is forced to ask what, aside from the fact that propagation of "slander" violates the Soviet sense of the truth, makes these Western forms of the struggle unacceptable? The answer lies in the peculiar way in which the Soviets relate the two forms of struggle. Desiring that "peaceful coexistence" prevail, they insist that this form functions properly only when the "acceptable" forms of ideological struggle are used. For instance, in referring to the conditions under which the cold war could be ended, Arbatov insists that "the renunciation of the propaganda of war and the hatred of other countries, slander and various subversive methods" is a necessary prerequisite. Only then, he continues, will "the inevitable struggle for people's minds . . . be waged precisely as a struggle of ideas, as a dispute between world views, by forms and methods that will not harm peaceful coexistence."[42] Mr. Mitin goes so far as to say that "such 'psychological warfare' is really incompatible with the principle of peaceful coexistence," that "it has nothing in common with the inevitable ideological struggle."[43] Essentially, then, the relationship between the two forms of struggle is a Soviet form of "linkage": if the West wants "peaceful coexistence," it must not engage in unacceptable forms of ideological struggle. But, since by definition the bourgeois imperialists do not know the objective truth, they are incapable of uttering anything but subversive slander. Therefore, under conditions of "peaceful coexistence" only the Soviets and other true Marxist-Leninists can properly engage in a policy of struggle.

In spite of this normative theory, the Soviets do accept the realities of the ideological struggle without severe theoretical dislocations. They acknowledge, for example, the struggle between opposing understandings of various concepts, including the ubiquitous "peaceful coexistence." As G. Trofimenko points out:

> The socialist understanding of the principles of peaceful coexistence and the bourgeois understanding of them are by no means identical, differing not only in nuances. In being compelled to agree to the concept of peaceful coexistence, some interpret it only as a commitment to observe the minimum mutual restraint necessary to continuing their conduct in the international arena in the spirit of the traditions of the classic "balance of power." One can hardly agree with such an interpretation of peaceful coexistence, by which the Soviet people and all progressive forces refer to a policy of active cooperation between states with different

social systems in order to insure a stable peace and their collective efforts to prevent a world war and strengthen international security. . . . There is and will continue to be an acute struggle over which of these understandings of this concept will triumph in the international community and its outcome will to a great extent be determined by the actions of the peace-loving forces and the degree of their resolve to repulse the circles primarily interested in making declarations on peace but not in peace as such.[44]

The Soviets acknowledge a similar conflict over differing interpretations of the concept of "collective security." As V. Sobakin observes: "The struggle over the question of what basis can and should be used for states' collective actions to insure general security is being waged not only between countries from opposed systems but also within the capitalist system, between individual bourgeois factions."[45] In this contest between the capitalists themselves, one side is said to advocate the pursuit of "collective security" through the conditions of "peaceful coexistence," while their opponents promote confrontation with socialism. Keenly aware of such "contradictions" within the capitalist camp, many Soviet analysts see those whose views coincide with theirs as an intrinsic and useful part of the broader ideological struggle.

Consequently, the Soviets seize the opportunity to exploit for propaganda purposes any thinking in the capitalist camp which is compatible with their own. Historically, this tendency has been manifested in the feigned relaxation of ideological rigidity in order to form a "popular front" with potentially useful political forces. We also see it in the selective appropriation of Western ideas and culture, a recurrent phenomenon that S. Mokshin explained in a 1973 article:

> The class approach to the question of the interaction of national cultures does not amount to dividing them into what is wholly acceptable and what is wholly to be rejected but teaches us how to set aside everything that is valuable, progressive, and revolutionary from that which is alien and reactionary, and to separate genuine values from those of a speculative nature.[46]

The economic struggle, like the ideological, has its acceptable and unacceptable forms. According to Arbatov, the unacceptable forms, which were frequently employed during the cold war, include: "embargoes, boycotts, diversions," as well as "blockade, [and] all possible kinds of trade restrictions and discriminatory practices."[47] Clearly, it is their restrictive impact on free trade which makes these forms of the economic struggle unacceptable. Thus, the Jackson-Vanik Amendment to the Trade Bill of 1974, which denies most-favored-nation status to the Soviet Union pending the liberalization of its emigration rights, constituted the continuation of unacceptable forms of economic struggle plus "unwarranted intervention into Soviet internal affairs."

As Arbatov pointed out in 1974, economic competition is the form of economic struggle acceptable to the Soviet Union: "In our way of thinking economic competition is also a form of struggle, but what distinguishes it is that it at the same time opens up the possibility of extensive cooperation." Such economic cooperation is seen as a means of cementing "peaceful coexistence," the form of struggle from which "everyone can profit... in comparison with what happens with the arms race and with indomitable hostility."[48] Ideally then, the

> economic struggle between the different social systems is a competition in the course of which socialism is intended to demonstrate and is demonstrating its superiority over the capitalist system. This superiority is expressed in the stable high rate and planned nature of the economic development of the socialist community, in the absence of man's exploitation by man, and in the economic and cultural burgeoning of all the peoples of the socialist countries.[49]

The economic struggle is thus perceived as an intrinsic part of the ideological and political struggles to win the "minds and hearts" of peoples around the world by convincing them of the superiority and benevolence of the socialist economic system.

According to D. Gvishiani, "The scientific-technical revolution is becoming one of the most important factors in the competition between the opposed social systems determining the historical prospects of social development."[50] In an attempt to explain this pervasive theme in Soviet political literature, Gvishiani writes that "the scientific-technical revolution is the fundamental, qualitative trans-

45

formation of forces of production, the transformation of science into a direct force of production, and, corresponding to this, the revolutionary change of the material-technical basis of social production, its contents and forms, the character of labor, the structure of production forces and the social division of labor." As such, the scientific-technical revolution "affects all spheres of life of the society, including the way of life, culture, and people's psychology."[51]

Like many other Soviet concepts, "scientific-technical revolution" has a one-sided quality that is misleading to Westerners. Taken at face value, the "scientific and technical revolution" appears to be a designation comparable to the "industrial revolution," the "space age," or something similar, but in fact this concept describes a process that, according to traditional Soviet theology, "scientifically" works for the benefit of socialism alone.* In Gvishiani's treatment of this theme, the familiar reciprocal relationship is again apparent:

> While exerting a growing influence on society's socioeconomic development, the scientific-technical revolution is itself conditioned by the specific level of this development. It has become possible thanks to the high degree of the socialization of production, that is, the process creating objective prerequisites for the transition from the capitalist method of production to the socialist. It has intensified the objective need for such a transition and, thanks to this, is becoming an important factor in the contemporary world revolutionary process.

More specifically, Gvishiani points out that "in accelerating the process of socialization of the means of production, [the scientific-technical revolution] deepens and exacerbates the contradictions inherent in capitalism, while at the same time engendering new contradictions that characterize the modern stage of its development."[52] Thus, the "scientific-technical revolution" is part of the struggle between the two systems: it strengthens socialism, socialism strengthens it, it weakens capitalism, and the stronger socialist camp is therefore able to struggle more effectively against its enemies.

Although scientific-technical revolution has a specific definition

---

*The view outlined here, it should be noted, is the *traditionalist* view, which, as we shall see in Chapter 3, is not shared by all Soviet analysts.

46

in the Soviet lexicon, the Soviets do use the term in a way that foreigners would understand. This "revolution" *is* referred to in the context of discussion about "scientific and technical progress." (Yet "progress" itself has its own Marxist, one-sided aspects.*) For example:

> The world competition between socialism and capitalism is currently becoming increasingly concentrated around the utilization of the opportunities opened up by scientific and technical progress. The monopolist bourgeoisie is striving to harness the scientific-technical revolution to its class interests and utilize the scientific-technical revolution to intensify its exploitation of the working people, increase its profits and strengthen its positions in foreign markets. . . . Bourgeois ideologists regard the scientific-technical revolution as a means with which to ease class contradictions, weaken the working people's political and economic struggle against domination by the monopolies and reinforce capitalism's positions in the competition with the socialist system of states.[53]

Despite this Soviet admission that scientific and technical advances do occur under capitalism, Soviet analysis would also seem to imply that science and technology have acquired some "revolutionary" properties that differ from those they possessed during the industrial revolution and the scientific revolutions. Or perhaps Soviet theoreticians are only implying that since science and technology have always been a force for social "progress," and since historical progress has always been pointing toward communism, science and technology have always been serving this ultimate goal.** Indeed, the industrial revolution did create the proletarian class, the chosen people of Marxist theology. In any case, however, traditionalist Soviet analysts like Yermolenko conclude that contrary to the designs of the "bourgeois ideologists," "the scientific-technical revolution is not only failing to cure capitalism's inherent social contradictions but is leading to their exacerbation and to the

---

*The idea of "peace" as illustrated on p. 39 has this same two-sided quality as do many other terms constantly used in the Soviet press.
**Of course, this raises one of the classic philosophical problems for Marxists: Since everyone is so "predestined" to follow the immutable course of history toward communism, to what degree do individuals possess free will? This question, needless to say, is not a favorite topic of discussion in Moscow.

emergence of new contradictions."[54] Somehow, then, capitalism cannot obtain any real benefit from the use of science and technology, because their "revolutionary" properties contradict the essence of capitalism itself.

Despite the "inexorable" course of "progress," the "inevitable" victory of the socialist system, and the deleterious effects of the scientific-technical revolution on capitalism, Leonid Brezhnev found it necessary to remind the Central Committee of the Belorussian Communist party that:

> The further intensive development of science and technology and the widespread introduction into production of the latest scientific and technical achievements [are] not just the central economic task but also an important political one ... [because] ... one of the main fronts of historical competition between the two systems lies precisely in this sphere—that of scientific and technical progress.[55]

Without specifying a reason, he went on to emphasize that "at the present stage, it can be said frankly, questions of scientific and technical progress are assuming crucial importance." Arbatov expands on Brezhnev's statement, attributing the growing importance of these factors to the fact that "the rate and depth of scientific and technical progress in our time are increasingly determining the course of the economic competition of the two systems." In addition, of course, "one of the inevitable consequences of the increasingly widespread scientific-technical revolution in our time is the intensification of the ideological struggle. Imperialism is trying to compensate for the weakening of its economic and political positions with ideological counterattacks in order to halt social progress and retard the development of socialism."[56] As a result, then, all the forms of struggle are linked; developments in one form affect those in all others. Again, Soviet analysts have created a multifaceted reciprocal relationship whose common theme is the erosion of the capitalist system at the hands of the socialist camp.

Since they viewed history as governed by the inexorable dialectic, Marx and Engels believed that the proletarian revolution would be a singular process that would occur almost simultaneously in most of the advanced capitalist states. Lenin's revolution, however, seemed to contradict this notion of a simultaneous and universal revolution, and in his "law of uneven social development" Lenin posited that since the "contradictions of capitalism" reach different levels of maturity at different times in different countries, the development of socialism among the different countries is not likely to happen "all at once." Does Lenin's theory deny the "international character" that Marx attributed to the revolution? Y. Krasin argues that it does not since "the socialist revolution in any given country results from the development of the entire world imperialist system."[57] He explains that the monopoly capitalists, having penetrated even the most remote countries, have created a worldwide web of economic and political dependence on imperialism. Consequently, since any proletarian revolution in one country is engaging in a struggle against an international phenomenon, it too assumes an international character. Consequently, such a revolution in a single country has an impact on the entire international position of the socialist community.

The Soviets view their position in the international system against this theoretical background. As Krasin points out, the first task before the Russian proletariat "was to save the 'island' of socialism in the stormy ocean of imperialism as a base for the further development of the world revolutionary process."[58] Lenin argued that, since it constituted such a base, the Russian proletariat must do its utmost to awaken and support revolutionary spirit and action in all other countries, thereby creating conditions in which the socialist community can expand and flourish, while the capitalist world shrivels, rots, and falls under the blows of world revolution.

Since the struggle between the two systems, as perceived by the Soviets, amounts to a "zero-sum game" in which a loss for one side represents a gain for the other, any movement that helps to erode the power of capitalism and imperialism represents a gain for the world socialist revolution. The manifold examples of such movements illustrate the scope of the worldwide struggle. The working class of the capitalist countries, for instance, "is waging a struggle against the domination of monopoly capital," and as M. Mitin points out:

Its most important demands in the struggle for social progress today are the establishment of democratic control over the economy, the nationalization of key sectors of production and the democratization of social and state life. To what extent this struggle will be successful depends on strengthening the positions of the Communist parties, consolidating the unity of the working class and creating a broad alliance of all democratic, anti-imperialist forces.[59]

Soviet commentators, ever sanguine, regularly extol the growth and achievements of this movement. S. Alexandrov and V. Yegorov, for example, note that the working class in the capitalist West

> has accumulated great experience in class battles, its political moral authority and its organization are constantly growing and the onslaught on the state monopoly system is increasing. The number of participants in strike battles and other mass demonstrations in the zone of developed capitalism alone amounted to 45 million people in 1973. The effectiveness of these demonstrations, is attested, for example, by the fact that the general strike by the British miners in 1974 made a considerable contribution to the government crisis and the resignation of the conservative cabinet.[60]

Similar movements that are considered part of the revolutionary process include those of "the millions-strong masses of the labor-peasantry of the capitalist and developing countries, the labor intelligentsia, students, and nonproletarian strata of the working people," all of whom are struggling against the "exploiters."[61]

Among the most important movements constituting the revolutionary process are the democratic and "national liberation" struggles and revolutions that occur in countries that are usually underdeveloped as a result, according to the Soviets, of colonial "exploitation" and which therefore do not have a large proletariat. As Alexandrov and Yegorov observe: *the struggle for national liberation in many countries has begun to develop in practice into a struggle against exploiter relations, both feudal and capitalist*" (emphasis in original).[62] Furthermore, the Soviets explain that it was these national liberation struggles that led to the collapse of the colonial system of imperialism. Socialist, and occasionally social-democratic movements may also serve the goals of the world revolution. Although the Soviets, as Communists, have many ideological differences with these groups, they often find them a useful element in the systemic struggle insofar as these groups constitute forces of anticapitalism or anti-imperialism. The Soviets also see them as potential allies of Communist parties in electoral politics through the formation of a "popular front."

Finally, there is the "vanguard" of the world revolutionary process itself—the Communist movement, which is constantly growing, as evidenced by Mitin's figures: "whereas in 1924, for example, there were 49 Communist and workers parties uniting 1.3 million people, today Communist parties are operating in 89 countries, and more than 50 million people are united in their ranks."[63]

Thus, the Soviets see many movements as useful parts of the worldwide struggle, all of which merge "into a single torrent of the world liberation movement,"[64] for, as Soviet theoreticians put it, "the revolutionary process is characterized by the broadening of its social base."[65] Despite the fact that individual movements are not led by the proletariat, they serve the communist cause because they help weaken imperialism. As a result, "the revolutionary process has acquired a truly worldwide nature in recent decades. It has embraced all countries, all continents and all peoples—large and small. Today there is no longer a region on earth where the struggle for the cause of social and national liberation has not been launched in one form or another."[66]

The Measurement of the Struggle

Soviet analysts use the concept of the "correlation of forces" to evaluate the relative strengths of the various parties to the worldwide struggle. Employing this concept, Soviet theoreticians can "measure" the two social systems against each other and weigh any of the smaller groups that oppose one another on a local level but still constitute elements of the broader struggle. "Correlation of forces" is a much more comprehensive and ambiguous term than the Western concept of "balance of power." Whereas "balance of power" generally refers to the balance of military forces which, of course, are dependent upon the relative strength of national economies, the "correlation of forces" is much more inclusive, comprising four main variables. As G. Shakhnazarov explains, in assessing the "correlation of forces," one must consider economic, military, and political aspects, as well as the quality of international movements:

A great multitude of criteria exists for an appraisal of the correlation of forces. If we are talking about the *economy,* one usually compares per capita gross national product, the productivity of labor, the dynamics of economic growth, the level of industrial production (especially in the leading branches), the technical equipping of labor, resources and the degree of qualification of the labor force, the number of specialists, and the level of development of theoretical and applied science. If we are talking about the *military* aspect, one compares the quantity and quality of arms, the firepower of the armies, the combat and moral qualities of the soldiers, the training of the command structure, the forms of organization of the troops and their experience in conducting military actions, and the character of the military doctrine and of the methods of strategic, operational, and tactical thinking. If we are talking about *politics,* one considers the breadth of the social base of state authority, the method of its organization, the constitutional order of relations between the government and the legislative organs, the possibility of making operational decisions and the degree and character of support by the population of internal and foreign policy. Finally, if we are talking about the appraisal of one or another *international movement,* one takes into account its quantitative composition, its influence among the masses, its positions in the political life of individual countries, its principles and norms of relations among its component parts, and the degree of their cohesion. [My emphasis][67]

Given the vast number of variables that must be considered when appraising the correlation of forces, any final assessment can only be an estimate. In spite of its purportedly "scientific" methodology, the correlation of forces is a highly elastic and subjective measurement. The following analysis of what Anatoly Gromyko (son of Foreign Minister Andrei Gromyko) and A. Kokoshin call the "foreign policy potential" of the United States is a good example of how Soviet analysts use this theory of the correlation of forces:

The combined resources that the ruling class, utilizing the state-monopoly mechanism, can allocate to the realization of its foreign policy may be called the foreign policy potential of the state. Such a "potential" indicates the need to distinguish between the *possible utilization* of this part of its resources and its *real appli-*

cation. Political, diplomatic, military, and ideological means are used in implementing foreign policy strategic plans. Changes in the *correlation of these means* with the aims and total volume of the allocated resources remaining the same can of themselves signify serious changes in foreign policy strategy.[68] [My emphasis]

Within this framework, Gromyko and Kokoshin proceed to explain how one must discover the "objective conditions" of the formation of U.S. foreign policy strategy:

> It is necessary to take into account such factors as the position of the United States in the contemporary system of international relations, the correlation of forces between the United States and the other main elements of this system, mutual relations with the principal subjects of international relations, and the state of Washington's foreign policy potential and its volume and structure.[69]

The analysis of the correlation of forces takes many forms, depending on which elements a given Soviet theoretician deems most significant, but several common themes emerge. In some cases the analyst may emphasize economic criteria—particularly in the context of some downturn or dislocation in the American economy which can be compared to contemporaneous Soviet economic "successes" to illustrate the "crisis" of capitalism. In other cases, the analyst may emphasize the degree to which the "national liberation movement" is victorious in a given area of the world— showing that the "shift" in the correlation of forces is away from imperialism toward socialism.

In addition to those themes mentioned by Shakhnazarov, the "scientific-technical revolution" is often cited as a basic element in the correlation. Thus, Soviet commentators often repeat Yermolenko's observation that "an attempt to adjust to the demands of the scientific and technical revolution under the conditions of a monopoly state leads to social antagonisms on an even bigger scale and with even greater acuity."[70] This line of argument leads to the conclusion that the more the "scientific-technical revolution" is used by the bourgeoisie, the greater its decay and therefore the greater the shift in the "correlation of forces."

The degree to which "collective security" prevails both regionally and globally provides another criterion for Soviet analysis of the correlation of forces. V. Sobakin observes that "the growth in the power of the socialist countries and in their international cohesion [i.e., "collective security"] and internal stability has been and remains the decisive factor insuring the effectiveness of the policy of peaceful coexistence, and consequently, the transformation of the idea of collective security from a possibility into a reality."[71] Here, of course, is another reciprocal relationship: the greater the degree of collective security, the more markedly the "correlation of forces" changes in favor of socialism, and therefore, the greater the degree of collective security.

"Peaceful coexistence," like "collective security," is a theme central to the assessment of the correlation of forces. In the Soviet theoretical lexicon, it is axiomatic that "any change in the correlation of forces in favor of imperialism would lead not to a reduction but to an increase in tension."[72] Conversely, any changes in favor of socialism diminish tension and strengthen the conditions for "peaceful coexistence." Once again, a reciprocal relationship is at work: a strengthening of "peaceful coexistence" implies that shifts have occurred in the correlation of forces which favor socialism, each of these shifts in turn strengthening "peaceful coexistence" until, presumably, imperialism is vanquished and "peaceful coexistence" simply becomes Soviet-style "peace."

A final criterion by which the Soviets measure the correlation of forces—one not formally acknowledged by Soviet analysts—might be called the "ideological criterion." This is the factor that the Soviets consider when they measure, for example, the ideological strength of a given country. They may ask, how strongly do the ruling circles of the United States hold their convictions as to the merits of the capitalist system? How willing are those ruling circles to defend their system—or ultimately—to use force to defend their system? In some ways, this sort of measurement constitutes an assessment of a nation's morale—the morale not only of its ruling classes but of its armies as well. Thus, any such ideological measurement represents an appraisal of a nation's will to employ the material forces at its disposal.

"Objectivity" is the one quality common to all these themes, for no Soviet theoretician could conceive that a real "measurement" of forces could be made from any other than "objective" criteria. And any "force" of a nonmaterial character, such as the morale of the general populace or the army, is necessarily seen as a direct function of such real factors. Thus, it is an axiom of Soviet political analysis that "changes in the political views of the capitalist powers' ruling classes have always been and continue to be determined not by abstract moral criteria but by absolutely real factors."[73] Reflecting the crudity of Soviet materialism, this idea, analyzed in light of the general one-sided quality of Soviet theoretical precepts, illustrates more about the Soviet political mentality than many other indexes. If one asks what makes so-called real factors real, the Soviet lexicon can only answer that these are the elements by which one measures the "correlation of forces." However, as our analysis has shown, "real factors," such as the military, the economic, and the scientific and technical, are "real" only for the "progressive" forces in the world: they work for one social system but not for the other. Thus, despite Soviet scholarship's strenuous exertions to explain this phenomenon scientifically, the irony exists that the "real" quality of these "real" factors ultimately depends on the abstract criteria of communist morality: only certain social elements can be "good" and therefore merit the divine sanction and assistance of history.

According to the bulk of Soviet press commentary, the beginning of the 1970s marked a major shift in the global "correlation of forces." At that time, of course, the Soviets reached a position of strategic parity with the United States, but, in the Soviet view, the period was marked by two other significant developments: (1) the worldwide erosion of "imperialist" positions (especially in Southeast Asia) as a result of the spread of socialism and the "national liberation movement"; and (2) the weakening of the capitalist system on account of the "deepening crisis of capitalism" and economic "contradictions" between the major capitalist states. Soviet commentators regularly described the resulting situation as "the change in the correlation of forces in favor of socialism" (or occasionally, "the *radical* changes in the correlation of world forces in favor of socialism").[74] Since statements of this sort have long been a part of Soviet rhetoric, and since there have been no recent references to a clear-cut "preponderance" of power on the side of socialism,* we must look elsewhere to ascertain whether and

---

*An important exception may be the statement by Andrei Gromyko (cited in Introduction, p. 17) referring to the "predominance of the forces of peace and progress."

to what extent the Soviets perceive one side to have strengthened at the expense of the other. It is the thesis of this book that the dominant group in the Kremlin indeed perceives such a change, and that evidence of the leadership's view can be found in Soviet analyses of the changes that this new "correlation of forces" has imposed on U.S. foreign policy.

In general, Soviet analysts point to changes in the priorities and methods of American foreign policy. For example, V. P. Lukin maintains that, throughout the 20th century, American policy was "globalist" in character but focused itself specifically in three major regions: Europe, East Asia, and Latin America—regions in which the United States strove to maintain either a "balance of power" or a hegemonistic advantage for its imperialist ambitions. However, with "the appearance and steady consolidation of the world socialist system" (phraseology that signifies a shift in the correlation of forces), the United States was forced to switch its focus from these aggressive and profiteering designs to the struggle against socialism, and so, "American-Soviet relations began to play the primary role."[75] In short, the shift in the correlation of forces had forced the United States to move from the offensive to the defensive.

According to the dominant Soviet view, this new world situation even tended to reduce the role of the United States in the capitalist world. Iu. P. Davydov observes that formerly, "drunk with its atomic, military, and scientific-technical power," the United States had undertaken "actively to assert itself in the role of world policeman, the leader of the imperialist camp. . . . It gave as its justification the fact that it was responsible for all other capitalist countries."[76] With the shift in the correlation of forces, however, the United States can no longer perform this job by itself, and thus, "in order to preserve itself as a global factor, . . . is forced to attract its allies to sharing the economic and military burden involved in the implementation of the imperialistic course."[77] In other words, the new world "realities" forced the United States to formulate a new strategic doctrine—the "Nixon Doctrine," with its provisions for the sharing of global responsibilities.

Having limited the opportunities for the United States to indulge its imperialist designs and reduced its strength relative to its allies and economic competitors, this new "correlation of forces" has accentuated the "continuing crisis of capitalism." With fewer opportunities to "exploit" Third World countries, the United States has been forced to compete even more strenuously for the remaining markets, thus creating deeper "contradictions" between itself and its capitalist allies. Hence, Georgi Arbatov speaks of the "costs to the U.S. monopolies of the new correlation of forces within the world capitalist economic system itself"—costs characterized by "balance of payments and balance of trade deficits [and] the weakening of the dollar."[78]

Now, Morton Schwartz is surely correct to observe that the Soviets *have* been talking about the "crisis of capitalism" since 1917. But such an observation should not be allowed to obscure the very significant changes in recent Soviet discussions of this crisis. For indeed, much of the recent Soviet discussion of the "crisis of capitalism" *is* different, not because of any change in its formulation, but instead because of the new context in which it is couched. This new context, which will be discussed in detail in subsequent chapters, includes analyses of both domestic and international repercussions of this "crisis": the domestic being the so-called problem of political priorities (which, in simple terms, amounts to a "guns or butter" debate of proportions unprecedented in modern American history), and the international being a global American retrenchment.

The Soviets also attribute the decline in the U.S. ability to realize benefits from the use of military force to the new "correlation of forces." In the dominant Soviet view, two major elements of the correlation of forces have worked to reduce sharply "the sphere of application of the enormous military might that the United States had accumulated in its pursuit of a 'position of supremacy.' "[79] The first of these elements is what the Soviets perceive as their own "major success" in increasing military strength, particularly the attainment of strategic parity, which they see as having forced the Americans to give up the recklessness that characterized U.S. policy during the years of American strategic superiority. The second factor that has limited U.S. military "adventurism" is the success of "external elements of the correlation of forces"— the "national liberation movement" and the worldwide spread of socialism. Thus, Soviet commentators argue that "in our time no force of arms is capable of turning back the development of countries and peoples that have cast off the fetters of oppression and that are building a new life."[80] This notion of what one might call "counter-historical" military force, of course, applies only to those forces attempting to restrain the inexorable development of history and not to those instrumental in its acceleration. The idea appears regularly in official Soviet publications, couched in such assertions as: "the importance of military force is, in its own way, becoming obvious," and "the impossibility of using it for political purposes is becoming increasingly clear.[81] Again, one might observe that such statements were part of the Soviet repertoire in the 1950s and earlier,[82] but again a distinction must be made between those statements and more recent declarations as to the limited utility of "imperialist" military power. In the 1950s Soviet commentators maintained that U.S. military power had been deterred or was of limited use in imperialism's attempts at expansionism.[83] But in the 1970s, in light of the victory of the "national liberation movement" in Vietnam, Soviet commentators could phrase their point more emphatically. In Arbatov's words: "Under conditions of the new correlation of forces in the world, the U.S. military might cannot guarantee it victory in a local war."[84]

The Soviet view holds that the bilateral agreements reached at the 1972 Moscow summit formalized the change in the world correlation of forces. The U.S. signature of agreements on the limitation of strategic arms indicated an American realization that it would be futile to compete with the Soviet Union in an arms race. The Soviet imagination was also capable of concluding that the United States might have signed these accords in the hope that they would restrain the growth of Soviet power. Indeed, only "objective factors" could possibly have impelled such an action on the part of American ruling circles—and what could be more "objective" than the vast growth in Soviet strategic power? The spirit of the 1972 agreements was epitomized, according the Soviet thinking, in the "Basic Principles of (Mutual) Relations between the Union of Soviet Socialist Republics and the United States of America."[85] This document officially enshrines the "Principle of Peaceful Coexistence" as the basis for mutual relations between the two powers, and thus, in Soviet eyes, is a proof that the correlation of forces has shifted in favor of socialism.* In an analysis of the summit ac-

---

*As stated in the text of the agreement: "They (the United States and the Soviet Union) will proceed from the common determination that in the nuclear age there is no alternative to conducting their mutual relations on the basis of peaceful coexistence."

cords, Arbatov duly observes: "The fact that the Leninist idea of peaceful coexistence takes the form of contractual relations between states can be considered as a true sign of the times, an important stage of changes taking place in the world, and the result of the active foreign policy of the Soviet Union and the entire socialist community."[86] In short, the adoption by the United States of the principle of "peaceful coexistence" is nothing but a victory for the Soviet Union and world socialism, whose combined forces have prevailed to institute globally the form of struggle which they deem most propitious.

The Conclusion of the Struggle: The Question of Soviet Optimism

Steeped as they are in the sacred texts of Marxism-Leninism, the Soviets display an unshakable belief in the inevitable victory of socialism, brought on by the "inexorable" forces of historical development. Armed with this faith, the Soviets maintain a constant optimism with regard to the continuing success of their foreign policy, which they see as the agent of these forces of "progress." This idea of inevitable victory has been a mandated theme of Soviet commentary since 1917, and expressions of optimism have always been the order of the day—even when prospects for the worldwide advance of socialism were bleakest.

An authoritative analysis of American foreign policy, written a year after the 1972 summit, provides an interesting example of this optimism: "It has become clear that in conducting a policy of antagonism with the Soviet Union, the United States is only weakening its own positions in relations with the other capitalist countries, at the same time losing the competition with socialism."[87] Faced with this prognosis, one is compelled to ask, whether the Soviet doctors would prescribe that the United States instead strengthen its position by conducting a policy of "detente" with the Soviet Union. Indeed, this is exactly the policy they recommend, in their continual exhortations for a mutual relationship under conditions of "peaceful coexistence." When one asks if this does not represent a contradiction in Soviet thinking, the answer is simply, no. The apparent contradiction is nothing but an expression of the fact that the United States has no exit: its defeat is inevitable regardless of the policy line it pursues. As Arbatov observes:

59

The nature of the main contradiction of present-day international relations by no means predetermines the forms in which it manifests itself and is resolved. . . . Although the main contradiction in international relations determines the content of the foreign policy pursued by countries belonging to different social systems, Marxist-Leninists are of the opinion that it cannot be resolved in the sphere of foreign policy (say, by one group of countries forcing other countries to adopt their social system). Here the decisive role is played by the inner processes of the class struggle in society in accordance with the objective laws of its development. Here the crucial point is that essentially it is an antagonistic struggle which leads not to any reciprocal drawing together or even fusion of the two systems . . . but to the victory of the most advanced system, socialism, and to the subsequent reorganization of all international relations in accordance with the laws of life and the development of the new society.[88]

This ritual optimism, which has been expressed both in good times and bad, is very difficult, if not impossible, to distinguish from genuine optimism. During some earlier periods, the Khrushchev era for example, precise predictions were often made as to when the USSR would reach higher stages in the dialectical process—stages representing *qualitative* changes. Since then, however, the Soviet leadership has been less inclined to make rash predictions, and recent expressions of optimism appearing during the early and mid-1970s therefore have been fairly ambiguous. These more general statements have not revealed any extant pessimism but neither have they offered much of a clue as to how Kremlin factions may differ regarding socialism's prospects for success. To gain some insight on how optimistic the Soviet leadership *really is,* and how others within the Kremlin may differ, we must examine the broader context and the patterns of analysis in which these statements appear.

Chapter 2

Domestic Determinants
of U.S. Foreign Policy

Any analysis of Soviet perceptions of U.S. foreign policy must take into account the special emphasis that the Soviets place on the domestic determinants of that policy. True to their Marxist-Leninist ideology, the Soviets see the policy of any capitalist state as a function of the interests of its ruling classes. As one commentator put it: "Bourgeois diplomacy . . . has served the interests of those classes that have their hands on the helm of state power."[1] In analyzing U.S. foreign policy, then, the Soviets must first ask who constitutes the ruling classes. The answer to this question has always been simple and reflexive—"the ruling class of the United States is the monopoly bourgeoisie"—but in recent years Soviet commentary has developed a more sophisticated response. While never denying the validity of the traditional formulation, it adds several qualifications that accord with changes in bourgeois society and in the world in general. As a result, the Soviet press has hosted a conflict between two contrasting views of the United States.

The first of these views is derived from and consistent with the traditional, and primitively orthodox Marxist analysis of capitalism. It has, as a rule, coupled its ritual optimism, born of the conviction that capitalism is on the decline, with cautionary warnings that this same capitalism will attempt to resolve its failings by continuing to follow a predatory course of imperialism and militarism. The second view, which might be termed the "realist" view, offers a more sophisticated analysis of the United States and the world political economy. This analysis is more "realistic" than its older counterpart in that it acknowledges the existence of political forces and trends that have come about, not in contravention to Leninist analysis, but in response to a changed world situation in which strategic parity now exists between the two antagonistic social systems. In contrast to the partisans of the traditionalist view, the "realists" have offered new interpretations of the active political forces in the United States, the "crisis of capitalism," and the foreign policies it spawns.

The Ruling Circles and Other Active Political Forces

Those Soviet analysts who subscribe to the traditionalist view have continued to claim that the U.S. ruling elite comprises "the monopoly families, the directors of the corporations, and the major military and political administrators." These monopolies consist of "some 500 corporations," and the most powerful of the controlling families are "the Morgan, Rockefeller, Dupont, and Mellon groups."[2] The major military and political administrators are characterized as mere servants of the class interests of the monopolies.

These theoreticians have arranged the monopolies themselves in a hierarchy of three main groups. The first group includes the "military-industrial monopolies, the main share of whose production constitutes the fulfillment of government orders for weapons." In the second group one finds those "monopolies with a high level of foreign capital investment or [those] oriented toward the sale of a considerable part of their output in foreign markets, by virtue of which they need corresponding political reinforcement for their interests in foreign countries." Third is the "group of companies, which because of its insignificant volume of foreign sales and investment, is interested primarily in the domestic economic stability of the country and less interested in foreign policy problems."[3] These categories are not seen as mutually exclusive, or even as necessarily competitive, although there may be "contradictions" among them. However, Soviet analysts do discern a hierarchy in terms of their "predominance" in the American economy, and certain monopolies may therefore influence foreign policy more directly than others.

The traditionalist theorists maintain that in recent years the military-industrial monopolies have exercised the greatest influence on U.S. policy making. Although "of the 500 largest U.S. corporations, only around 50 are closely tied to military business," these corporations grew tremendously during the Vietnam War and thus "they have a very high concentration level and have very large opportunities for directly influencing an important U.S. department such as the U.S. Department of Defense."[4] Since these firms are dependent to a large degree on government contracts, Soviet analysts can identify an important reciprocal relationship between them and the state: "The state has been ever more active in promoting the concentration and centralization of capital, which accelerates the growth of the monopolies."[5] The essence of "state-monopoly capitalism," this mutual relationship

> is expressed in the long-established system of relationships between the major financial magnates and the bourgeois governments, in the constant support given by big business to the whole bureaucratic and military political machine and, conversely, in the assistance given by the bourgeois governments to private capital in its operations at home and abroad, in the choice of top government executives and government officials, etc.[6]

It is this system, then, that the traditionalists among Soviet theorists see as perpetuating the paramount influence that military-industrial monopolies exert on U.S. policies.

These monopolies are primarily interested, of course, in expanding the sale of armaments. In light of this exigency, Soviet commentators note that "the development level of the armed forces and armaments has very often been determined by American generals on the basis of subjective assessments of the degree of 'threat.' In these questions, the Pentagon has acted as Supreme Court, judge, and indisputable authority."[7] The source of a particular threat, or the nature of the tension involved, is of little consequence to the military-industrial monopolies, according to Soviet thinking. In 1969, for example, M. Sturua observed that although "we often write of the stock exchange as the true economic barometer of one or another capitalist state," every sign of a peace settlement in Vietnam "has caused a rise of stocks on Wall Street." Asking if this were not a contradiction, he asserted that, no, any war money made by manufacturers of conventional arms will go to nuclear missile manufacturers in peacetime.[8] This line of argument helps these analysts explain the functional importance of the "Soviet threat": in the words of one of them, "playing on the notorious 'Soviet threat' has served and continues to serve as an effective means for exerting ruling-circle pressure on the U.S. public and Congress."[9] Traditional Soviet thinking on the military-industrial complex also leads analysts to emphasize "its desire to intensify or at least maintain international tension" anywhere in the world, in order to "give a more rapid boost to foreign markets for military production."[10] The monopolies, however, cannot stoke international tension by themselves, but must secure the help of the Pentagon, which sends its military missions abroad to help foreign countries plan their armed forces and thus promotes the sale of American weapons. As summarized by one of these traditionalist commentators:

> Business wins relatively stable foreign orders worth billions with corresponding enormous profits. The Pentagon also benefits: the increase in military production output (for foreign orders) leads to lower prices, so the Pentagon can purchase considerably more arms for its own armed forces. In addition, according to the calculations of the military departments, weapons sales are also likely to strengthen U.S. military-political positions abroad.[11]

Of course, since Soviet observers of this type see that these phenomena are "no accident," it follows that the generals, the Pentagon, and the national security apparatus are simply in the service of the monopolies.

The second group in the hierarchy of monopolies—those dependent on foreign operations—is seen as enjoying the fastest growth. Gromyko and Kokoshin have noted that "the growth of these operations is double the growth of domestic industrial production in the U.S. and significantly exceeds the growth of the volume of government expenditures." Alleging that "the sum of the U.S. monopolies' profits from military production and the export of capital constituted over 50 percent of their total profits by the beginning of the 1970s," these same analysts concluded that "this [profit] forms the main material basis of the interests of the ruling class in the conduct by the United States of its foreign policy."[12]

In contrast to the traditionalists, the more sophisticated realist theorists acknowledge the existence of other important factors that influence the American system. Specifically, they have reinterpreted the significance of public opinion, elections, the press, government decision makers, and academics, while reassessing the nature of the "crisis of capitalism" and the methods by which the ruling class copes with it. This reappraisal has amounted to a major revision of the usual Soviet thinking, the upshot of which has been a view of American strengths and weaknesses which differs considerably from that of the traditionalist school.

The contrast between the traditionalist and realist schools become quite apparent when one compares their analyses of public opinion and elections. On the one hand, the traditionalists see public opinion as having little or no influence on major policy decisions since "everything the U.S. does is determined and must be determined only by the interests of the real bosses—the large monopolies."[13] In this view, elections are merely *pro forma,* a sham: "The bourgeois electoral system lets no one escape from the vicious circle where everything revolves around the big money of big business and where it is predetermined who will reach the 'corridors of power." The pathway to those corridors is forbidden to the ordinary man."[14] This view does not deny that congressmen are representatives, but its real emphasis is on *whom* they represent. Referring to a change in congressional attitudes toward East-West trade, E. Shershnev observes: "What brought political dividends to senators and congressmen yesterday, today no longer enjoys popularity among *those who really finance elections*" (my emphasis).[15] Thus, political representation is merely servitude to capital; and insofar as public opinion exists it is a function of manipulation by the monopolies, with whose interests it therefore coincides.

The realist school, on the other hand, entertains the view that public opinion really is influential in the United States. V. Matveyev's subtle acknowledgments of U.S. public opinion are quite representative of the realist approach:

> Sentiments in favor of improving relations with the Soviet Union and other socialist countries have begun to intensify in the United States under the influence of the failures of Washington's aggressive course. . . . Some figures in the U.S., adopting the old anticommunist position, are concerned about the increased might and economic capabilities of the Soviet Union, and are intimidating the *ordinary citizen* with the "Soviet danger" and calling for the con-

tinuation of the "from a position of strength" policy. . . . It is not surprising that such a recommendation is increasingly engendering active *protest* in the U.S. itself. In the minds of *ordinary Americans* the question arises completely logically: "If the 'from a position of strength' policy has failed before, why should it be crowned with success now, with a changed correlation of forces?" . . . There were figures . . . who raved about a crusade against socialism. Now such appeals are *scarcely taken seriously*. It is not by chance that during this year's presidential election campaign [1972], the theme of improving relations with the socialist countries is being used by all contenders for the presidency without exception in order to increase their chances. . . . In light of the *moods of the American public,* it is becoming increasingly difficult to speak directly against the normalization and development of these relations. [My emphasis][16]

Another analyst, Iu. A. Shvedkov, goes so far as to examine the individual strata of the American public, an approach that would seem to assume that they have some sort of political influence:

For the first time, it is not only for narrow segments of the population—for example, small businessmen, farmers, provincial politicians—but also for broader public circles, including university intellectuals, student groups, and some of the monopoly bourgeoisie, that foreign policy has begun to seem too expensive; it is necessary to pay for it with the lives of young Americans and high taxes. The involvement of broad segments of the public in the discussion of the questions of foreign policy represents a factor which, for the time being, remains in effect in the United States. . . . President Nixon and his advisers, undoubtedly, have shown a great amount of attention to these moods, and that is not by accident. The American public, as is well known, does not have any great influence upon current foreign policy making.[17]

While clearly admitting that public opinion is influential, Shvedkov simultaneously reminds the reader that it lacks "any great influence" in policy making. His emphasis is crucial, for it prevents him from having to weigh the relative influence of these various segments of the public—a form of analysis that might violate the ideological strictures within which he is constrained to work.

Another observer, however, notes that an entire foreign policy initiative, the Nixon Doctrine, has been aimed "not only—and perhaps not so much . . ."at the solution of international problems in and of themselves, as at the mollification of American *public opinion,* at lessening the pressure that the aggravated domestic problems exert upon the administration, and at preventing the consequences of those moods, which might be detrimental to the party that is in power" (my emphasis).[18] The "detrimental" consequences referred to are, of course, the loss of power to the other bourgeois party, a threat on which G. Trofimenko elaborates:

> The optimum policy for any government of a bourgeois country is either to ignore public opinion or to create an artificial climate of support for official policy in the country by means of the propagandist manipulation of public opinion. However, as has been shown by the American people's reaction to the aggression in Vietnam, the possibilities for such manipulation are not infinite. Moments arise when the split between the sentiments and feelings of broad public circles and official policy prove so deep, that a bourgeois government, wishing to remain in power, has either to correct official policy or to resign from power and hand over the reins of government to another grouping (party) of the ruling class.[19]

Several years later, the same commentator made this point even more sharply:

> The ruling classes of the West have been forced to consider, to a greater degree than before, the opinion of the popular masses. It is not by chance that in 1970, at the height of the mass antiwar demonstrations, the U.S. vice-president said in all seriousness, "Will the government of our country remain in the hands of its elected officials or will it pass into the hands of the people on the streets?"[20]

There is some evidence that these more sophisticated views (which in 1971 could almost be characterized as avant-garde) were, by the mid-1970s, becoming something of a commonplace in the Soviet press. The preceding quotations are taken from lengthy articles by Soviet specialists on the United States—logically the first to take a more subtle and complex approach to their subject. But by 1975 one can find A. Krivopalov writing the following in a very small and routine news article from the daily government newspaper: "Under pressure of U.S. public opinion, the Senate has passed and sent to the President for signature a bill under which appropriations for military construction are reduced by $500 million compared with the sum requested by the government."[21]

Given this range of views, one can conclude that Soviet analysts believe that the greatest power of American public opinion is its ability to force changes either in the policy of the ruling party or in the configuration of circles which holds power. At the same time, however, the Soviets see the bourgeois nature of the American system as limiting the potential influence of public opinion, for, short of revolution, the public can only force changes in the means and methods of ruling class policy. Thus, although public pressure may have forced the U.S. government to adopt a new foreign policy doctrine—one with a lesser degree of overt aggression—Soviet commentators repeatedly insist that the basically exploitative and aggressive nature of the bourgeois system of government is unchanged.

Studying these statements about American public opinion, one notes a marked tendency to recognize the influence of public opinion when that opinion coincides with Soviet interests and the Soviet foreign-policy line. In all of the examples discussed here—detente, defense spending, and Vietnam—the American opinions cited dovetail with the aims of Soviet policy. Since such coincidence is generally the case in Soviet commentary on U.S. public opinion, one can generalize that even the realists among Soviet observers continue to tailor their analyses to the interests of the Soviet state. Only rarely do Soviet analysts portray the American masses as something other than "progressive" in spirit. One interesting example is this admission, printed in an October 1972 *Izvestiia*, that the American public revealed two tendencies toward the Vietnam War:

Everyone is dissatisfied with the war. . . . Despite the dissatisfaction, the polls show that it is precisely R. Nixon whom the majority of Americans are prepared to give "another chance." Precisely to Nixon, and not McGovern, who proposes immediately to stop the bombing, to withdraw from Indochina, and to deny support to the Saigon regime. A paradox? Yes, for those who know about the antiwar protests and not about the average American. In the American's eyes, the war is a minus for the Republican candidate but even a greater minus for the radical antiwar program of the Democratic candidate since the latter's policy is a retreat from chauvinistic concepts and conventional rhetoric about "American honor" and "loyalty to its allies" (Saigon puppets). "They [average Americans] do not like war but neither do they like defeat," . . . says S. Alsop.[22]

Other examples of the "nonprogressive" attitudes of the American electorate are cited in the Soviet press, but many of these are explained as a function of the "bribery" of the masses by the ruling class and the inculcation of the infectious mentality of "consumerism."

The new realist assessment would seem to revise the traditional ideological explanation. After all, if the only effective political force in a capitalist regime is the bourgeois ruling class, does not the admission of the political influence of public opinion constitute a major ideological departure? The answer to this is decidedly negative. The realist assessment of public opinion does constitute a revision but it is perfectly consistent with a major line of orthodox Marxism-Leninism—namely, that the masses' role in policymaking is increasing throughout the world, and that the influence of the "workers movement is growing inexorably everywhere." The Soviets' view of the increasing importance of international propaganda,[23] their actual dissemination of such propaganda, and their substantial commentary on the antiwar movement in the United States constitute both theoretical and practical testimony in support of the ideological acceptability of this line. The new, more sophisticated analysts of U.S. policy are thus not less ideologically pure than the traditionalists, at least in their treatment of public opinion. They are simply more realistic; they have been able to describe an American political process with much greater accuracy while remaining faithful to a conception of history that is predicated on the axiom that the influence of the masses is increasing.

Still, the realists do not go too far. As the above quotations testify, they are reluctant to view public opinion as anything more than a tool, however useful, of the ruling class. They simply cannot abandon the idea that this class, so long as it exists, will be the force that decides state policy. In accordance with this view, these analysts conclude that most of the struggles in bourgeois society occur between segments of the ruling class.

The Soviets observe that such "domestic struggle becomes exacerbated" during election years, when "many problems are uncovered and come to light."[24] However, as Arbatov notes, a student of the United States "is always in a contradictory position" when viewing American elections, for, while a real struggle *is* occurring, the observer also notes that "an empty duel rages between political rivals, and the public is showered with such a torrent of political speeches, documents, and statements that it becomes particularly difficult to discern the pivotal salients of the real struggle taking place in the country and within its ruling circles."[25] Primary among the distracting elements that make it so difficult for Soviet observers to distinguish the outlines of the "real struggle" is the duel between the Republican and Democratic parties. Soviet analysts, both traditionalist and realist, see the differences between the two parties as negligible and essentially limited to tactical considerations. As Arbatov notes:

> The real differences between the platforms of the two principal bourgeois parties and their presidential candidates are, as a rule, relatively hypothetical, and this is understandable. If one disregards pre-election rhetoric, it is usually a question of nuances in the methods and forms utilized to pursue the uniform two-party policy of the ruling class, forms and methods which do not leave much scope for displaying the personal views and inclinations of any given candidate.[26]

Anatoly Gromyko, a traditionalist, puts it similarly:

> While the aim . . . to retain and strengthen American imperialism's positions in the world . . . is the long-term and sole aim of the entire ruling class in the United States, and of the bourgeois parties and bourgeois states which serve it, disagreements can exist within the various groupings of the ruling class as to the means and methods by which this end may be achieved. These disagreements are manifest in one form or another in the struggle between the two main bourgeois parties—Republican and Democrat—and between the factions in these parties for the right and privilege of serving the interests, including the foreign policy interests, of the ruling elite.[27]

Thus, both parties are depicted as bourgeois parties that serve the interests of the ruling class. The dynamics of this process were detailed in a 1972 article by Nekrasov and Kolesnichenko:

> Concealing, on account of class solidarity, those provisions of the draft budget which openly show that its main purpose is directed toward the creation of favorable conditions for big business and the stimulation of big capital, the Democrats at the same time denounce the buildup of military expenditures. . . . The concept of the foreign policy "from a position of strength" is being rejected now in America by those strata of the population who still quite recently looked upon it more or less calmly. Even among the ruling circles of the U.S., dissatisfaction with the dominance of militarism in the country's economy is intensifying. "The policy of 'from a position of strength' is destructive," stresses Senator J. W. Fulbright. . . . However, in practice, the Democrats limit their criticism of the economic policy of the Republicans: they did not advance a constructive program for the recuperation of the American economy. Life has often shown that the Democrats, like the Republicans, are a party of big business, and upon assumption of power, quietly forget their campaign promises, discard their campaign slogans. and faithfully serve the interests of capital.[28]

In this connection, the Soviets also observe that the Republican and Democratic parties do not follow consistently divergent policies. In reference to certain of Richard Nixon's domestic policies, for example, his "New Economic Policy," Arbatov notes: "Under pressure of necessity he has repeatedly abandoned the traditional planks of Republican political philosophy and has adopted and implemented many tenets taken from the political platform of his rivals."[29]

The theory that both parties serve only the interests of capital is further buttressed by the Soviet view that the ruling classes have no substantial *organized* opposition in society. Although the working class is seen as a natural opposition, its official representatives, in this case George Meany and his AFL-CIO, are considered "loyal allies of the ruling circles" and "lackeys of imperialism."[30] Furthermore, the trade-union bosses are said to "struggle for the continuation and intensification of the arms race, persuading the workers that if it were not for this, they would be unemployed."[31] Thus, with the exception of such mass protests as the movement against the Vietnam War, the people as a whole are often seen as too helpless to combat the ruling forces. This helplessness is manifested, the Soviets argue, in the apathetic attitude toward elections among Americans, "who do not see real opportunities for their hopes to be realized."[32] As usual, the Soviets do not ascribe this situation to an "accidental" turn of events, but blame this apathy on the calculations of the ruling classes. On the eve of the 1976 elections, V. Sisnev wrote that "the possibility is being predicted that only a small proportion of adult Americans will turn up at polling stations on November 2 and that the majority in favor of one side or another will be negligible. But in this event, everyone will lose except his majesty, capital."[33]

The orchestration of political campaigns as a whole is also seen as the work of the ruling classes. Not only are they the ones who "really finance elections," but they also are seen as deceiving the public about the real nature of political struggles. Again Sisnev's article sets forth the typical Soviet view:

> Battles of words between the aspirants to the White House are served up every day by the mass media like communiques from theaters of combat operations: the voter must see that an earnest political duel is taking place, in which the rivals rain blows on each other without mercy. The clanking of armor and the warlike cries must distract the spectators from the thought of why, exactly, are lances being broken and what difference is there in principle between the warring parties?[34]

Despite the plethora of references to this "empty duel," Arbatov (who often indulges in such descriptions himself) cautions that "it would be wrong" to conclude that "the entire polemic, the entire struggle taking place within U.S. ruling circles is unimportant and amounts to no more than a mere personal competition between pretenders, or attempts to deceive the public."[35] Rather, he says, "there is a struggle in progress"—but a struggle that is animated by the "more complex contradictions" within the ruling class which are in turn determined by various aggravations of the domestic economic situation and developments in the international arena. Specifically, Arbatov sees a struggle over "national priorities," over "the issue of what is to occupy the predominant place in U.S. policy and of which problems and tasks are to receive the major resources and efforts."[36] This struggle, which is seen as having engendered a

72

major rift within the American ruling class, will be discussed in connection with our analysis of the Soviet concept of the "crisis of capitalism."

Soviet analyses of the press and its control by the ruling class also illustrate the contrast between the two Soviet assessments of American political forces. According to the traditionalist Soviet line, there is no true "freedom of the press" in the United States. Freedom of the press belongs to those who own the press—the monopoly capitalists—and "the press serves as a reliable instrument in the hands of monopoly capital and governments that are obedient to monopoly capital."[37] Given this basic outlook, Soviet analysis enjoys exposing various connections between the monopolies, the government, and the press. The CIA, as part of a government ostensibly "obedient" to monopoly capital, is thus depicted as heavily involved in the media: "It became known that at least 29 percent of the CIA's secret operations over the course of a number of years had been conducted in the sphere of mass information and propaganda."[38] When confronted with disclosures in the American press as to the "criminal activity" of the CIA—an organization that could presumably prevent such embarrassing revelations—a Soviet commentator could only muster (or perhaps bluster) this response: "These dirty deeds of U.S. intelligence became well known not thanks to the 'freedom of the press' in the United States, but, it may be said, despite it. And it was not for nothing that the journalist Daniel Schorr, who was the first to dare to come out in a newspaper with the details of the secret investigation, is being threatened with severe punishment."[39] In the traditionalist view, then, the press is a pliant instrument in the hands of a homogeneous ruling class. Revelations, like those about the CIA, are aberrations; generally they concern acts of malfeasance which will be severely punished by this class.

In contrast, the realist school has advanced a more sophisticated analysis. Again in reference to the revelations about CIA practices, Shvedkov explains:

> The scandalous exposures of Washington's policy, which were expressed first in the publication of the secret Pentagon documents on the war in Vietnam and then the protocols on the White House meeting during the conflict on the Hindustan peninsula, are by no means random initiatives by individual persons. These "bureau-

cratic scandals" are above all the results of the keen rivalry in the ruling clique of Washington, a result of the struggle for power and influence.[40]

This explanation clearly implies that the American press is not simply another tentacle of the only octopus on the block, but that it sometimes serves as an instrument for the sallies of political rivals. By implication, then, the realists among Soviet analysts attribute greater independence to the press than do those who see it simply as an appendage of the monolithic ruling class.

A similar difference exists between traditionalist and realist analyses of the role of individual decision makers and the government bureaucracies to which they belong. The traditionalist view has long held that since all American political leaders owe their positions to the influence of their monopoly-capitalist patrons, these leaders will, as a rule, loyally serve their class interests. Independent political action is interpreted as a temporary divergence from ruling class interests, for, according to the traditionalists, U.S. decision makers must work to serve the ruling class interest over the long term if they are to guarantee the survival of the social system. In this view, then, no leader can be truly independent, for the prolonged exhibition of such independence will incite the ruling class to expel the offending leader and rectify the situation.

In contrast, the realist analysis admits that truly independent policy makers can and do exist in the United States. For example, as Inozemtsev explains, "contradictions" may arise between the monopolies and the state because "the state has a measure of independence" which may allow it to act against the interests of the monopolies, especially when there is a conflict between national and local interests.[41] The realists also point out that the institutional powers of an office such as the presidency give its incumbent considerable independence.[42] Furthermore, they observe that government bureaucracies may possess discretionary powers that can be exercised independently not only of monopoly control but even of presidential influence.[43] Again, however, one must note that this realist approach often tends, like most Soviet propaganda, to contain a substantial normative element. When Soviet commentators cite a given president's act as "independent," there is generally a direct correspondence between those acts and the foreign-policy interests of the Soviet Union.

The same pattern emerges when one examines Soviet perceptions of the American academic world and the products of American scholarship. Traditionalist commentators have long portrayed American scholars and researchers as the paid "lackeys" of big capital, applying this caricature to all the various "bourgeois ideologists" and "Sovietologists." In their view, these "lackeys" are not only paid to rationalize the aggressive policies of "imperialism" but also used in international propaganda and psychological warfare to "subvert" the thinking of people around the world. With the intensification of the "domestic struggle" in the United States, however, Soviet realists have noted that many academics have protested the more nefarious tactics of the bourgeoisie and the military-industrial complex, adopting an especially vocal stance on Vietnam and such strategic arms issues as the ABM. The realist analysts no longer attack such scholars as academic prostitutes but instead speak approvingly of their "independence." Again, however, one notes that the greater the coincidence between the opinions of American scholars and the aims of Soviet foreign policy, the greater the degree of "independence" attributed to them by Soviet analysts.

Internal Contractions and the Crisis of Capitalism

The study of "contradictions" is the primary method by which Soviet analysts rationalize and reconcile the inconsistencies of Marxism-Leninism and its misinterpretations of politics, economics, and society. "Contradictions" include both the situations of social antagonism postulated by Marx and Lenin and any inconsistency in the general theory brought on by new and unforeseen historical circumstances. The use of this "technique" of "contradictions" analysis is a tricky business, however, for while it allows a broader scope for the imaginations of "creative" Marxist-Leninist analysts, it does not delineate the permissible limits of interpretation, a step beyond which would constitute "revisionism"—a grave and punishable ideological sin. Nevertheless, this technique is indispensable to Soviet analysts, for without it, they would be hard-pressed to explain innumerable situations plausibly.

Taken together, the contradictions of bourgeois American society constitute what the Soviets are fond of calling the "crisis of capitalism." Though the "general crisis of capitalism" comprehends both domestic and international contradictions, this section will be restricted to those of a domestic nature—contradictions that the Soviets believe to be crucial to the general nature of American society, and therefore, to its foreign policy. Indeed, Soviet analysts see this link between domestic political forces and U.S. foreign policy as the most intriguing variable of analysis, for, in their view, the domestic nature of American society not only predetermines its foreign policy, but its foreign policy is often part and parcel of domestic political struggles, the result being the often incomprehensible "zigzags" that mark American behavior in international affairs. These "zigzags" (which, of course, are characteristic of all human behavior, political or otherwise), constitute an irksome obstacle to the rigid patterns of Marxist-Leninist "scientific" analysis, with its vaunted ability to predict the flow of social processes. Thus, the sophisticated Soviet analysts, in particular, resort to rationalizing such "zigzags" as "contradictions."

In orthodox Marxist-Leninist theory the principal contradiction in capitalist society is that "between the social character of production and the private capitalist form of the appropriation of its results."[44] This contradiction, of course, explains both the "exploitative" nature of bourgeois society and the "antagonism" between labor and capital. The traditionalists see the "workers' movement" and the "strike movement" as a direct consequence of this antagonism. This view leads Soviet analysis into a blatant self-contradiction, for they view the leaders of the American trade unions as allies and servants of the bourgeoisie. Still, Soviet analysts constantly assert that real workers' movements exist in the United States and that they are developing independently. Indeed, the traditionalist theorists seem dogmatically bent on convincing themselves that these "movements" exist as such.

Soviet statisticians dutifully compile data on the outbreaks of strikes throughout the capitalist world, the sum of which constitutes the so-called strike movement. As Boris Ponomarev, chairman of the CPSU Central Committee's International Section, declared in January 1974: "Every day brings fresh news of the growth of the strike struggle. Strikes are developing into demonstrations and meetings, into occupations of enterprises, and into acute conflicts between national trade centers and governments."[45] Although Ponomarev was probably referring to strikes that had recently occurred in Western Europe, his remarks reveal the general theoretical context with which the Soviets treat contemporary capitalism. By implication, the United States is among those capitalist states that will be subject to inevitable and intensified contradictions. In any case, many Soviet commentators[46] tally the numerous "strike battles" in the United States, concluding that the results of such conflict between labor and capital are, in the words of one traditionalist commentator:

> the erosion of the old "worker aristocracy," changing the position as well of those strata of workers in a more privileged position, and shattering the myths, cultivated for many years in the West, on the "mass consumption" society and the "conflictless" development of a "neocapitalist" system. . . . There is an ever increasing expansion of the strata of workers whose level of class and political consciousness is growing more rapidly than previously, and opportunistic prejudices of the "pragmatic," Gompers type are being surmounted.[47]

The economic manifestations of the crisis of capitalism are described by the traditionalists as occurring in a recurrent pattern: depression, recovery, and boom. There are many causes for this pattern, but the most basic is the so-called crisis of overproduction, a phenomenon described by Marx and still considered universally valid by both schools of Soviet analysts. This "crisis of overproduction" is the result of the entire dynamic of capitalism as described in *Das Kapital* and other writings, and is akin, incidentally, to the Keynesian concept of "underconsumption." Essentially, the process is based on the production of "surplus value," the harnessing by capital of the forces of production (i.e., labor) such that they produce above and beyond what is "necessary."[48] Marx explained that "the worker receives means of subsistence in exchange for his labor power, but the capitalist receives in exchange for his means of subsistence labor, the productive activity of the worker, the creative power whereby the worker not only replaces what he consumes but gives to the accumulated labor a greater value than it previously possessed."[49] The continuing accumulation of surplus value, which of course entails the exploitation of the worker, is the basis for the growth of capital, the portentous consequences of which Marx expressed as follows:

The more productive capital grows, the more the division of labor and the application of machinery expands. The more the division of labor and the application of machinery expands, the more competition among workers expands and the more wages contract. . . . The working class gains recruits from the higher strata of society; a mass of petty industrialists and small rentiers are hurled down into its ranks. . . . That the small industrialist cannot survive in a contest one of the first conditions of which is to produce on an ever greater scale, that is, precisely to be a large and not a small industrialist, is self-evident. . . . Finally as the capitalists are compelled, by the movement described above, to exploit the already existing gigantic means of production on a larger scale and to set in motion all the mainsprings of credit to this end, there is a corresponding increase in industrial earthquakes, in which the trading world can only maintain itself by sacrificing a part of wealth, of products and even of productive forces to the gods of the nether world—in a word, crises increase. They become frequent and more violent, if only because, as the mass of production, and consequently the need for extended markets, grows, the world becomes more and more contracted, fewer and fewer new markets remain available for exploitation, since every preceding crisis has subjected to world trade a market hitherto unconquered or only superficially exploited.[50]

As Marx and Engels wrote a year later, in their *Communist Manifesto*:

It is enough to mention the commercial crises that, by their periodical return put on its trial, each time more threateningly, the existence of the entire bourgeois society. In these crises a great part not only of the existing products, but also of the previously created productive forces, are periodically destroyed. In these crises there breaks out an epidemic that, in all earlier epochs, would have seemed an absurdity—the epidemic of over-production. Society suddenly finds itself put back into a state of momentary barbarism; it appears as if a famine, a universal war of devastation had cut off the supply of every means of subsistence; industry and commerce seem to be destroyed; and why? Because there is too much civilisation, too much means to subsistence, too much industry, too much commerce. The productive forces at the disposal of society no longer tend to further the development of the conditions of bourgeois property; on the contrary, they have become too powerful for these conditions, by which they are fettered, and so soon as they overcome these fetters, they bring disorder into the whole of bourgeois society, endanger the existence of bourgeois property. The conditions of bourgeois society are too narrow to comprise the wealth created by them. And how does the bourgeoisie get over these crises? On the one hand by enforced destruction of a mass of productive forces; on the other by the conquest of new markets and by the more thorough exploitation of old ones. That is to say, by paving the way for more extensive and more destructive crises, and by diminishing the means whereby crises are prevented.[51]

These passages are quoted at length because they amount to a precis of the existing Soviet interpretation of the most basic economic problems of capitalism. The grudging admiration that Marx and Engels express for the powers of economic growth under laissez-faire capitalism is also reflected in contemporary Soviet thinking, though ironically, the traditionalists have been comparatively silent on this score. Whereas the traditionalists consistently disparage or deny the strengths of capitalism, the realists are more true to the views of Marx and Engels. While continuing to condemn the immorality of capitalism, they have not let their self-righteousness blind them to its real strengths. Thus, these realists recognize the regenerative power of the capitalist system and illustrate it through their frequent analyses of the boom-and-bust cycles of American economic history.[52] Similarly, they are willing to acknowledge the high levels of American production and of scientific and technical progress, a subject to be treated in detail below.

One should not conclude, however, that the realists believe that the concept of the "ongoing crisis of capitalism" is nonsense or has outlived its usefulness. Rather, their more realistic observations of the American economic system are the product of a more sophisticated method of analysis which carries with it, of course, a greater credibility. The realists may admit to those aspects of capitalism which work toward its survival, but they analyze its weaknesses with equal sophistication. Thus, Soviet realists have conducted quite plausible analyses of two related aspects of the latest stage in the crisis of capitalism—the international monetary crisis that was marked by the breakdown of the Bretton Woods system, and the subsequent, unprecedented rise of "stagflation," a phenomenon that empirically invalidated the body of economic thought by which the American economy had been run for some forty years.[53] These events are of "crisis" proportion from any ideological perspective, yet the Soviet realists have analyzed them without resorting to the undocumented and polemical prognoses of capitalism's imminent collapse which are the standard fare of most traditionalist Soviet tracts.

In sum, then, Soviet analysis suggests that capitalism, while inherently self-destructive, is capable of some regeneration, though these recuperative powers lessen as the cycle of boom and bust recurs and capitalism confronts the growing economic and military might of the socialist community. Nevertheless, the crises that capitalism inflicts upon itself (and the world) remain the subject of intense scrutiny and criticism by the Soviets. Even though the "scientific" techniques of Marxist-Leninist analysis can predict the path of capitalism's development, capitalism's internal contradictions can lead to unpredictable results. The convulsions of capitalism may produce a communist revolution, a Hitler, or something as yet unforeseen. For all the certainty of their "scientific" methods, then, Soviet analysts must maintain a constant vigilance.

Coping with the Crisis of Capitalism

In addition to scrutinizing the crisis of capitalism, the Soviets have paid close attention to the efforts of the ruling class to cope with the crisis. Orthodox criteria, as usual, have established the framework for all analysis, but within those limits we can again discern different schools of thought.

The traditionalists have likened the severity of the capitalist economic crisis of the 1970s to that of the Great Depression of the thirties,[54] arguing, of course, that this situation fosters "the development of the material prerequisites for socialism."[55] One of these prerequisites is the activation of the forces of the workers' movement, precisely the group that the traditionalists see as allied with the Soviet Union and the socialist community of states in the great worldwide struggle for socialism. In the traditionalist Soviet view, the onslaught of workers' demands affects American foreign policy, forcing the monopoly bourgeoisie to attempt to "fortify its economic and military positions, extend the basis for its social maneuvering, and improve the means of ideological indoctrination of the masses."[56] The last of these tactics, the intensification of the ideological indoctrination of the masses, entails procedures that we have already discussed: the manipulation by the monopolists of both the press and various academic "ideologists." In addition, however, the ruling classes are said to resort to three main methods in their attempt to fortify their economic and military positions: the use of the "scientific-technical revolution," the use of "militarism," and the increased use of the state.

According to recent Soviet theory, the general crisis of capitalism has become so severe that the ruling class has had to employ, more than ever before, the fruits of science and technology to strengthen and perpetuate its economic domination. As Inozemtsev explained in his book on contemporary capitalism, the monopoly bourgeoisie is impelled "to the most extensive development of scientific and technical progress and its use for its own ends, whether the self-seeking ends of maximizing monopoly profits and superprofits, or the more general aims of the bourgeoisie as a whole linked with the preservation of capitalism as a system."[57]

This emphasis has, in the Soviet view, not always characterized capitalism. Indeed, Soviet analysts detect two opposing attitudes toward science and technology under the capitalist system—one that favors progress and one that tends toward stagnation. Traditional Soviet analysts have held that the latter attitude often has predominated, turning to Lenin for their explanation, as in this quotation from a recent Soviet text: "Since monopoly prices are established, even temporarily, the motive cause of technical, and consequently, of all other progress disappears to a certain extent, and further, the economic possibility arises of deliberately retarding technical progress." Thus, as the textbook's author concludes, "the capitalist monopolies, who gain monopoly superprofits by establishing monopoly prices, often prevent the introduction of new machines."[58] Moreover, these same monopolists are seen as limiting and even reducing output and delaying the introduction of important inventions for years. As one commentator observes elsewhere in the same text: "alongside the rapid introduction of many scientific and technological innovations, the powerful monopoly unions are hiding patents by the hundred in their safes."[59]

The realist theorists, in contrast, have advanced a new analysis—one that stresses the rise of the world socialist community and the intensification of the struggle between this community and capitalism as factors influencing a shift in the capitalists' approach to science and technology. Admitting that stagnation was once a frequent characteristic, and that scientific and technical progress was seen primarily as a function of competition between monopolies, the realists argue that "today it has become literally a matter of life and death both for the monopolies and for capitalism as such."[60] Inozemtsev attributes this change to "capitalism's fear of lagging behind, being defeated in the economic competition with socialism, and finding itself in an unfavorable position in terms of military-industrial potential."[61] Thus, in the contemporary era, the monopoly capitalists are seen as irrevocably committed to maximizing the potential of the scientific-technical revolution.

Soviet analysts also disagree as to the effectiveness of the bourgeoisie's attempts to exploit science and technology. The traditionalists, on the one hand, see the adoption of the scientific-technical revolution as exacerbating capitalism's inherent contradictions and even creating new ones. According to F. Konstantinov, contemporary capitalism, by using the results of scientific and technical progress, "has become even more antipopular, antihumane, and inhuman, causing a growth in the struggle of the working class and a stormy movement of protest by youth against bourgeois society, in which the science and technology created by man's genius are turning against mankind and becoming a force that is increasingly alien and hostile to it."[62] These remarkable comments are entirely in accord with Marxist-Leninist orthodoxy. As Konstantinov explains, the fundamental source of this "evil antihumanism" lies not in science and technology per se—this is alleged to be the explanation put forward by bourgeois ideologists—but rather in "the social attitudes of capitalist society, where the main motive and incentive force of monopoly activities is the acquisition of maximum profit, and where man is the instrument and the means of achieving this aim." Konstantinov goes on to argue that

> modern forces of production are becoming increasingly powerful and production is becoming increasingly collectivized, combining tens and even hundreds of thousands of hired laborers in the enterprises of the gigantic corporations and conglomerates. At the

same time, private ownership of the means of production and the gigantic profits of a small group of capitalist magnates accentuate even more the incompatibility of the social nature of production with private means of appropriating its results.

The realist theorists may at first seem utterly traditional in their emphasis on the contradictions that the scientific-technical revolution brings to capitalism. But, as we shall see, their analysis ultimately diverges from the traditionalist view in certain important particulars. One realist analyst thus sounds quite traditional when he observes that the introduction of scientific and technical achievements, by substituting machines for men, creates unemployment. He finds that "in many industrialized countries some categories of workers cannot find jobs because they lack the necessary general education and are incapable of rapidly adapting to the almost ceaseless changes in the technology and organization of production."[63] This situation in turn creates an "acute contradiction between the rapidly growing demands on the working people's skills and education made by scientific and technical progress and the general education and vocational training system, with its social and class barriers, characteristic of the bourgeois countries." This new contradiction, of course, contributes to the growing anger of the working class and sharpens its hostility to the monopolists.

Though such "scientifically" derived arguments contain a certain logic and plausibility, they always lead to the same conclusion: capitalism is in a "no-exit" situation. Even when an escape from the current, seemingly fatal contradiction is discovered, Soviet analysts, both traditionalist and realist, will claim that it is only temporary and the result of further "contradictions." We have seen, for example, that the argument of insufficient education is used to postulate the exacerbation of class contradictions. Nevertheless, Inozemtsev himself notes that because of the demands of scientific and technical progress, education is being promoted in the capitalist world and especially in the United States.[64] This development is, of course, a function of the effort by the monopoly capitalists to adapt the scientific and technical revolution to bourgeois reality and thus avoid the sharpening of internal contradictions. Observing this same phenomenon, however, Yermolenko argues that this effort "to raise the educational level of a certain section of the working people" and "increase the proportion of intellectuals among the total number of people at work" is, "to a certain extent, . . . also changing the class structure of bourgeois society." He concludes that "the number of skilled workers is rising as is the workers' general educational standard, and the ranks of the working class are being supplemented by a considerable number of people originating from among the intelligentsia and the middle classes, a process which has helped to raise the working classes' awareness and its role in society and the anti-imperialist struggle."[65] According to this view, then, increased education raises the political consciousness of the working class, thereby intensifying the class struggle. Thus, either way, through more or less education, the contradictions are exacerbated.

The capitalist adoption of the scientific-technical revolution has also led to environmental pollution and the "ecological crisis," an effect that the Soviet realists also express in terms of a contradiction:

> the contradiction between the new prospects for the use of natural resources and for transforming nature in the interests of man and of society as a whole, prospects which are opened up by science and technology, on the one hand, and on the other, the threat of environment pollution arising from the domination of private property, under which the drive for profit is the overriding consideration.[66]

The same commentator stresses the international implications of this contradiction, arguing that "when one country pollutes the atmosphere or the seas and oceans, it has a negative effect on other countries." The ecological crisis thus gives the popular forces of international socialism yet another target on which to focus their struggle against capitalism. In addition, Soviet analysts note that the ecological crisis has spurred a severe domestic reaction. As Arbatov observes, "It is not by accident that the concept of 'zero growth'— that is, remaining at the given level both of economic development and population size—has emerged and gained certain credence in the West as a special kind of reaction to these negative consequences."[67]

Despite agreement on many points, however, the realist school has made some observations that militate against the traditionalist emphasis on the deleterious consequences of capitalism's adoption of the scientific-technical revolution. The realists recognize, for example, that when confronted with the rising "workers' movement," their "strike struggles," and their concomitant demands for a better life, the monopoly bourgeoisie feels constrained to implement measures that will mollify the workers and guarantee the survival of the system. Furthermore, the realists believe that in such situations the scientific-technical revolution can be used to advantage by the capitalists. As Inozemtsev explains, "Only through the wide use of scientific and technical achievements can monopoly capital now reduce its labor costs and create material possibilities for its policy of social maneuvering. Higher productivity through the use of improved and more efficient hardware and further intensification of labor make it possible not only to maintain but even to boost capitalist profits while allowing some increase in wages."[68] In striking contrast to the traditionalist view, then, some realists believe that the capitalists *can* exploit the scientific-technical revolution to bribe the workers while fortifying their own positions of power.

The realists' discussion of "creation versus destruction"[69] also demonstrates their belief that the capitalists can use science and technology successfully. This concept refers to the dichotomy between the unprecedented, creative potential of science and technology and the possibility that this potential will be diverted to purely destructive, military purposes. Inozemtsev argues, for example, that "imperialism tends to distort the very substance and idea of progress, converting great scientific discoveries and the vast potentialities of modern technology into sources of evil."[70] Even as they condemn the "evil" of militarism, however, the realists implicitly admit that capitalism has managed to use science and technology to strengthen its position.

Soviet traditionalists, in addition to treating militarism as a function of the scientific-technical revolution, see it as yet another method by which monopoly capital fortifies its economic and military positions against the onslaught of the workers' movement and the growing power of the socialist community. As Lenin once noted, in an oft-repeated remark: "Militarism is the weapon used by the ruling classes to suppress any kind (economic or political) of proletarian movements."[71] A. Migolat'ev applies this formula to American society in a manner that clearly demonstrates the traditional Soviet point of view: "It is well known . . . that in the United

States, militarism is the weapon for suppressing the working class, who are increasingly actively developing the struggle not only for their economic needs, but also for political rights. Militarism is used as a means of terror against the 25 million-strong Negro population."[72] Thus, though militarism is primarily an aspect of foreign policy, it has a domestic side as well—one which, according to Soviet analysts, contributes to the "contradictory" nature of American society and, as a result, conditions its foreign policy behavior.

A primary goal of militarism, according to the traditionalists, is to create gigantic profits for the monopolies of the military-industrial complex. These profits are seen not only as perpetuating the existing complex, but strengthening its positions through an intensification of the monopolization process. As Iu. Bobrakov observes, "Militarism . . . is becoming a constant and 'chronic' factor in the entire financial system of the bourgeois state." As such, militarism is said to be dependent upon "the development of the monopolies and the intensification of their domination in the economies and policies of the capitalist states. State-monopoly development is accompanied by the growing concentration of colossal financial resources in state hands and the subordination of the use of these resources to the same aims as the state itself serves."[73] Such an analysis posits the existence of two reciprocal relationships: first, while the military-industrial complex requires more militarism, militarism, in turn, requires a greater growth of this complex; and second, while the monopolies with vested interests in militarism require the increased cooperation of the state and its vast resources, the state, attempting to fulfill its obligations to the ruling class by increasing its sponsorship of militarism, requires larger and more concentrated monopolies in order to handle the volume of the vast financial inputs necessary for production. The net result is an increase in militarism and a growing concentration of monopoly power.

In the traditionalist point of view, contemporary militarism also seeks to provoke and maintain international tension. Such tension not only ensures a continuing demand for the products of the military-industrial monopolies, but also sustains a climate for carrying out a general policy of "imperialism," from which all the other monopolies foresee broader benefits.

Soviet analysts agree that these domestic aspects of militarism stimulate their own contradictions in both the foreign and domestic spheres, but in turning to the specific nature of these contradictions, we again find that the traditionalists and realists are not in full agreement. Both sides do accept what Arbatov terms the "dialectic of militarism," a phenomenon first observed by Engels, who wrote that "militarism conceals within itself the embryo of its own destruction . . . [and] will perish on the strength of the dialectic of its own development."[74] Arbatov expands on Engels' dictum, pointing to the tension between the tremendous growth of military expenditures by bourgeois governments and their employment of mass armies that will sooner or later "refuse to pay for the policy of the oppressors with heavy sacrifices and deprivations."[75] In the case of U.S. militarism, Arbatov maintains that such a mass army has already borne out Engels' prediction. "It is not by accident," Arbatov concludes, "that in light of the experience of the Vietnam War, the United States embarked on a major reform in military building which essentially signified a return to a professional, hired army."[76]

The two Soviet schools of thought do disagree, however, on the ultimate utility of militarism for the capitalist system. The traditionalists have argued that the monopoly capitalists, unanimously agreeing that a militarist policy is beneficial to them and helps to secure their power, will continue to pursue such a policy as a matter of course. In short, traditionalist theory has always held that capitalism and militarism are inseparable.

The realists do not concur with this analysis. Instead, they maintain that the policy of militarism has produced such acute contradictions within the capitalist ruling class that it can no longer be seen as the automatic corollary of capitalism. These analysts do describe militarism as the cause of the arms race, which of course yields great profits for the military-industrial monopolies. Nevertheless, they argue that the arms race has failed to fulfill its purpose of economically straining the socialist community, even as it has had grave consequences for the United States, including: "the growth of inflation and unemployment in the country and the further sharp exacerbation of the dollar crisis in the international arena."[77] Indeed, as another realist commentator emphasizes, "The acute monetary crisis is deeply rooted in the internal processes in the U.S. economy, above all the spiralling inflation and the mounting militarization, which has exceeded the capabilities of even the richest capitalist country."[78] This monetary crisis (the breakdown of the Bretton Woods system and the subsequent devaluations of the dollar) forced the Nixon administration to resort to emergency measures to stabilize the monetary situation—measures that, however, "make imperialism's internal and external contradictions even more complex since they have not been accompanied by a renunciation of the arms race."[79] Arbatov summarizes the realist position, claiming that "military expenditure can no longer be viewed as an unmitigated blessing, as a stimulator of the economy, as a means of saving it from crisis and as an instrument for pumping assets into the monopolies' safes. In particular, it has become obvious that, having reached a certain level, this expenditure is leading inevitably to a slowing down in the rate of economic growth and to an acceleration of inflation."[80]

These severe economic dislocations, in turn, have prompted a massive public debate over America's "national priorities," and led to the emergence of an opposition that, in Arbatov's view, comprises both the public in general and that segment of the ruling classes for whom "the link between the aggravation of domestic problems in the country on the one hand and the imperialist course of United States foreign policy, the Vietnam War, and the arms race on the other has become an indisputable fact in this situation."[81] Clearly, Arbatov attributes the predominant role in this opposition to this segment of the ruling classes and their interests. He points out that the deleterious economic effect of militarism "is inevitably taking its toll on the revenues of corporations, with the sole exception of that group of corporations working chiefly on military business." Furthermore, Arbatov emphasizes the way in which the enormous U.S. military expenditure, "by increasing the prices for American products through inflation and taxation, is making them uncompetitive on the world markets." As a result, these same ruling circles are beginning to resent the fact that America's capitalist allies, which spend a smaller proportion of their GNP on military needs, are thereby able to beat the United States in the competition for world markets. When Arbatov does mention the general public in connection with the opposition to militarism, he assigns it an ancillary role:

> The U.S. monopoly bourgeoisie is becoming increasingly sensitive not only to direct threats to its profits but also to more oblique

threats to its omnipotence engendered by the aggravation of the economic, social, and political difficulties in the United States and by the upsurge in opposition feeling in the country caused by these difficulties. Hence the opinion, which is being voiced increasingly clearly, about the necessity for increasing the meager allocations for solving the many internal social problems and about the necessity for urgently "putting our own house in order"; if only for the sake of long-term global interests.[82]

In sum, Arbatov argues that the imperatives of profit and global interests, much more than any increase in public pressure, have led to the emergence of a substantial faction within the ruling class which believes that "in order to continue playing its hegemonic role in world capitalism, America needs a stable and strong home front."

Arbatov also maintains that this new faction within the U.S. ruling class is more realistic in its assessment of the new correlation of forces that results from the rise of the military might of the socialist community of nations. As a consequence, it has realized the "limited nature of the role of military strength in the modern world and the futility of turning military might into a fetish to which economic and domestic policy interests are sacrificed." Simultaneously, a growing segment of this faction is finding that the tension aroused by the arms race with the socialist world interferes with the conduct of peaceful and mutually beneficial economic relations with these states.

The policy of militarism, then, rather than fulfilling the ambitions of the ruling class, has spawned new contradictions—in foreign relations, in economic and social stability, and in the very cohesion of the ruling class itself. The last of these contradictions has become, in the view of the Soviet realists, the essence of the new domestic struggle in the United States—the struggle that, in Soviet terminology, pits the forces of "realism" versus the forces of "reaction." This struggle is most clearly expressed, of course, in the debate over detente with the socialist community—the proponents of detente being realists, whereas its opponents represent the forces of reaction.

It is true that in earlier periods Soviet commentators also made reference to differences between elements of the American ruling class. During Khrushchev's tenure, for example, Soviet commentary remarked on the existence of a few "sober-minded," "realistic," or "reasonable" men in the American power structure.[83] In that period, "realism" was understood to include: (1) the realization that in the nuclear age, all sides share a common interest in avoiding the use of war as an instrument of policy; (2) the awareness that socialism is the wave of the future and the willingness to accept its arrival without much resistance; and (3) a commitment to pursuing American national interests under conditions of mutual deterrence in such a way as to maintain, not disrupt, the existing international system (for certain Soviet theorists, this type of American behavior was desirable because it made possible both struggle and cooperation between the superpowers—a situation more propitious for Soviet interests than struggle alone).[84] Only the first of these attributes of more "realistic" behavior had an empirical basis: under conditions of mutual deterrence, the United States *did* recognize that it could no longer rely as much as previously on the use of military force.[85] The second and, to some degree, the third aspects of this notion of "realism" were, as William Zimmerman has concluded, largely functions of Khrushchev's efforts to "prettify imperialism"—an ideological imperative imposed on the Soviet leader now that nuclear weapons appeared to vitiate the possibility of the achievement of revolution through war. This situation severed revolutionary theory and practice and, as Zimmerman explains, "In order to retain the inevitability of revolution under atomic age conditions, under post-imperialism, if there were no policy alternatives to bring reality into conformity with theory, Khrushchev had to prettify imperialism."[86] Furthermore, it might be noted that Soviet commentators were not unanimously convinced that Khrushchev's assessment of American "realism" had any empirical foundation. Indeed, since the Kennedy administration had proceeded in its actual policies to discredit this Soviet notion of American "realism," Soviet commentary felt compelled to diminish the claims it had been making on the new and favorable balance of power which was supposedly bolstered by the fatalism, passivity, and accommodationism of American "realists."[87]

The "realism" that Soviet commentators discern within the American ruling class in the 1970s contains the essence of the old Khrushchevian definition, but is based on a much more consistent and well-documented pattern of empirical analysis. First of all, this "realism" is viewed as a function of both the newly diagnosed domestic components of the "crisis of capitalism" and the policy of militarism. Thus, Soviet realists describe American "realists" as being aware that the capitalist economy cannot provide both guns and butter (the "problem of political priorities," unprecedented in the postwar period) and that the arms race and foreign military adventures are counterproductive. Furthermore, the Soviets see American "realism" as a function of a split in the ruling class—a split that is deeper and wider than any seen before. Soviet commentary is quite clear on this score, enumerating, for example, the different types of monopolies which have stakes in particular policies. In light of all this, these recent analyses have been able, as Khrushchevian commentary was not, to base their conclusions about American "realism" on "objective" criteria. Using these criteria, Soviet analysts also have been able to diagnose certain changes in the ideological strength of the American ruling class. Seeing that substantial segments of this class acknowledge the new incapacities of the American economy and the futility of the arms race, these Soviet analysts have concluded that a certain erosion of faith in American capitalism has taken place. This erosion, combined with new self-doubts about the universal applicability of the American path of development (see p. 192), constitutes what the Soviets see as a change in the ideological correlation of forces in American society— a change that has international repercussions.

The last of the methods by which the monopoly bourgeoisie strengthens its positions and extends its basis for "social maneuvering" in the struggle against the threat of "progressive" movements is the increased use of the state. Soviet analysts—it is primarily the realists who examine this issue—see several factors as contributing to this development. As already mentioned, the bourgeois state is pressed to provide more education to satisfy the imperatives of the scientific-technical revolution. Simultaneously, the state is called upon to implement the policies that are the basis for the policy of militarism: it must supply statements by the Pentagon's generals that corroborate its assessments of the "Soviet threat"; it must draw up government contracts by which it invests its vast resources in the large-scale construction of armaments; and it must implement imperialist foreign policies. At the same time, the ruling class has harnessed the state, manipulating it to fulfill its conflicting goals in the struggle over national priorities. Among these goals is the solution to the host of problems which the Soviets characterize as the "acute sociopolitical crisis" in America—problems such as unemployment (especially among the black population), inflation, the ecological crisis, the energy crisis, and the growing demands of the working people for better health care, old age security, and a life free from exploitation. These are problems that segments of the ruling class feel must be solved in order to perpetuate the capitalist system.

Such problems, of course, are seen as inherent in capitalism and, in addition to the particular causes mentioned above, Soviet analysts attribute them to the impossibility of a "balanced development of the [capitalist] economy in the interests of the whole people."[88] Faced with this contradiction, the ruling class has attempted to substitute state intervention into and regulation of the economy for "balanced development." This policy is largely accomplished by the redistribution of income, as manifested in the increased growth of the state budget as a percentage of the national income. As one traditionalist analyst cautions, however:

> The national income is redistributed in the interests of the monopolies. But it must be remembered that it is not redistributed in the interests of individual monopolies or even financial groups. Certainly state subsidies, interest-free loans, and similar privileges are granted to monopoly companies. But, budget policy promotes the interests of the entire financial oligarchy, the ruling elite of the capitalist class, and not necessarily the current interests of this elite, but their basic long-term interests.[89]

The scientific-technical revolution also impels the monopolies to resort more frequently to state regulation of the economy. According to Inozemtsev, this revolution

> urges the need to tackle economic tasks of vast proportions, like the creation of a fundamentally new economic basis, development of the resources of the world's oceans, preservation of the environment, urban transport development, creation of much better machinery for the management of the whole economy, etc. This requires nationwide control over the distribution of national income, investments and planning of the economic system.[90]

Finally, the struggle against socialism contributes to this increase in the monopolists' use of the state. Since the Soviets are convinced that socialism is the superior economic system, they see monopoly capitalists as constrained to adopt any measures, including socialistic techniques, to compete in this struggle.[91]

While admitting that this growing state intervention has solved some of the economic problems of capitalism and has influenced the shape of the general economic structure, Soviet realists maintain that it has not been able to overcome the "anarchy of production" or cope with the allegedly deleterious "spontaneous forces" of the market place.[92] Indeed, this increased use of the state has led to the emergence of new contradictions, including clashes between "private monopoly elements" and "state elements" that are attempting "to regulate the economy from one center."[93] Such contradictions are inevitable, according to the Soviet realists, because the state retains a measure of independence which, under certain conditions, it can exercise against the interests of the monopolies.

Another contradiction arises from the need for centralized control of redistribution, investment, and economic planning which results from the scientific-technical revolution. Such centralization, for which there is allegedly an "objective need," cannot be fully realized as long as private ownership remains,[94] and, as a result, the people as a whole cannot benefit from the fruits of scientific and technological progress. Finally, to increase the centralization of the state control of the economy is "to intensify the socialization of production,"[95] a process that ultimately weakens the very foundations of capitalist society. In the end, then, even the realist analysis returns to an emphasis on the original and fundamental contradiction of capitalism, a contradiction that can only become more aggravated.

Both schools of Soviet analysts believe that, in the midst of the multifaceted crisis of capitalism, many monopolies are continuing their exploitative activities with a vengeance. Among the most aggressive are the oil companies, which, through "covert machinations" and "speculative operations," "are taking advantage of their dominant position in the energy market to inflate artificially the prices of petroleum products and gain illicit wealth."[96] These actions, not the restrictions imposed by the oil-producing countries, are seen by Soviet analysts as the fundamental cause of the energy crisis in the United States and other industrialized capitalist countries. Nowhere does Soviet commentary hint at such alternative explanations for this crisis as government price controls and regulations. Instead, as A. Grigoriants insists, "The monopolies' machinations are so obvious that U.S. congressional committees have been forced to investigate them."[97]

The energy crisis is thus viewed as another corollary of capitalism, indeed, a symptom of its inherent malaise, a phenomenon that, in Grigoriants' words, "did not engender but only exposed and exacerbated the chronic flaws of the capitalist economy." This same commentator observes that the United States is engaging in two tactics to deal with the energy crisis: "accusing the oil producers of responsibility for all the West's ills," while "striving to transfer the weight of the burdens that have arisen onto its partners and competitors and put its own trade and economic affairs in order." But, no matter what Washington does, he concludes, its policies "will lead to a new exacerbation of the contradictions in the world of capital." Indeed, the 1974 flareup between the United States and the EEC over the latter's attempts to reach independent accommodations with the Arab oil producers was interpreted as an illustration of such contradictions. Thus, T. Kolesnichenko attributed the EEC's dissatisfaction with U.S. policy to the fact that "the U.S. oil monopolies are continuing to profit from the Near East conflict."[98] The attempt to reconcile this line with American support of Israel has led to some mercurial leaps on the part of Soviet intellectual and journalistic imaginations, which in the end can explain the situation only by talking about still more "contradictions."

This same crisis of capitalism, according to Soviet analysts, has spawned a moral, spiritual, and political crisis in the United States—a crisis manifested in the "spiritual decline, increased crime and corruption" that characterize American society.[99] Politically, this crisis is expressed in the attitudes Americans have adopted toward presidential elections. Noting that "bourgeois propaganda" only managed to attract one third of the voters to the primaries, N. Kurdiumov cites a satisfactory explanation for such apathy from the *Wall Street Journal,* to which he adds a few embellishments of his own:

94

A vast number of Americans are indifferent about who wins the battle for the White House. . . . Alienation and cynicism are everywhere as a result of the deepened crisis of confidence in the authorities caused by the U.S. war in Vietnam, the "Watergate affair," and the economic crisis. All this [let's add the scandalous exposures of the sinister activities of the FBI and CIA] has opened the eyes of a great number of Americans to the true state of affairs.[100]

Kurdiumov finds additional symptoms of this crisis in "mass drug addiction," the "cult of violence," conflict of interest cases involving government officials, and the "wave of pornography." Further aggravating the general disarray is the attitude of the giant monopolies, which have adopted as their guiding principle the "cynical saying" that "What's good for General Motors is good for the United States." Kurdiumov and other analysts thus depict a pattern in which each symptom becomes a crisis unto itself, turning back and nourishing the crises that gave it birth. As capitalism spreads its morality, "it mutilates and corrupts people's minds and hearts, . . . driving a growing number of Americans to the conclusion that the cause of the crisis is the system of class exploitation which has legitimized economic and social inequality. In its report to the 25th CPSU Congress, the Central Committee distilled the essence of this line of argument when it concluded that "capitalism is a society devoid of a future."[101]

While some factions of the monopoly bourgeoisie have tried to solve the crisis with palliatives, most of which only aggravate contradictions, and others have continued to ride roughshod over the "true interests of the people," some have made concerted efforts in Ponomarev's words, "to set up the forces of reaction against the upsurge of revolutionary forces."[102] Militarism, discussed above, is but one of the forms that such efforts may take. Ponomarev, true to his traditionalist outlook, asserts that "big capital is bringing all methods into play—reform maneuvers, manipulation of the public with the mass media and direct repressions. The stronger the shocks in the capitalist camp, the more clearly its sores and defects are revealed, the more frenzied become its slanderous attacks on socialism." Finally, he raises the possibility of the rise of "neofascist elements" in the capitalist world. As the head of the 1970s equivalent of the Comintern, Ponomarev must prepare his charges for the

95

worst and incite them to prosecute their struggle with vigor. In none of his speeches does he mention the possibility of there being any recovery from the crisis, or benevolent developments emanating from the capitalist ruling classes. Though his personal opinion may differ from his public statements, Ponomarev paints the blackest possible picture of capitalism and, obviously, he has a reason for doing so. The picture he creates cannot but reinforce the general Soviet perception of the evils of American policy and the irreconcilability of the struggle between the two systems.

Arbatov, a more realistic analyst of the United States, implies that these same contradictions may have positive as well as negative consequences:

> We [we Marxists] are well aware that every crisis in bourgeois society may have various political results. The crisis of the "thirties" produced Roosevelt and his "New Deal" in the United States and Hitler, fascism and war in Germany. I do not mean by this to draw an exact parallel and assert that the present difficulties in the capitalist world will pave the way for fascism, although they could strengthen the pressure of reactionary rightwing trends; I would like instead to emphasize that we well understand the complex and contradictory nature of events taking place.[103]

(The implication here is not only that Roosevelt produced the New Deal instead of a war, but also that he officially recognized the Soviet Union for the first time—an act to which Soviet leaders remain very sensitive.) Another point of view, one that illustrates the breadth of perspective in Soviet thinking on monopoly capital's possible responses to crisis, is raised by A. Bovin, who writes that "it is entirely probable that capitalism will be able to overcome the present period of crises and upheavals."[104] Significantly, however, Bovin gives no explanation as to why or how this recovery might take place, leaving one to assume that his reasoning draws on the standard Marxist notion of the capitalist boom-and-bust cycle. Bovin's optimistic assessment is corroborated by Inozemtsev, who predicts that the West's economic prospects are improving, despite problems with raw materials, currencies, and unemployment.[105] Although his analysis is quite realistic, Inozemtsev's explanation still draws on the orthodox Marxist explanation: he claims that the West is getting over yet another "crisis of overproduction" and is heading for more balanced growth.[106]

Such expressions of confidence in the West's ability to recover, however, have become rather rare in Soviet commentary, and when made they carry even less assurance than during the Khrushchev period, when various Soviet economists generally concurred with U.S. economists in their growth-rate projections for the American economy.[107] There is, of course, copious documentary evidence to account for the diffidence of realist analysts regarding the West's recuperative powers. Although, like all Soviet analysts, the realists must and do subscribe to Marx's theory of the boom-and-bust cycle, their own diagnosis of the many new aspects of contradiction in current capitalist society must make them wonder whether a new "boom" can occur. These new contradictions—especially the increased use of the state and the consequent bureaucratic ossification (a phenomenon intimately familiar to the Soviets)—raise doubts as to the viability of the old laissez-faire techniques that produced the booms of the past. (After all, it was the power of laissez-faire capitalism which Marx so admired.) Furthermore, if a boom were to occur under such conditions, Soviet analysts would quite probably find that their orthodox formulas could not explain its real causes to their satisfaction. In any event, Soviet analysts have covered all bases in preparation for whatever denouement may emerge through the channel of American foreign policy as a result of the continuing crisis of capitalism. Throughout, their optimism for the prospects of socialism stands out as unflagging, and is in fact bolstered by their persistent emphasis on the problems of the United States and the West. These problems, after all, which together indicate the dynamic breakdown of the system of state-monopoly capitalism are "of primary importance for the development of the world revolutionary process."[108]

A comparison of the two main points of view expressed by Soviet analysis can tell us a great deal about how they measure the correlation of forces. As is evident, our reliance on the traditionalist view alone does not fully reveal the actual measurement by which the Soviets make their policy decisions. Traditionalists have issued fairly uniform commentaries on the correlation of forces for decades. Their consistent view is that capitalism always seems on the verge of imminent collapse. Meanwhile, their almost religious faith in the eventual triumph of socialism never ebbs. For the most part, their analysis is indistinguishable from propaganda.

The realists, in contrast, offer a much more detailed picture of the factors they weigh in assessing the strengths and weaknesses of American capitalism. While they acknowledge that the American economy has genuine capabilities, the realists also discern real and unprecedented weaknesses. They distinguish the relative powers of various U.S. political forces, but see a real split within those forces which has fragmented the former U.S. consensus on foreign policy. While cataloguing such quantifiable indexes of American strength as the economy, the realists also weigh more subtle, qualitative factors, such as the ideological commitment of the American ruling class, which they believe to be declining. Given its willingness to allow for American strengths, the realist analysis of American weaknesses becomes more credible than that of the traditionalists. Though the realists may not have determined that this recent American decline is irreversible, they see that, for the time being, it as quite real and rooted in objective factors. How this relative weakness manifests itself in the international arena is the subject of the following chapters.

Chapter 3

General Ends and Means
of U.S. Foreign Policy

The Ends of U.S. Foreign Policy and Their Determinants

There is no debate in the Soviet Union about the nature of the
fundamental ends of U.S. foreign policy and their basic determinants. In essence, U.S. foreign policy is said to reflect "the interests
of the dominating class, . . . the monopoly bourgeosie. It inevitably
bears the imprint of this class's aspirations in the most varied
spheres: economic, social, domestic, political, military, and ideological. Its main concern—to retain and strengthen American imperialism's positions in the world—also predetermines its very long-term
features and its continuity through different historical stages."[1]
These class interests constitute what the Soviets see as the "determinants" of U.S. foreign policy. Although the Soviets see these
domestic determinants as the mainspring of American foreign policy,
they also maintain that capitalism's international dimension—imperialism, with all its attendant effects—is both a determinant of
foreign policy and an end in itself. Like all other capitalist phenomena, however, imperialism is deemed to be ridden with contradictions, among them being the rise of anti-imperialist movements.
Since such movements, themselves the expression of an "objective
law of social development," emerge as primary constraints on U.S.
foreign policy, Soviet analysts number them among the crucial
determinants of that policy.

These observations raise a question that is akin to the classic
problem of whether national interests or communist ideology guide
Soviet foreign policy: to what extent do the Soviets perceive that
ideas and values (or, ideology and ideals) constitute determinants

of U.S. foreign policy? Soviet answers to this question prove to be much more straightforward and self-assured than the confusing array of conflicting responses found in the corresponding Western analyses of Soviet policy. In short, class interests are deemed the primary determinant of U.S. policy; ideals and values play a determining role only insofar as these class interests constitute the ultimate value and ideals. Other ideas have only a subordinate role in the policy-making process, figuring as means to achieve the ends of the ruling class. Soviet analysts, then, broadcast a picture of a basely philistine American ruling class for which ideals and principles are tools used in the cynical manipulation of the people.

This image provokes speculation on the extent to which the Soviet view of their own political reality conditions their perception of how things work elsewhere. If in fact the class interests of the "new class" (the CPSU and its managers in government and industry) are the primary determinant of Soviet policy, and if their ideology is a cynically manipulated rationale and weapon, then, given the totalitarian control of alternative sources of knowledge, the Soviets' view of the world may indeed be so constricted that they can only believe that other societies work in the same fashion. This situation would explain Soviet reluctance to ascribe much independence to American public opinion in the formulation of policy.

Given this general and constantly repeated assertion of class interests as the determinants of policy, one can see that Soviet analysts believe American foreign policy to have three main goals. First, and most basically, it seeks to perpetuate the domestic power of the American ruling class. Second, it strives to maintain the means of that power by perpetuating the capitalist system both domestically and internationally. Finally, American foreign policy works to fortify American power positions abroad, a policy that, in turn, helps it to attain its other basic goals. Indeed, all three goals are interdependent, but, as the following analysis shows, the Soviets perceive the last to be the most flexible—at once the most ambitious and the least essential, and therefore the most expendable. Soviet analysts see the "true nature" of American capitalism—its wildest aspirations, its capabilities, and its limitations—reflected in the international arena, and it is thus in discussions of this third goal that one finds clear expressions of the difference among Soviet analysts.

The most striking difference is in their conflicting assessments of

American ambitions. In a fairly traditionalist analysis, for example, Anatoly Gromyko wrote in early 1972 that "the U.S. ruling elite has begun openly to lay claim to command over the destiny of the world." These pretensions were said to arise from "dreams of a world 'after the American fashion.' "[2] Even as Gromyko wrote, however, such comments gradually began to disappear from the Soviet press. This trend might be explained by the fact that in 1972 the Kremlin was determined to avoid unnecessarily incendiary propaganda that could jeopardize the then inchoate detente. It is also possible, however, that the traditionalist approach had come into direct conflict with the increasingly sophisticated realist analysis of American foreign policy, which at that time appeared increasingly dominant in the theoretical and scholarly journals. Although these realists shared the traditionalist conviction that the American ruling class would always harbor global ambitions, they had begun to feel that the "change of the world correlation of forces in favor of socialism" had forced the United States to adapt its foreign policy to new realities. As a result, the maximalist ambitions of the American ruling class were increasingly irrelevant to the analysis of current international politics.

Arbatov explained that such adaptation can be accomplished in two ways:

> One of them is adaptation primarily in methods and forms which provides for the quest for more refined and more cunning methods of bringing about the same reactionary domestic policy and the same foreign policy course. . . . The other trend, in addition to the improvement of methods, provides for a certain amount of adjustment of the policy itself, consideration of the realities of the modern world not only in form, but in essence (of course, within definite limits restricted by the framework of the bourgeoisie's class interests), and partial concession by the bourgeoisie for the sake of saving the whole—their domination.[3]

Soviet analysts observed that, during the 1970s, U.S. policy makers used a combination of these methods.

From the Soviet point of view, the second method is the more desirable; indeed, it is a method they find fit to encourage through their own foreign policy. Still, as Arbatov notes elsewhere, a "class approach" (in this case, of course, the "working class") to this question demands understanding that however much imperialism may adapt to new "objective" conditions, its fundamental and oppressive nature does not change. At the same time, he cautions against ignoring the positive aspects of imperialist adaptation, arguing that any substantial adaptation by the bourgeoisie implies "concessions forced by the forces of peace and progress."[4] Since such concessions, even though only partial, are what the working class and the socialist countries have long been striving to secure, they assume an enormous significance for Soviet realists: "They can signify the difference between fascism and bourgeois democracy, for all the shortcomings of the latter. They can also signify the difference between war and peace."[5]

In the 1970s, however, Soviet analysts saw U.S. foreign policy as tending to emphasize the first method of adaptation—changing its means of achieving basic objectives. The realists explained this emphasis by arguing that it is only in the last resort that the ruling class will have recourse to changing the goals of its policy. Through the mid-1970s, the realists had not detected sufficient evidence to demonstrate that the ruling class was driven to such adaptations. As an example, Arbatov observes that if one looks at American domestic policy, one sees that the emphasis is not on finding real solutions for the most acute problems, but on implementing new methods of political control: improving the administrative apparatus, searching for the most effective means of struggle against the opposition, or combining ideological influence with repression.[6] This pattern, he claims, is even more evident in foreign policy, where the imperialists constantly change their methods of attaining unchanging objectives. Not surprisingly, then, Soviet analysis focuses primarily on the means of American foreign policy, not only because they constitute the nuts and bolts of the ongoing policy process, but also because close attention to them exposes "the maneuvers of the bourgeoisie and its demagogy."[7] By analyzing this focus, one can reach a better understanding of the Soviets' general world view and their assessment of the correlation of forces in the struggle between the two social systems.

The Means of U.S. Foreign Policy

Ideological Means

One thesis of this study is that the Soviets see the realm of ideas as the greatest threat to their power and legitimacy and, as a result, they devote the most attention to this component of foreign policy. They know that, try as they may, they cannot exercise ultimate control in this sphere, for the "scientific" postulates of Marxism-Leninism have not yet figured out how to eliminate completely the private ownership of thought. Nevertheless, fully cognizant of the importance of thought-control in their own calculus of power, the Soviets may, through a process of projection, see American and other capitalist ruling circles as equally reliant on ideology, equally insistent to command the means of its dissemination (through capitalist ownership of the news media), and equally committed to the "brainwashing" of their people. Parenthetically, it is in considering this aspect of American society that the Soviets blunder into perhaps their greatest misperceptions: however assiduously Soviet analysts may read the "bourgeois press," thereby exposing themselves to the multiplicity of ideas expressed therein, they continue to stress that a monolithic "bourgeois ideology" predominates. It prevails primarily because it is constantly and successfully proselytized by the monopoly bourgeoisie in a disingenuous campaign of indoctrination by which one class-conscious class maintains power over another. The end result of this campaign is the weakening of working-class consciousness. This emphasis on the degree to which "class consciousness" constitutes a real factor in American politics is perhaps the point on which the Soviets diverge most dramatically from American self-perceptions.

Both traditionalists and realists believe that this American manipulation of ideas is a crucial means of U.S. foreign policy and that it serves three primary purposes: (1) it is a means to justify and rationalize various policies; (2) it can serve as a means of ideological struggle and thus constitutes a weapon of foreign policy; and (3) it constitutes a source of new strategy and tactics. Manipulated in these different ways, ideas are seen as the essence of different American foreign policies. When trying to discern the nature and motivation of a given U.S. policy, Soviet analysts examine either its ideological underpinnings or the way ideas are employed as instruments of the policy itself. A study of Soviet analyses of various American ideas can, therefore, increase our understanding, not only of how the Soviets read changes in American policy, but also of how Soviet traditionalists and realists differ on issues that both deem crucial.

103

Soviet analysts are convinced that a significant part of the American foreign policy process involves wielding ideas to justify policy actions, and they have written copiously on this subject. As a result, Soviet analysts are strikingly familiar with the diverse schools of American political and philosophical thought—in sharp contrast to their American counterparts, who are comparatively unfamiliar with the variety of Soviet writings. There can be little doubt that such an intensive focus on this one aspect of American policy is, at least in part, the product of Soviet ideological insecurity and the consequent compulsion to engage in ideological struggle. Indeed, this emphasis has been virtually institutionalized as a component of Soviet writings on American foreign policy: invariably, the "works" of some "bourgeois" author, who is often alleged to "aspire to the role of 'theoretician of international relations,' " are cited as crude attempts to justify one or another U.S. policy and pronounced too lame to withstand "scientific" communist scrutiny.

The Soviets have devised several classifications of arguments by which the Americans are said to justify their policies. We turn first to the category of arguments directed to the more general means and ends of American policy, a category within which the Soviets include several types of arguments: those which try to justify the "policy of force"; those which try to justify the "policy of status quo"; and those which attempt to rationalize the growing "realism" and weakness of American policy.

Among the arguments that attempt to justify America's so-called policy of force, those belonging to the school of "political realism" are said to be especially influential. As B. A. Shabad observes: "The doctrine of political realism is the one usually resorted to for the purpose of justifying power politics."[8] Noting that "political realism" describes an attitude toward a number of concepts central to politics and international relations—concepts such as power, interest, will, human nature, and others—he concludes that its attitude toward "interest" is primary, the real cornerstone of the "doctrine." "Abstract 'interest,' " Shabad continues, "is reduced to the use of naked violence, extended to all social relations." On the basis of this analysis Shabad argues that "political realism" is ultimately "based on the old worn thesis that violence is the main instrument of politics." It is a doctrine that "transfers the basic premises of the theory of violence to the sphere of international relations."[9] Such reasoning leads Shabad to assert that "the aggressive foreign policy of imperialism is invariably treated [by political realists] as the inevitable product of 'political reality,' human nature, and the character of international affairs."[10] In short, he concludes, the "doctrine" of political realism is nothing more than "an apology for the use of violence as a means of halting socio-historical progress."[11]

The concept of the U.S. "national interest" that is derived from this doctrine of political realism is subject to similar analysis. In an article devoted exclusively to this concept, V. I. Krivokhizha argues that, as used in the United States, the idea of "national interest" is in fact equivalent to the "class interests" of the "ruling class."[12] She observes that American political commentators are aware of this fact and are simply being disingenuous when they use the term: "The specific character of the treatment of the concept of the 'national interest' in general and regarding the USA in particular, consists of the fact that the overwhelming majority of American bourgeois authors identify the nation with the state, thereby denying the former's class nature."[13] Krivokhizha's clear implication is that since the state represents only the "ruling class" and not the entire "nation," the interests of nonruling classes are not part of the "national interest." As a result, "national interest" can be invoked both to mask and to justify the perfidious methods of force employed by the American ruling class.

The Soviets make a considerable effort to prove not only the existence but also the necessity of the alleged links between "political realism" and "violence," and between the idea of the "national interest" and the "policy of force." Krivokhizha gives a good illustration of such efforts as she quotes a passage by Robert E. Osgood:

"The fundamental question in the field of foreign policy which seriously arose before the United States after two decades of the cold war, consists of what are the vital national interests of America and how should it use *military power* [*voennuiu moshch'*] to secure them." [My emphasis][14]

What Osgood really wrote, however, was:

What are America's vital interests and how should it use its *power* to support them? This is the fundamental foreign policy question facing the United States after two decades of the Cold War. [my emphasis][15]

Needless to say, this imaginative misrepresentation did not occur by accident. It is part and parcel of a ubiquitous form of Soviet analysis which, spurred by the exigencies of the ideological struggle, finds it necessary to twist foreign statements making them conform to and confirm the Soviet view of the basic pattern of international relations. And clearly this tactic is not confined to the kind of crude misquotation cited here—it is evident in most Soviet analyses of Western ideas.

Another influential group of arguments said to justify America's "policy of force" are subsumed under the general heading of "conservatism" or "neoconservatism." Shabad, for example, characterizes conservatism as an "attempt to cloak neo-fascist ideas, political reaction and aggression in more respectable garb, and sanctify the policy of counter-revolutionary force on the basis of extra-temporal, and hence, supra-class conservative principles."[16] He argues that "neo-conservatism aims to justify the policy of violence in international relations by the 'divine sanction' of the religious-idealist world view, trying to present it as having nothing at all to do with political reaction, as an external, extra-temporal phenomenon." Such a "metaphysical approach" thus conceals the real purpose of policy, which is to preserve social and national inequality; for, as Shabad notes elsewhere, the central idea of conservatism is that "before creating something new, existing values must be 'conserved.' "[17] In addition, he maintains that conservatives will agree only to changes that improve the social institutions of the capitalist system, and that "this can be done, in their opinion, by means of reform, but not by means of revolution."[18] In light of all this, Shabad concludes that "for the solution of twentieth-century problems it ["contemporary bourgeois conservatism"] prescribes one of the time-hallowed recipes of the exploiter classes: the use of force— police coercion at home and military aggression abroad."[19]

There are many other, less well-developed arguments that the Soviets interpret as attempts to justify the so-called policy of force. Of particular interest to Soviet commentators are the theories of "social dynamics" which, in Shabad's words, "purport to analyze the mutual influence of various social factors" in order to justify the role of power through a more "subtle, covert method."[20] Such theories are also accused of ignoring the "class content" of social phenomena, especially as they describe the relations between the capitalist and socialist systems as a "power conflict."[21] Thus, the basic feature and error of these theories is their tendency to "reduce the social conflict exclusively to a military one,"[22] and to "present military force as the foundation of foreign policy in general."[23] This concentration on the "power" element of politics is viewed as the link between bourgeois theory in general and the active policy of "militarism." As A. Migolat'ev observes:

> Other bourgeois theoreticians, while recognizing the connection between militarism and politics, ignore the class content of the latter and consequently, also ignore the social and political essence of militarism. In this case, militarism amounts to a policy which attaches "disproportionately great importance to military preparations." The advocates of such a view identify militarism with any developed military organization, with an army as such, irrespective of which class is in power. This is fundamentally incorrect.[24]

Soviet analysts conclude that, given their reductive emphasis on power, these theorists of "social dynamics" ultimately justify a policy of force through "their absolutization of the role of force in social life in general," and through their shameless "appeal to spare no expense on military ends and to conduct comprehensive preparation for total war."[25]

"The idea of the fatal inevitability of war" is yet another of the arguments which Soviet analysts claim that the Americans use to justify their "policy of force." This argument is a means by which the "U.S. militarist circles" seek "to impose their will in international relations,"[26] and its corollary is the "doctrine of preventative war," used for similar purposes. Also alleged to provide theoretical justification for U.S. aggression is the "so-called theory of foreign policy blackmail," which entails "balancing on the brink of war."[27] Additional theories of the same type include: the "diplomacy of force," the theory of "psychological intimidation," and theories of limited and local war.[28] Soviet analysts see some theories as attempts "to represent militarism as an innocent, purely professional, and strictly parochial phenomenon, independent of politics and class wishes." In fact, of course, these theories are "an attempt to absolve from responsibility the ruling classes and the ruling circles in capitalist states who are guilty of disseminating militarism and its pernicious consequences."[29] Other theories, which posit that war is a function of human psychology or derived from instinctive animal behavior, are also cited as active "apologetics in defense of militarism,"[30] regardless of whether they are coined by "bourgeois political theoreticians," psychologists, or anthropologists.

The Soviets see many recent acts of American "aggression" as having been justified by the invocation of the "domino theory." This well-known theory is of special interest to Soviet commentators, for it lends a certain Western "second" to the Marxist axiom that the expansion of communism is a historically inevitable process. Insofar as the domino theory voices Western fears, it reinforces Soviet optimism and delights Soviet analysts, but since it is also a "justification" for the Western policy of force, the domino theory must be subjected to the scientific criticism of "creative Marxist thinking." Asking whether this theory is indeed "correct," Soviet analysis concludes that it is not. G. Trofimenko begins his criticism by conceding that "the rapid process of national liberation did in fact take the form of a 'chain reaction' as an increasingly large number of countries escaped from the fetters of colonialism, and it may be said that this process has now mainly been completed with the collapse of the last colonial empire—the Portuguese Empire."[31]* However, he goes on to argue that while the "figurative comparison" is correct, the fallaciousness of the theory lies in the fact that it tries to present "a natural process engendered by objective conditions" as being "contrary to nature" or "inspired from without." Thus, says Trofimenko:

> Since revolutions, as the U.S. strategists asserted, are "made to order," why not try to make counterrevolution to order as well? If the partisan liberation movement is the "work of the hands of Moscow," then it is possible to organize with the same success a counterinsurgent movement—"counterinsurgency"—and to export from Washington forces of this nature to a "trouble spot" to struggle against a "communist plot."[32]

According to this line of argument, then, bourgeois ideologists have

---

*One of the standard techniques of Soviet propaganda is distraction. Mr. Trofimenko employs this technique quite routinely as he conveniently neglects to note that the Soviet Union is the last colonial empire.

developed a "philosophy" that purports to justify the "interference of U.S. imperialism in the affairs of other countries" and a major component of the "policy of force." In the Soviet view, however, the U.S. experience in Vietnam is irrefutable proof of the bankruptcy of this so-called philosophy. In Trofimenko's words, "precisely because a national liberation movement is not a 'plot by a handful of people' organized from outside, but a profoundly national, mass movement generated primarily by the working people's dissatisfaction with existing economic, political, and social living conditions, the U.S. strategy of 'counterinsurgency' suffered an inglorious defeat."

Finally, there is the "alleged Soviet threat," of all these "theories" the one to which Soviet analysts devote perhaps the greatest attention. In their view, Washington invokes the specter of the "Soviet threat" to rationalize almost every evil that emanates from its foreign policy. When this "theory" is combined with the general nostrum that American "weakness is a threat to peace," it amounts to the most insidious justification of that American notion that U.S. policy must be conducted "from a position of strength."[33] Soviet analysts, therefore, constantly denounce the theory of the "Soviet threat" while extolling the virtues of the "peace-loving" policy of their own Party and country. As Arbatov notes: "The chief weapon of the opponents of change remains, however, the intimidation of the public with the myth of the 'Soviet threat,' thus whipping up a war psychosis aimed at substantiating the expansionist policy and the further acceleration of the arms race."[34] Anatoly Gromyko, however, notes that this weapon has its limitations: "The Soviet Union's peace-loving program is attracting the fixed attention of the American public, which is succumbing less and less to the brainwashing with myths about the 'Soviet threat.' "[35]

There are still other concepts, often expressed by U.S. policy makers, which the Soviets see as sharing one common denominator: they all attempt to justify the American "policy of the status quo." The phrases "world stability" or a "stable and constructive world order" represent one of these concepts. "It has long been known," writes one Soviet commentator, "that the United States approaches the definition of the concept of 'stability' from the viewpoint of preserving reactionary antipopular regimes against the will of the peoples of these countries."[36] For the Soviets, then, the American notion of "stability" is simply a justification for maintaining the status quo no matter how odious it may be. As such, it is part and parcel of "conservatism" and its "reactionary" nature.

Related to "stability" and allegedly helping to maintain it in practice is the concept of "equilibrium," which Zbigniew Brzezinski has expressed as a "symmetry of power." The Soviets are particularly critical of this notion, for, as Anatoly Gromyko writes (in reference to Europe), " 'symmetry' implies nothing but 'the further integration of Western Europe and its close cooperation with the United States' in order to isolate the former from socialist Europe."[37] He continues by arguing that

> the line aimed at the further consolidation of U.S. influence in Western Europe is based on the need to counter "the other Europe," whose alleged sole aim is "to weaken Western unity." Thus the favorable tendencies in the relations between European countries and the weakening of the U.S. administration's influence on the foreign policy of such major West European states as France, Italy, and to a certain extent the FRG compel the U.S. foreign policy theorists to seek a new justification for the main U.S. aims in Europe.

In this case, of course, the American justification is that "symmetry" and "equilibrium" must be maintained for the sake of "stability." And the very process of justification is reinforced by another American ideological tactic—the camouflaging of a given policy's true nature. As Gromyko concludes, "It is necessary to make special mention of the intensification of the ideological implications of Washington's renovated foreign policy concepts. U.S. imperialism's foreign policy theorists are striving as painstakingly as possible to blur the expansionist and reactionary nature of this policy."[38] The U.S. attempt to maintain equilibrium in Europe thus "blurs" the policy of the "status quo," itself a deliberate misnomer that attempts to conceal a policy that Soviet experts define as "expansionist"—presumably because it attempts to expand imperialist influence at the expense of "progressive" forces of "national liberation" in Western Europe. Extending this line of reasoning, one could argue that the very maintenance of power by the currently constituted American government is "expansionist."

The last of the major arguments that the Soviets cite as justifica-

tions for the "policy of the status quo" is the American interpretation of the concept of "peaceful coexistence." As L. A. Leont'ev
explained in 1971:

> Frequently, the ideological standard-bearers of American imperial-
> ism pretend to support peaceful coexistence between nations with
> different social systems, but in so doing they interpret peaceful co-
> existence as maintaining the status quo. In other words, they at-
> tempt to create the impression that in adopting a policy of peaceful
> coexistence, socialist countries should abandon political, economic,
> and all other support for the just national liberation struggle of
> nations, should in some way become guarantors of the status quo
> throughout the world, guarantors of the inviolability of obsolescent
> regimes and of the survivals of colonial domination. It is super-
> fluous to mention that this is a gross distortion of the policy of
> peaceful coexistence.[39]

Finally, the Soviets turn to the ideological means by which the
Americans in the 1970s justified their policy of "realism." Since
this U.S. policy corresponds to the Soviets' own concept of "realism," it represents to them a departure from some of the more
"troglodytic" policies of anticommunism and its methods of force.
However, recognizing the continuing influences of such "cruder"
sentiments, and understanding that this fact implies a debate among
various alternatives in the U.S. foreign policy establishment, Soviet
analysis may more properly be said to perceive an American need
to *rationalize* rather than *justify* the new policy. Here, "rationalize"
implies a need to feel more comfortable with a situation that is
less than optimal—the situation being the increasing weakness of
the United States, and capitalism in general, in the international
arena as a result of the change in the "correlation of forces." More
correctly, then, the Soviets would say that the United States seeks to
rationalize its admitted weakness, the manifestation of which is the
policy of "realism."

Soviet analysts have not identified many such rationalizations of
this policy of "realism," a situation that they probably attribute to
the reluctance American analysts must bring to this unpleasant task.
The American concept of "multipolarity" has been cited as the
principal example of such rationalizations. G. Trofimenko observed
that

in fact, the "multipolarity" concept is primarily a recognition by U.S. theoreticians of the limited nature of U.S. imperialism's potential in the modern world. . . . It embraces: a recognition of new "centers of power" in the capitalist world (such as the European Economic Community or Japan); a realization of the well-known lack of convergence between the interests of the United States and the policies and interests of many of its chief capitalist allies, even with regard to the socialist countries; and an understanding of the fact that the U.S. "strategic nuclear missile force" is not automatically a political influence and that in the majority of conflict situations in the "third world" it does not even constitute a real threat.[40]

In a related vein, Anatoly Gromyko described the emergence of this concept as a function of "interimperialist contradictions,"[41] while Arbatov referred (in 1972) to the breakdown of the assumption that the United States has "one and only one enemy in the shape of the USSR":

It has become clear that the U.S. is encountering numerous dangers and problems unrelated to the traditional 'bipolar' confrontation, dangers and problems emanating from many allies, from neutrals, and chiefly, from the development of objective processes that cannot be accommodated in the straightforward and primitive concepts of anticommunism. Whereas these traditional American concepts once prompted such a clear and traditional course of action—a buildup of military strength and its direct or indirect utilization —under the new conditions, and for the first time in many years, an urgent need for a *realistic* policy has arisen. [My emphasis][42]

Since the Americans nowhere refer to what the Soviets see as one of the "true" reasons for this policy of realism—"interimperialist contradictions"—Soviet analysis can only regard the concept of multipolarity as a euphemism that rationalizes what some Americans at least "recognize" as the real situation.

The concept of international "interdependence" is the other such rationalization noted by Soviet analysts. This concept, according to A. Sergiev, was born during a period of "gradual weakening of U.S. preponderance" and was designed to serve several goals: to remind America's "imperialist partners" of their commitments to the United States; to set up an imperialist united front to oppose the demands of Third World states; and to make these states "agree to a compromise with imperialism under the slogan of the 'common destiny' of the bourgeosie of the developing nations and the main capitalist countries."[43] Sergiev argues that, in spite of these efforts to "undermine the solidarity" of the developing countries in their "anti-imperialist struggle," the very fact that this concept of interdependence was set forth reflects "an understanding of the changed alignment of forces in the world in favor of socialism." In short, the American theorists, beginning to recognize their country's growing weakness, sought to rationalize this development by propounding a doctrine that would permit them to minimize adjustments to the "new realities" of the world while preserving the essentials of the capitalist system.[44]

The one means of American foreign policy that the Soviets see as especially influential among the imperialists (the advocates of the policies of "force" and "status-quo"), is the ideology of "anticommunism." They take pains to point out that this ideology is not a general "American" phenomenon, but a weapon that the American "ruling class" can use specifically in the "ideological struggle" and generally as a tool of foreign policy. Soviet analysts generally characterize this instrumental use of ideology as a strategy of "psychological warfare," meaning that these are tactics deemed impermissible in a world where the ideological struggle should conform to the norms of "peaceful coexistence" (see page 42). The Soviets are convinced that the imperialists attach great importance to the conduct of this "psychological warfare," citing as evidence not only the Western countries' utilization of the NATO framework to pool their efforts in the sphere of ideology, but also the fact that " 'psychological warfare' has become a very important integral element in NATO's activity."[45] Soviet analysts classify these anticommunist ideas into two broad categories: those which are meant to discredit and weaken communism, and those designed to mask the true nature of capitalism while dressing it in a more acceptable costume.

The Soviets believe that the theoretical discrediting of communism is one of the chief preoccupations of the bourgeois ideologists who serve the American foreign policy process. Among the concepts that these ideologists have concocted for this purpose, the Soviets argue, is that of "totalitarianism." This concept which, according to an editorial of the CPSU's theoretical journal *Kommunist*, was originally a description of fascist regimes, has been unfairly applied to socialism. As the editorial inveighs: "By readdressing the term 'totalitarianism' to the socialist system bourgeois propaganda has resorted to a dirty trick and thereby perpetrated a most vile forgery. . . . The concept was based on the cynical calculation of taking advantage of the individualist psychology of the bourgeois man in the street and his instinctive fear of collectivism."[46]

Another bourgeois tactic is to "distort not only the political but also the socioeconomic content of socialist democracy."[47] Such distortion is perpetrated in several ways, among them being glorifications of bourgeois democracy. As the *Kommunist* editorial declares:

> The bourgeois concept of democracy, which has long borne the imprint of deep-seated degeneracy, is a tool in the struggle to maintain and consolidate the dictatorship of monopoly capital and an instrument for the splitting, undermining, and suppression of genuinely democratic movements. The system of bourgeois democracy includes the practice of a formal "guarantee of the freedom of the individual" which is characterized by every possible limitation, even to the point of abolishing constitutional guarantees. But what have bourgeois ideologists to do with facts! Closing their eyes to all this, they grieve over the "imperfection of socialism," and dream of altering socialist democracy to their own bourgeois style.[48]

This type of distortion is also perpetrated by analyses that portray the Soviet state as a one-party system with no political competition. Soviet commentators, however, maintain that this is "the only argument" of the bourgeois theoreticians; and since it ignores the fact that "the establishment of the one-party system in the Soviet Union was the law-governed result of the specific historical features of the revolutionary process in our country"—a process that eliminated the oppression of one class by another—they conclude that such an argument has a "completely bankrupt nature."[49]

Another Soviet argument is that social science theory has been manipulated to create distortions of socialism. Thus one commentator, writing in a 1976 Soviet text on the varieties of anticommunism, argues that "the stillborn hopes of the 'experts on communism' for a relatively swift and easy disintegration of socialism found their theoretical expression in the form of further borrowings from bourgeois sociology."[50] One of these theories of "bourgeois sociology" is identified as the "structural-functional method," which "falsifies the actual dialectics of the base and superstructure and studies the superstructure idealistically, without taking the social character of the base into account." Yet another example is "elite theory," which is linked to the theories of the "postindustrial society" and the "technetronic age." In the Soviet view, elite theory leads to the serious imbalance that characterizes most imperialist analysis of the USSR, resulting in

> the interest shown by the imperialist ideologists in scientific, technical, and creative intellectuals and in functionaries of the Party and state apparatus. The working class is regarded by them, if it at all comes into the field of vision, mainly as an object of social development. They largely ignore the fact that in socialist society the working class is the most organized class which is most closely linked with socialist public property, that it creates the largest portion of all the material values, comprises most of the working people and bears the largest responsibility for the destiny of the whole society. The growth of the collective farm peasantry is also represented by the "experts on communism" as not meriting attention.[51]

A similar distortion of communism is also detected in many works in the field of economics. Anticommunist economic theories allegedly employing "idealistic and metaphysical methods," are said to "pursue the common purpose of misrepresenting the social content and popular character of the socialist system."[52] This misrepresentation is accomplished by belittling the economic achievements of the Soviet Union, comparing them unfavorably with American economic performance, and declaring that the socialist countries must pay a prohibitive price for every economic achievement.[53] The Soviets maintain that this "theorizing" is based on the alleged bourgeois claim that "state-monopoly capitalism" is an "optimum economic system,"[54] an assertion that they see as a "falsification of the very concept of 'optimum.'" As one commentator explains:

> They [bourgeois theorists] usually interpret "economic optimum" as meaning the fullest utilization of limited resources for the "maxi-

mum usefulness." Although this "deideologized" interpretation of the concept reflects some common elements inherent in production at any of its historical phases, it is formally abstract. It circumvents the basic question of society's socio-economic structure, which is what determines the social content of of the term "optimum" and the social conditions of its realization. True optimal development presupposes not only the choice of methods for the attainment of the aims of production, but also the choice of these aims.[55]

Thus socialism, allegedly the only system that creates the social conditions for the most efficient use of resources in the interests of society, is seen as best equipped to ensure the economic optimum.

Some economists, those of the neoclassical orientation, are alleged to "misrepresent" socialism by regarding "general economic principles of the socialist economy as functional forms inherent in society at all stages of development, regardless of the socio-economic system.[56] Among the neoclassicists are the champions of "economic psychology," who are criticized because "they argue that socialism simply does not have specific categories and laws on the grounds that economic categories spring from human psychology which does not depend on the specifics of a socio-economic system."[57] Using the concept of "psychical energy" to replace that of labor, they attack the "labor theory of value" in Marxist-Leninist economics. Since, in the Soviet view, they "regard value as 'absolutely rational and not ideological,' " these economists are accused of using the "deideologization" of political economy "as a means of attacking the central Marxist-Leninist idea, namely, that of the historic role of the working class as a leading force capable, in alliance with the other toiling people, of destroying capitalism and building a new, genuinely humane and just society." Working from such concepts, "the economico-psychologists maintain that 'the mental progress of the individual, and not the class factor' is the basic law of economic development."[58]

Another group, the neoliberal school, "preaches that objective economic categories and laws cannot exist in a planned, consciously directed socialist economy."[59] Furthermore, this group denies "the objective character of commodity money relations under socialism," and refers to socialist economy as "a 'command economy' deprived of 'objective economic expediency.' " Such views are accompanied by "deliberately spurious interpretations of the economic reforms

116

carried out in socialist countries" and recommendations that social- ist countries reject the "etatist principle" and adopt a structure of "market socialism."[60]

A group of economists occupying an intermediate position be- tween the above-mentioned groups is said to acknowledge "the ob- jective character of some categories of socialism." However, these economists, referred to as "proponents of socio-economic conver- gence," allegedly transplant these aspects of socialism into what they see as an "ideal" society—one that the Soviets view as "funda- mentally nonsocialist."[61] Their "convergence theory" is especially irritating to the Soviets, who note that, since it is "a typical theoreti- cal expression of how the minds of a large segment of the bourgeois intelligentsia work," its "polymorphous character" and "the ap- parent credibility of many of its arguments made it a dangerous ideological and theoretical threat to Marxism."[62] Indeed, so con- cerned are the Soviets that almost every article about the "ideo- logical maneuvers of the anticommunists" contains some reference to this "notorious" theory, a phenomenon notable enough to prompt, in turn, a separate American study on the Soviet views of convergence.[63]

As the Soviets see it, the convergence theory posits that "the scientific-technical revolution allegedly erases the difference be- tween the two opposing socioeconomic formations and leads to the emergence of a sort of hybrid society which transpires on investiga- tion to be the same old capitalism."[64] Thus, like elite theory, it is related to the theories of the "postindustrial society" and the "tech- netronic age"—theories that are said to concern "capitalism's ability, utilizing the achievements of the scientific-technical revolu- tion, to create its own version of 'heaven on earth.' " Advocates of the convergence theory are also said "to hold that the Soviet Union owes its recent economic successes to the 'transplantation' of some elements of the Western economy to socialism."[65]

According to the already cited editorial in the September 1973 *Kommunist,* the propagation of this theory has three aims, and thus merits "a prominent place in imperialism's foreign policy ideology." First, its exponents seek "to embellish capitalism and to convince the popular masses that capitalism is not really so bad if it devel- ops along the lines of 'approximation' and 'merging' with socialism. Their task is to save the bourgeois system from revolution." Second, they "strive to denigrate and compromise socialism, to disarm ideologically the public of the socialist countries, to shake its confidence in the triumph of communist ideals, and to divert the masses toward a search for 'compromises' at the cost of renouncing first some and ultimately all the fundamental principles of socialism." Third, "under the guise of the 'supra-class' nature of ideology," the exponents of convergence try "to wring from the Communists recognition of the 'legality' of the bourgeois orders, ideas, and principles that have long been doomed to destruction by the entire course of history."[66] Thus, the convergence theorists "try to 'prove' the lasting nature and unshakability of capitalism by 'smoothing over' the irreconcilable contradictions between labor and capital and between the peoples of the developing countries and imperialism with its policy of colonialism and neocolonialism, and by 'smoothing over' the contradictions between the two world social systems— the capitalist and the socialist."[67] In addition, *Kommunist* argues that on the basis of this theory, "imperialism tries to dictate its interpretation of the policy of peaceful coexistence and its 'schedule' and scheme for implementing it."

The Soviet views of the convergence theory are especially significant because they show us not only how the Soviets see the American "misperceptions" of reality but also, given the Soviet conviction that this theory has such a large American following, the extent to which such misperceptions are thought to infect the American world view. As *Kommunist* observes, "the 'convergence' concept is a *reactionary utopia*," whose utopianism "lies in the attempt to unite what cannot be united, to implement what cannot be implemented, and to turn back the course of history."[68] The theory is also said to lead to a distorted interpretation of shifts in international relations. Such shifts "are portrayed as the first steps along the path of the actual 'merging' of the two opposing social systems and the slackening and virtual ending of the class struggle in the international arena."[69] In addition, the editorial accuses the advocates of convergence of "consigning to oblivion" all the USSR's efforts to win recognition of the principles of "peaceful coexistence," alleging that they reduce to purely "utilitarian motives" the efforts of the socialist countries to implement the peace program advanced by the 24th CPSU Congress." For example, *Kommunist* continues, the advocates of convergence insist on ascribing to "economic difficulties" the Soviet Union's attempts to establish a dialogue with Western countries." Another example is the identical tactic used by the Maoists, namely, the exaggeration of "the legend of the 'plot of the superpowers' to the detriment of other countries." What the Maoists are referring to is the alleged collusion between the United States and the USSR for purposes of global condominium, an effort that, of course, denies the fundamental contradiction between the two social systems.

In light of their analysis, the Soviets claim that the convergence theory is "the only ideological weapon" in the bourgeois arsenal—curiously, however, it is not the only "weapon" about which such a claim is made. Though the Soviet claim acknowledges that, as a "weapon," this theory must do some damage,[70] Soviet analysts nevertheless allege that the widespread acceptance of the convergence theory "is evidence of present-day anticommunism's *defensive* posture in the face of the mounting achievements of the forces of socialism" (my emphasis).[71]

Integrally linked with the convergence theory is what Soviet analysts call the "deideologization" of social awareness. Yermolenko characterizes this tactic of Western commentators as the active dissemination of "fairytales" which claim that "scientific and technical progress demands that ideology be replaced by structures free of class positions and value judgments," and that "broad theoretical schemes of historical development are losing all significance."[72] Whereas some adherents of "deideologization" are seen to be simply overly enthusiastic about the growing role of scientific and technical progress, and others are judged to be suffering from a misunderstanding and underestimation of the socio-philosophical analysis of reality, another group is accused of having a completely different objective: "In proclaiming 'the end of all ideology,' they are thinking primarily about putting an end to working-class ideology" and fomenting an "erosion" of Marxist-Leninist ideology through a promotion of a "conflict between ideologists and 'technocrats.' "[73] Such plans for "erosion" are seen as based on totally illusory notions about the true nature of the "scientific-technical revolution." Since the anticommunists allegedly falsify the "social content" of this "revolution,"[74] they promote the idea that "political and ideological processes, which must gradually lead to the restoration of the capitalist class structure, superstructure and ultimately, relations of production, spontaneously develop in the socialist states parallel with scientific and technical progress."[75] This argument points up the close link that Soviet analysts see between "deideologization" and convergence; a relationship that is exemplified with special clarity by the theory of the "convergence of ideologies." In response to one Western analysis of the alleged convergence of liberalism and Marxism, M. Mitin observes: "Every word here is a lie. Marxism-Leninism is a scientific ideology expressing the fundamental interests of the working class. It cannot associate itself with the views of the bourgeoisie, under whatever mask they may be presented."[76]

Soviet analysts classify bourgeois ideological maneuvers against the USSR and the Soviet "brand" of communism as another arm of the ideological strategy of anticommunism, one of its main components being the "falsification of the role played by the CPSU" in Soviet society.[77] Among these "falsifications" are distortions of the results, character, and methods of the Party's work, as well as allegations that the Party is not only no longer needed as a leading force due to the development of the scientific-technical revolution, but that, indeed, it has become an obstacle to further development.[78] Another example of such "falsification" is the attempt to ascribe "false" motivations to the work of the Communists and thereby to deny that Marxism-Leninism serves as a theoretical guide to Party activity.[79] In Western commentary of this sort one finds the Party's policies analyzed in terms of "practical needs," "traditional national interests," the "desire to retain power," and the notion that the society is dominated by an "elite group" or "class"—all examples of what the Soviets term "subjective factors," factors that bear no relation to the scientifically interpreted laws of history.[80] The basis for all these falsifications is the bourgeois contention that Marxism-Leninism is "unscientific," and in attempting to substantiate this argument, bourgeois ideologists have produced the most strenuous and unscrupulous of their anticommunist efforts, including: the portrayal of Leninism as a specifically Russian doctrine, the depiction of Marxism as a faith or religion, and the presentation of Marxism-Leninism as "disintegrating," "pluralistic," "obsolete," "inhumane," "antidemocratic," or "utopian."[81]

Another aspect of the attempt to discredit the USSR ideologically includes all the "falsifications" relating to the already discussed notion of the "Soviet threat." Examples include "the clumsy asser-

tion that the 'Soviet presence' in Europe is allegedly a manifestation of 'traditional imperialism,' "[82] and other accusations of Soviet "hegemonistic ambitions." Soviet analysts also refer to the
bourgeois "propaganda" argument that the purpose of the Communist Party of the Soviet Union has been first to seize power in one
country and then to export communism with the goal of establishing worldwide communist rule.[83] Also cited is the related argument
that since the Soviet Union has become a "mighty industrial power,"
it pursues "expansionist" aims. All of these arguments elicit the
scorn of Soviet commentators, who point out that such "myths"
have been "exploded" by the Soviet policy of "peace" and the
"peace program" advanced by the 24th CPSU Congress.[84] Like so
much of "bourgeois thinking," these arguments ignore the "class
basis" of Soviet foreign policy and attempt to debase its high ideals,
treating them as mere ploys of "power politics."

Soviet analysts claim that a similar falsification of Soviet foreign
policy principles is perpetrated in the field of "bourgeois" interna-
tional-relations theory. For example, it is alleged that Western
analysts refuse to classify wars as just and unjust, a refusal by
which the bourgeois ideologist attempts "to place the aggressor and
the victim of aggression side by side to justify plundering, unjust
wars, and to whitewash those reactionary forces that even today
are inclined to suppress the people's liberation movements by means
of armed struggle."[85] Once again, bourgeois analysts concoct such
specious arguments by ignoring the "class basis" of both the aggressor and the victim. It is further argued that this line of thinking promotes the "fallacy" that the Soviet Union pursues its policy with
the aid of the threat of war.

Particularly irritating to the Soviets is the attitude that Western
analysts have adopted toward Moscow's claim that the relations
among the nations of the world socialist community conform to
the high ideals of "proletarian internationalism." Indeed, the "men-
dacious" bourgeois theorists assert that relations among socialist
countries are characterized by exploitation, imperialist rule, and
subordination of the economically weaker states to the stronger
ones—policies that the Soviets insist are the predominant characteristics of capitalism.[86] Thus, the argument continues:

*The anticommunists regard the entire world through their own
prism,* with the result that some see in the new inter-state relations

only what they call an artificially created "military and political bloc," others see in them relations of the "ruling metropolis" and "subject satellites," and still others simply call the socialist community a "communist empire." [My emphasis]

Another brand of anti-Sovietism—that which expresses itself in the bourgeois attacks against detente—stems from the already mentioned bourgeois distortion of the idea of "peaceful coexistence." Arbatov notes that the main line of these attacks comprises "attempts to prove that only the Soviet Union and the other socialist countries are deriving benefit from detente, while the West constantly remains on the losing side."[87] From the Soviet point of view, of course, nothing could be further from the truth; detente is a function of "peaceful coexistence," which is itself a form of the struggle for progress, and "progress" is a phenomenon from which everyone must benefit.

The final example of anti-Sovietism which receives prominent attention in the Soviet literature is the U.S. "human rights" campaign. In this regard, Kudinov and Pletnikov, writing in 1974, declared that "Anticommunist propaganda spares no efforts in order to blacken socialist society and portray the imaginary suppression of the rights and freedoms of the individual. . . . This slander is extensively employed in order to hinder the growth of the force of attraction of socialism in the nonsocialist part of the world and to cause distrust and even open hostility toward the new social system."[88] Soviet analysts condemn as "hypocritical"[89] the attempt to cloak the campaign to defend human rights in arguments about "freedom of the individual." In their view such arguments ignore the "class" implications of the concept of freedom. Once again, bourgeois analysts refuse to ask: "Which of the classes has freedom?" or "Is there freedom from the exploitation of one class by another?" An honest answer to these questions shows, in Mitin's words that "the workingman's true freedom is attained in the class struggle."[90]

Another concept frequently utilized by American foreign policy makers and intolerable to the Soviets is that of the "free exchange, or free flow, of ideas and information." Soviet analysts have variously described this concept as "a cover for 'psychological warfare' against the socialist countries," a justification for "electronic imperialism" and "subversion,"[91] and a "demand for the right to interfere in the internal affairs of other countries."[92] Particularly offensive to Soviet analysts are U.S. notions as to the sources of this "free flow" of ideas. In the words of Zasurskii, "In all the capitalist countries the press is in the hands of the big monopolies, and radio broadcasting and television are the property of major concerns or of bourgeois states."[93] The nature of the source renders the entire flow suspect in Soviet eyes. Zasurskii argues that information disseminated by many Western newspaper and magazine associations, as well as by radio and television, by no means corresponds to reality and there are numerous examples of this. . . . In the United States less than 21 percent of the population trusts the information in the newspapers." This talk about information flow, then, is nothing but the monopolies' defense of their own class interests. As Zasurskii concludes: "Bourgeois theoreticians do not hide the fact that the press, radio, and television serve the aims of manipulating public opinion. They justify their activity in every way by referring to the 'freedom of speech,' which is actually the freedom for the capitalists to carry out propaganda in their own interests." And what is the stuff of this propaganda? According to Korobeinikov,

> The output of the mass information media of the capitalist countries frequently represents nothing other than an apologia for violence, cynicism and pathological perversions. Such works of "mass culture" contradict, for example, the principles of socialist culture and are incompatible with the nurturing in the individual of lofty moral qualities and the enrichment of his spiritual world.[94]

Insofar as the American "bourgeois state" is its source, the flow of ideas advances American foreign policy interests.[95] As such, Soviet analysts view it as a means for the "ideological infiltration of the Soviet Union and other socialist countries with the view to undermining their ideological-political unity and 'eroding' the socialist system from within."[96] The U.S. "propaganda machine" will stop at nothing in its campaign of "bourgeois chauvinistic ideology": "The U.S. military clique utilizes the movies, radio, television, and press organs to implant a spirit of militarism, glorify the cult of violence, and to create an atmosphere of malevolence and mistrust

123

toward other countries and, primarily, toward everything social-ist."[97] The American government continues to support Radio Free Europe and Radio Liberty, which are "continuing the anticommu-nist and anti-Soviet slander campaign."[98] When in 1973 Congress appropriated new funds for these stations, which are said to "be-long to the CIA," one Soviet commentator noted that the 313 representatives and 76 senators who voted this support "must have known what they were doing: they were essentially voting against the relaxation of tension."[99]

Yet another major component of the American ideological strat-egy includes all those tactics that can be subsumed under the "strat-egy of building bridges." The Soviets argue that this strategy, origi-nally devised by Zbigniew Brzezinski, entails:

> using the easing of international tension and the promotion of com-mercial, scientific, and technical relations with the East European socialist countries for ideological subversion in these countries, whipping up nationalistic feeling and encouraging revisionist ele-ments. By bringing sustained, differentiated ideological, political, and economic influence to bear on the socialist countries, the im-perialists strive to divide them in their attitude to various eco-nomic, political, and international problems and subvert the social-ist community.[100]

In this case the Soviets allege that the main tactic is to exact a price for the benefits of economic, scientific, and technical cooper-ation with the West—namely, to compel the East European states to loosen their links with the Soviet Union. The anticommunists combine this tactic with assertions that the Soviet Union is exploit-ing its East European satellites, and thus pursue a policy of "selec-tive coexistence."[101] Altogether, these tactics seek "to bring about ideological changes that will eventually lead to political changes."[102]

Viewed as the primary American policy line toward the social-ist community during the 1960s, this strategy was still in force during the 1970s, but with a few amendments. The most basic change was the adoption of "a more differentiated approach to individual socialist countries and individual categories of the popu-lation."[103] This change in turn spawned various tactical initiatives, including: the "liberalization of socialism," the use of "reformism," the doctrine of "peaceful penetration," the use of "social democratization," the use of East-West trade and other exchanges for sub-version, and the use of "creeping counterrevolution." Soviet analysts noted changes in the rhetoric of American policy as well: from "bridge building" to "verbiage" about "a new strategy in the interests of peace"[104]—a strategy that nevertheless seemed to incorporate most of the essential elements of bridge-building.

Soviet analysts see the convergence theory as the theoretical foundation of the bridge-building strategy,[105] and, as a result, the general strategy is said to include the various bourgeois efforts at "reformism," the "liberalization of socialism," or "social democratization." In short, the bridge-building strategy encourages the socialist system to accomplish its part of the convergence process by becoming more democratic through establishment of a multiparty system and the adoption of a less draconian stance in its human-rights policy. As the Soviets see it, "The renunciation of the principles of socialist management, the restoration of bourgeois democracy, and the abolition of the leading role of the Communist party—this is what all the anticommunist recipes for 'humanization,' 'democratization,' and 'liberalization' of the socialist system boil down to."[106]

Soviet analysts see the "doctrine of peaceful penetration" as an integral part of the general bridge-building strategy. M. Mitin refers to this "doctrine" as one of the forms of the convergence theory, the supporters of which "try to use every opportunity to break the unity of the fraternal countries of socialism by kindling nationalist trends in them."[107] Kudinov and Pletnikov, however, have a broader sense of the motive behind this "doctrine," observing that it seeks to make active use of the atmosphere of relaxation and the expansion of East-West cooperation in many fields "for the export of bourgeois and petty bourgeois ideology."[108] These writers allege that the anticommunists intend "to legalize bourgeois propaganda in the socialist society and to use all available means of ideological influence in order to erode, loosen, and undermine the foundations of socialism from within."

East-West trade is one of the primary means of perpetrating such subversion. The Soviets detect a conscious effort on the part of Western traders to encourge a "commercial way of thinking"[109] and to resurrect the concepts of a private entrepreneurial economy,[110] while pushing the socialist countries toward adoption of some form of "market socialism."[111] Bourgeois ideologists, it is argued, hope that increased commercial contact, the attendant growth of scientific and technical cooperation, and the resulting use in material prosperity will create an atmosphere in which the people of the socialist countries will develop "property-obsessed, consumer-minded instincts that will push communist objectives and moral principles into the background."[112] Other qualities allegedly "distinctive" to the capitalist way of life, are introduced through this same pattern of subversion. They include: "extreme individualism, violence, unspirituality, and self-interest," as well as "everything that constitutes the basis of the narrow-minded ideology of the so-called consumer society"—qualities that are all "aimed at blunting the class-consciousness of the working people."[113] The use of increased cultural exchanges and the promotion of tourism is seen as a natural concomitant of this kind of "subversive" activity.[114] In this regard, however, Korionov observes that not all forms of international exchange (nor of ideological struggle in general, for that matter) are equal:

> When Soviet people repulse the ideological saboteurs, certain bourgeois press organs try to interpret this as the USSR's reluctance to agree to develop cultural, scientific, and social ties with Western countries. Lies and slander! We are firmly convinced of the correctness of our path and our Marxist-Leninist ideology. Therefore, we have nothing to fear from the expansion of contacts and the exchange of spiritual values and information, which are natural under the conditions of the relaxation of tension. We are sure that such an exchange will serve to spread the truth about socialism.[115]

As has been mentioned briefly, nationalism is identified as one of the main ideological weapons in the arsenal of American foreign policy. According to one commentator, "the main function of nationalism, whatever its form, is to split, divide, and fragment the international working class and also the advanced contingents of the national liberation movement."[116] Since the Soviet Union and the socialist community of states constitute the main bastion of the working class and provide the primary support for national liberation movements, they naturally have become the targets against which the anticommunists wield the "bourgeois concepts of nationalism," attempting "to hinder the objective, all-sided integration of the community of socialist states, break their unity and cohesion, and emasculate proletarian internationalism as the paramount principle of relations between socialist countries."[117]

Soviet analysts have found that bourgeois groups of differing political persuasions employ particular variations of this basic strategy. Thus, the "moderate conservatives" advocate provoking a "mass rejection of socialism" by stimulating "nationalist tendencies" that will ultimately push the East European countries back to capitalism without violence or war. Bourgeois "liberals" tend to argue that socialism should be encouraged to evolve toward "national communisms," preferring this outcome to policies that might risk an "internationalist" "world revolutionary reconstruction."[118]

Zagladin's authoritative text on this subject maintains that the theoretical basis for this strategy of "reliance on nationalism" lies in the perversion of one of the principles of Marxism-Leninism itself, namely, the "contradiction" between the "universality" of communist ideology and the fact that each communist party must consider the characteristics of its particular nation. Whereas Marxism-Leninism postulates that social development advances from this contradiction toward "universality," the bourgeois ideologists allegedly see the same contradiction but conclude that it is evolving toward "national communism." As one analyst observes in the Zagladin volume, " 'National Marxisms,' it is said, are bound to compete with each other in proving that they are the only authentic variety. Unification of Marxism is said to be impossible because the national interests of different socialist countries collide and will continue to collide."[119] Thus, when discussing the socialist community of states, "imperialist ideologues" refer to "Moscow's hegemony" while sparing no effort "to find objective points allegedly favoring a pro-Western orientation in some socialist countries."[120] Part and parcel of this tactic is the bourgeois propaganda about the economic "exploitation" of the East European states by the Soviet Union, a campaign designed to stir up national enmities. Soviet analysts argue that whereas bourgeois ideologists previously besmirched the true nature of the socialist community's economic success, they now see that these "falsifications" crumble upon collision with "reality," and as a result are forced to follow a different course. Gambling on nationalistic feelings, these bourgeois ideologists "hypocritically" acknowledge the economic achievements of socialism, thus creating "a semblance of 'objectivity.' With this gimmick the bourgeois ideologists are trying to turn the pride that the people of the socialist countries take in their achievements into nationalistic conceit."[121]

As a final illustration of their argument that bourgeois ideologists will go to any extreme in their campaign to inflame nationalist prejudices, Soviet analysts point to the "slandering" of Soviet nationalities policy by anticommunist theorists. Maintaining that the national question is fatal, that today is the "age of nationalism," and that nationalism is an everlasting and independent phenomenon that transcends all other ideological systems and loyalties, these bourgeois theorists attempt to show that the Soviet policy of national integration has been a failure and that the persistence of national discrimination and inequality throughout the Soviet republics dooms it to still more severe setbacks. Confronted with this argument, however, Soviet analysts manifest a noticeable discomfort. As one commentator concedes: "Nationalism represents a special danger for the process of the revolutionary transformation of the world."[122] Such an admission is a noteworthy contrast to the smug scorn that characterizes most Soviet views of American analysis and strategy.

Finally, the Soviets consider the exploitation of ideological diversity—especially among left-wing ideologists—to be one of the crucial ideological means of American foreign policy. By using the same tactic that they employ to exploit nationalism, namely, to "split, divide, and fragment" the international workers movement, the socialist community of states, and the national liberation movements, the anticommunists allegedly seek "to disorient people ideologically and distract them from Marxism-Leninism."[123] This tactic is supposedly implemented by manipulating all the varieties of "opportunism," a notoriously ambiguous Soviet term that denotes the adoption of "wrong" or "unscientific" ideologies for whatever political purposes. According to the Soviet lexicon, "opportunism" may be of a rightist or leftist nature and includes all sorts of "revisionism" and "reformism." "Ultra-left extremists," "right social democrats," and other assorted "radicals" may be included among the "opportunists."[124] Indeed, any group that professes Marxism-Leninism but does not follow Moscow's interpretation may be accused of opportunism. All of these "revisionists" are said to have "accumulated a stock of falsificatory ideas, forms and methods of subversive activity within the Communist and workers' movement," thereby enabling "the forces of anticommunism [to use] opportunism's ideological and tactical arsenal for their own unseemly purposes."[125] The American reliance on the "Peking leadership's hostile actions" against the USSR is a primary example of such bourgeois exploitation of opportunism.[126] The Soviets argue that the anticommunists will exploit any statement from Peking which suits their purposes and thus they embrace with "great joy" every Chinese polemic against Soviet "social-imperialism."[127] Since bourgeois propagandists are "ready to make use of anything that comes to hand and invent anything in order to question the moral political unity of Soviet society," they are quick to indulge in infamous "exaggeration" of the "verbiage" of Academician A. D. Sakharov—a subject treated in the revealing editorial in the September 1973 *Kommunist*. While the bourgeois press is accused of treating Sakharov as the spokesman for some kind of "opposition" to Soviet policy, Soviet analysis proceeds to counter all his arguments, denouncing them as an "eclectic jumble of 'imported cliches' dragged out in anti-Soviet propaganda exercises," and declaring that "Sakharov has not found and could not find either understanding, or much less, support among Soviet people." As he has supposedly found support only "outside our country," he is said to be a "tool in the hands of the enemies of socialism."[128]

Another favorite tactic of bourgeois ideologists is to distort and exploit any apparent schism in the world Communist movement. For example, the ideological battles between West European Communists and the Soviet theorists over the primacy of the "dictatorship of the proletariat" are said to have produced a new anticommunist theory. This theory posits the existence of two types of communism—the Western and the Eastern—and recommends that the bourgeoisie "support 'Western communism' against 'Eastern communism of the Soviet model.' "[129] Related to this theory are the "insinuations to the effect that Communist parties are 'degenerating,' " including claims that some Communist parties are no longer innovative or revolutionary, that they have diluted their ideological traditions, and that the revolutionary standard has passed to "more ideologically volatile and activist groups."[130] The anticommunists then place their hopes in such volatile groups, activating "all the former ideological tendencies that have long since been refuted by life itself—Trotskyism, Menshevism, anarchism, and so forth."[131]

The final result is the creation of a "united ideological and political front of anticommunism, reformism, and revisionism."[132] Especially interesting to Soviet analysts is the fact that such fronts often form in connection with the "inflaming of nationalist prejudices." As Kudinov and Pletnikov maintain, "concessions to nationalism and direct adoption of nationalist positions now often constitute a sign under which right and left opportunism unite." Thus, Soviet analysts have discovered links among most of the varieties of anti-Sovietism and anticommunism, which in one way or another are exploited as ideological weapons of the American foreign policy process.

In 1969, at the Moscow international conference of Communist and workers' parties, Leonid Brezhnev said: "Imperialism cannot count on success by openly stating its real aims. It is compelled to create a whole sytsem of ideological myths that blur the real significance of its intentions and dull the people's watchfulness."[133] Brezhnev's statement expresses the essence of the second goal of the ideological manipulations that characterize American foreign policy. Alleging that a growing number of people in the West are "doubting and reappraising what were formerly considered to be capitalism's inviolable values—the principle of private ownership, bourgeois democracy, and so forth," the Soviets maintain that "the open defense of these 'values' is proving to be a fiasco."[134] As a result, anticommunism increasingly has "to hide behind pseudoliberal phraseology, to create myths, and to resort to various types of subterfuge to conceal its real essence."[135]

Soviet analysts have written extensively about the various forms of such concealment. There is, for example, the policy of "controlling conflicts" which is viewed by the Soviets as a justification for maintaining "world stability" and the status quo.* Since the policy calls for the use of "international mechanisms" in controlling conflicts, the Soviets see it as a mask for what they term the "strategy of collective colonialism." As A. Baryshev sees it, "This strategy is now [1969] clearly being given priority over 'unilateral actions' by the United States in intervening in the affairs of sovereign countries and peoples, inasmuch as these 'unilateral actions' have failed dismally."[136] Baryshev's point, then, is that given these failures, the

---

*For further discussion of "controlling conflicts" see below, page 182.

United States has embraced such implements as multilateral aid, international economic organizations (which further the goals of capitalism), and regional organizations to exercise a policy of "colonial exploitation." Even direct military intervention is carried out under the respectable cover of international cooperation. As Baryshev concludes, the United States, operating "under the guise of assisting in strengthening the capacities of certain regional organizations in carrying out 'investigations' and 'supervision of peace' in the corresponding regions, . . . intends to utilize these organizations to interfere in the internal affairs of these states."[137]

Diversionary tactics are another form of concealment prized by anticommunist policy makers. One example of this method, cited by Iu. Nalin, was the concerted effort to publish Alexander Solzhenitsyn's *Gulag Archipelago* simultaneously in many Western countries. Nalin notes that simultaneously in all NATO countries there began a "clamorous campaign" to show how this book confirmed Western theses about the absence of rights in the USSR and the persecution of dissenters. Observing that while this clamor was meant to "disorient" the masses during a period of exacerbated domestic problems and sociopolitical conflicts, Nalin concludes that its primary aim was "to divert world public attention from the crimes and terror of the fascist junta of Chile."[138] Such an explanation reveals a Soviet conception of the bourgeoisie as a group that is driven by "nationalist-chauvinist" ideas, but that is also flexible and wily enough to utilize methods of "interimperialist" cooperation to guarantee its survival.

Soviet analysts agree that the "whitewashing" of capitalism is another important tactic in the American ideological strategy. Here again the Soviets find a whole repertoire of anticommunist themes, though they devote their principal attention to the notion of the "transformation" of capitalism. Since it is allegedly "impossible and dangerous" to champion capitalism under its own name, "its high priests have begun to propound the theory that capitalism is 'disappearing.' "[139] Among the variations that bourgeois ideologists play on this theme, Soviet analysts list the following: that the nature of capitalism has been regenerated, that the exploiting substance of bourgeois society has been modified, and that capitalism has surmounted social injustice. One of the principal bourgeois arguments for the changing nature of capitalism is summarized by Soviet analysts in the phrase, "transformation of private capitalist property."[140] The Soviets explain that the bourgeois analysis of this transformation emphasizes the separation of management from the ownership of property, as well as the process by which the diffusion, "democratization," and "socialization" of property are allegedly reshaping the nature of private property, stripping it of its former character as a means of exploitation. The Soviets see these arguments as attempts to conceal what Marxist-Leninist analysis recognizes immediately: that property is increasingly concentrated in the hands of the monopoly capitalists. In the words of one commentator, "They [the bourgeois ideologists] are trying to make people believe that inasmuch as the bourgeoisie is being 'progressively removed' from power and steadily losing control of the implements and means of production, there is no longer any sense whatever in fighting the capitalist proprietors."[141]

Bourgeois ideologists also explain the modifications of capitalism by pointing to the "transformation of the social structure of capitalism" through the "deproletarianization" and "integration" of professional groups, which are giving rise to a "new" society free of class distinctions, and therefore, without social contradictions.[142] This theory is allegedly put forth to refute the Marxist-Leninist idea that social contradictions and antagonisms are increasing in capitalist society, and thereby to stave off revolutionary thinking.

Finally, the Soviets cite the bourgeois theory of the "transformation of the state" into an organ that serves the interests of the whole of society—the "welfare state." The anticommunist aspect of this theory is "its attempt to disprove the Marxist-Leninist theory that the bourgeois state is an instrument of class rule and of the suppression of the working masses."[143] The bourgeois ideologists are depicted as exploiting the idea of "political pluralism" in their attempt to convince their audience that the state takes the interests of the working people into consideration. Furthermore, they argue that the welfare state is able to assure full employment, equitable distribution of incomes, participation in decision making, and improved living conditions. Kortunov maintains that these arguments have one common denominator, namely, the idea "that modern capitalism is, properly speaking, no longer capitalism and that it has been 'transformed' under the influence of industrialization and scientific and technical progress into a society that is allegedly closer to socialism than socialism itself."[144] To all these arguments, however, the Soviets reply simply that this alleged transformation "proves to be nothing more than the formation of a system of state capitalism."[145] All the talk about a new "bureaucratically administered society" is characterized as the interjection of "elitist technocratic concepts" whose "class meaning is no secret": they simply serve "to camouflage the domination of monopoly capital and its complete economic and political power."[146]

As the bourgeois theorists exploit the idea of "transformation," Soviet analysts observe that they use various concepts and approach the problem from various directions, thereby attempting to create the impression "of the broad range of public opinion allegedly inherent in the 'free world' in contrast with 'totalitarian' socialism, which preaches only one world outlook."[147] The promotion of such ideological pluralism is, of course, interpreted as just one more tactic in the ideological struggle to conceal reality. Thus, it is said that

> the abundance of anticommunist concepts in their most diverse variations is caused by other factors and pursues completely definite aims. The point is that as ever increasing numbers of social strata join the liberation struggle against capitalism, anticommunism, in addition to opportunism, becomes increasingly multifaceted and splits into a multiplicity of directions. This process objectively reflects, on the other hand, the heterogeneity of the forces participating in the revolutionary process, and on the other hand, the ruling classes' subjective aspiration to conquer the consciousness of various social strata and to inculcate anticommunist prejudices in various social groups in capitalist society.[148]

When listing the efforts to improve the appearance of capitalism, Soviet analysts give particular emphasis to two other activities of bourgeois ideologists: the search for scapegoats for the failures of capitalism, and attempts to work out new doctrines to cure the ills allegedly inherent in capitalism's contradictory nature. The main scapegoat that the bourgeois ideologists have found is the scientific-technical revolution. In this connection Yermolenko notes the "attempts to 'free' capitalism itself from any responsibility not only for the antihumanist utilization of many scientific and technical

133

achievements but also for all its contradictions in general, and to shift this responsibility onto the scientific-technical revolution."[149]* Having shifted the blame from capitalism itself, these ideologists then set out to frame new doctrines to explain away the remaining contradictions. Among their solutions is the doctrine of the "humanization of labor" and the organization of more "human relations" between businessmen and workers. As N. Bogomolova notes, the "human relations" doctrine "is designed to undermine the labor movement from within in an attempt to integrate it into the capitalist system." This doctrine is said to entail the use of "subtle psychological methods to create among workers the illusion that in present conditions employers and workers can become 'equal partners' with common interest in the success of 'their' factory and in the establishment of 'good human relations.' "[150]

At this point the reader may ask what these matters have to do with American foreign policy. From an American perspective such a question is logical, and indeed may be buttressed by Bogomolova's observation that "the 'human relations' doctrine stands apart from other pro-capitalist theories on account of the fact that it is concerned not so much with general socio-economic and political concepts but rather with devising concrete methods for ideological 'conditioning' of workers in the factory." Nevertheless, it is important to remember that from the *Soviet* perspective such apparently "domestic" questions have international implications. Thus, both a so-called struggle for national liberation in a small country in the Third World, essentially a domestic struggle for power, and the dynamics of the "class struggle" within the United States itself are seen to have implications for the correlation of forces between the two social systems. The "human relations doctrine," an alleged attempt to mitigate "contradictions" between labor and capital and "prevent workers from coming under the influence of communist ideas," can therefore be seen as a tool of the bourgeoisie in the ideological struggle against the *international* workers' movement."

---

*It is interesting to note that whereas the Soviets see some bourgeois ideologists using the scientific-technical revolution as a scapegoat, others, as was mentioned earlier, are seen to employ it as the source of salvation—the vehicle by which capitalist "contradictions" may be eased. According to orthodox Soviet thinking, this dichotomy in attitudes illustrates the ineluctable quandries that capitalism encounters when faced with the "objective" and "inexorable" forces of social development.

It amounts, according to the Soviets, to another of the "camouflaged forms of exploitation and oppression of the working people . . . in order to keep the masses under its ideological and political control as far as possible."[151]

The Soviets categorize the use of ideas as a source for new strategy and tactics as the third main ideological means of American foreign policy. Though this category appears equivalent to the notion that "American ideology serves as a guide for action," Soviet analysts never put it in those terms because they do make a certain distinction between the "ideology" and the "interests" of the American ruling class. Since "anticommunism," the ideology of at least the reactionary, "unrealistic," military-industrial segment of this class, is directed *against* the forces of "peace and progress," it serves primarily as an auxiliary of the *interests* of the ruling class (or at least those of its "reactionary" factions).* As a result, this ideology cannot be the guiding force of American policies. Moreover, to attribute such qualities to it would, in the Soviet mind, dignify it as a possible "alternative" to Marxist-Leninist ideology—an implicit conferral of legitimacy that would carry most unpleasant connotations. Ruling class interests thus remain the true determinants, or "guide," to American policy. Nevertheless, in serving these interests, American ideology is seen as a source of new strategies that are often implemented in the context of "imperialist" policy.

In the development of "imperialism's long-term, comprehensive political strategy," the "bourgeois social sciences" are held to play a growing role. As a result, one commentator notes that "state-monopoly capitalism's need for recommendations founded on knowledge of the actual situation is fostering the numerical growth of specialized research centers. In the U.S., over 200 centers devise imperialism's strategy and tactics."[152] Especially influential, according to the

---

*One should be sensitive, here, to the differences between the traditionalist and realist schools. On the one hand, so long as it refuses to discern significant differences between factions of the American ruling class, the traditionalist school will continue to identify anticommunism as *the* ideology of a monolithic ruling class. Soviet realists, on the other hand, recognizing differences between such American factions, associate overt anticommunism largely with that segment of the class that is most "unrealistic" and imperialistic, and find a noticeable dilution or weakening of anticommunist sentiment among the American "realists."

Soviets, are the centers for the study of communism, which are used both to "evolve diverse and more flexible concepts of anti-communist ideology" and to work out "diverse forms, methods, strategies and tactics of the imperialist struggle against socialism."[153] Also cited frequently are the "innumerable Zionist organizations" in the United States, which are "helping to devise anti-communist strategy and spread anti-communist propaganda."[154] Soviet analysts claim that the "ideological orientation" of most of these centers is controlled by "monopoly capital" through the system of foundations. In these centers, as one analyst notes:

> anti-communist theorists draw up not only situation reviews but also long-term forecasts and formulate conclusions and recommendations providing the "scientific" basis for global anti-communist policy and propaganda. For instance, no sooner had Peking broken the unity of the socialist countries and begun to pursue a policy hostile to the Soviet Union than the Columbia Research Institute on Communist Affairs, headed by Zbigniew Brzezinski, began drawing up recommendations on the forms and methods of stimulating the "erosion" of socialism.[155]

As the Soviets saw it, the new world situation engendered by the Sino-Soviet rift provided a cue for the bourgeois strategy mills, which immediately began to churn out new, anticommunist variations on the traditional concept of the "balance of power," eventually producing the concept of "three-sided diplomacy," or the "triangular relationship." In 1973, V. Lukin observed that "now, according to the opinion of U.S. theoreticians, the side that displays the greatest flexibility and skill in applying the 'objective rules' of 'three-sided' diplomacy will find itself in the most favorable position."[156] In the Soviet view, of course, the "objective rules" to which Lukin refers are not objective at all, but a product of bourgeois (i.e., unscientific) ideas and the actual U.S. policies based on those ideas. As Lukin illustrates:

> Attempts to devise formalized "rules" of this kind are typical, for example of Z. Brzezinski: "In the triangular system of relations it is most profitable to have better relations with the two other participants than these latter two have with each other. Basically, this rule has been the guideline in Washington's relations with Moscow and Peking from the very emergence of the Sino-Soviet conflict."

General Ends and Means of U.S. Foreign Policy

The changes in the world situation brought on by the "change in the correlation of forces in favor of socialism" were seen, especially by Soviet realists, as yet another challenge to bourgeois theorists. Since, in the Soviet view, these changes were the function not only of the rise in the power of socialism, but also of the "exacerbation of interimperialist contradictions," bourgeois ideologists were forced to develop the concept of "multipolarity." In the late 1960s, Lukin noted in an earlier article, "there appeared the first works whose authors attempted to prove that the buildup of military might no longer resulted in a proportionate increase in global influence, that new centers of political attraction had sprung up in the world, that the world was becoming multipolar, and that these circumstances should be reflected in American global strategy."[157]

In the Soviet view, these "ivory-tower research projects" combined with the pressures of the new world situation to produce the "Nixon Doctrine"—the new foreign policy doctrine of the United States. "The Nixon Doctrine," says Lukin, "was born at the juncture between those two tendencies—the regional and the global, the pragmatically vital and the *a priori conceptual* (my emphasis).[158] Lukin's statement is noteworthy as an illustration of the fact that Soviet realists acknowledge that *some* bourgeois ideologists are sufficiently independent from the capitalist socioeconomic base to produce, *"a priori,"* a "realistic" assessment of the worldwide correlation of forces. This assessment, when combined with the interests of the "realistic" faction of the ruling class, led to an ideological justification and a set of policy guidelines for this new doctrine.

Soviet analysts attributed conceptual origins, although of a less "independent" nature, to many more American strategies, doctrines, and tactics. Examples include the policy of "containment," the strategy of "building bridges," the policy of "collective colonialism," and more recent ideas such as "trilateralism." At the root of each of these policies Soviet analysts see a corresponding concept—theories of Soviet "imperialism," the "convergence" theory, Western notions of "collective security," and "multipolarity"—and, in turn, each of these concepts is said to derive from a fundamentally anticommunist frame of mind.

The pattern of Soviet analysis, then, is remarkably consistent. The bulk of this analysis is the work of traditionalist Soviet theorists who see the sinister hand of the anticommunist American ruling class behind every idea that emerges from the scribblings of "bour-

geois ideologists." Their efforts to monitor and "expose" the falla-
cies of these bourgeois ideas are, of course, a mandated ritual of
their profession. They are motivated partly out of a general perception that any idea emanating from the capitalist United States has
an insidious angle to it. They also may be driven out of a sense
of political or ideological insecurity—especially in light of their comments on such ideas as "bridge building." Here, traditionalist analysts may very well feel that the Soviet political and ideological hold
on the East European satellites is dangerously tenuous, a sentiment
that could explain the particularly defensive tone of so much of
their rhetoric.

A number of realist analysts such as Trofimenko or Arbatov
participate in this ritual as well, and much of their analysis accords
with that of their traditionalist colleagues. There are, however, real
differences between the two schools, and it is noteworthy, that, by
and large, the realists choose not to engage their traditionalist comrades in debates on these subjects. What a traditionalist commentator may identify as a sneaky attempt to disguise the true nature of
capitalism—for example, theories such as that of the welfare state
—a realist analyst might well construe as a step toward greater
"realism." Nevertheless, in contrast to the traditionalist concern for
identifying most every Western idea as anticommunist, the realists
have managed to ferret out a couple of crucial American ideas that
they see as expressing the American "realist" faction, and therefore
supporting their conclusion that there is indeed a split in the American ruling class. However few they are in number, these ideas—
particularly that of multipolarity—are especially significant, because, as the Soviet realists see it, they represent a significant American analysis of the correlation of forces which, not accidentally,
accords with their own.

Economic Means

According to the Soviets, the economic means of American foreign policy are the central foundation of "imperialist" policy in
general, for these means are an intrinsic part of the economic interests of the "ruling class"—interests that ultimately dictate the
form and content of all policy. Since Soviet analysts define American foreign policy as coterminous with the policy of the American
ruling class, we must remember that they see both state policy and

"private" initiatives as determined by the interests of the ruling class. Private operations which extend overseas, after all, are conducted not by the petite bourgeoisie but by the "monopolies." As the Soviets see it, "some 25 major monopolies account for more than 50 percent of the total private American capital invested abroad."[159] To the Soviet mind, then, whether the monopolies conduct business by themselves or use the state to serve their purposes, the effect is the same. Although the realist analysts have discerned differences between the interests of different monopolies—some with foreign economic interests and others primarily concerned with domestic commerce—both traditionalists and realists are in substantial agreement as to the economic methods pursued by the imperialist, foreign-oriented faction. What follows is a brief look at the Soviet consensus on these methods.

Soviet analysts deem the "export of capital" to be the primary method of imperialist economic policy. The purpose of this policy is to remove "surplus" capital, which has accumulated in the form of "excess profits," from the metropolitan country (here, the United States).[160] As one commentator explains: "A 'surplus' of capital forms not because it is not needed by society, but because the capitalists can find no application for it. 'Surplus' capital begins to form when the effective demand in a given country for a particular line is satisfied."[161] Such "surplus" then seeks profitable application in other countries. To Soviet analysts, the very existence of this process indicates that capitalism is unable to utilize resources in the interests of the "whole society": priorities for the use of capital are not set by the "people" and their needs but by the profit-seeking imperatives of the "monopolists." In addition to increasing profits, the export of capital helps to secure the raw materials and food needed by the metropolitan country and contributes to the construction of an international economic system "which enables the monopolies of a few developed countries to dominate over the peoples of the world."[162]

There are basically two types of export capital: productive capital and loan capital. Productive capital is used in the acquisition of "productive, commercial, financial, transport or other enterprises," as well as in the establishment of foreign branches of domestic monopolies, and, according to Soviet analysis, it "always leads to the emergence of foreign property in the importer country, and to the creation of a nucleus of influence for the imperialist monopolies."[163]

139

Distinguishing between "direct" and "portfolio" investments, Soviet analysts note that the vast majority of American investments abroad are direct, a fact that indicates the "annexationist character of American export capital."[164] Loan capital constitutes the lending of capital to foreign entrepreneurs or governments while requiring interest payments. The export of loan capital (on which the receiving foreign entrepreneur or government must pay interest) is seen as a successful means of pushing domestic "overproduction" ("surplus" commodities) onto foreign markets, and thereby helping "to delay economic crises in the metropolitan countries."[165] The Soviets argue that one corollary to both these methods of capital export is capital protectionism—the erection of "barriers against the penetration of 'alien' capital into monopolized production spheres."[166] The utilization of all these methods enables the monopolists to pursue both their domestic and foreign interests without obstruction.

Soviet analysts maintain that the export of capital produces two types of "economic relations": first, "the struggle between the monopolies of the main capital-exporting countries for more profitable spheres of application for their capital," and second, "the exploitation of peoples in the capital-importing countries."[167] The "acute competitive struggle" between the imperialist monopolies has led to "clashes" of an "incredibly violent and destructive" nature, the enormous costs of which have prompted the monopolies to come to terms and divide up markets and spheres of influence. As one commentator puts it: "So, to end competition among themselves the biggest monopolies in the imperialist countries divide the world economy among themselves and share out the world markets for specific commodities."[168] The "exploitation" of the peoples of the capital-importing countries occurs, according to the Soviets, because the monopolies "take out of such countries profits higher than the new funds they invest in their economy."[169] Frequently citing Lenin's dictum that "the export of capital is parasitism squared," Soviet scholars argue that this policy is designed to "take over the domestic markets of other countries,"[170] to sap these countries of the fruits of their labor, and, in doing so, to dominate them completely. In the past this policy was carried out in the form of "colonialism," but, according to the Soviets, it continues to thrive, changed only by its adoption of the more "subtle" and "covert" methods of "neocolonialism."

The attempt to realize their "dirty deeds" causes the monopolies to turn to the state, whose main service is to protect monopoly interests through the use of force. One Soviet analyst observes that "the accumulation of capital invested by the monopolies in different areas of the capitalist world makes it necessary to safeguard that capital by force of arms,"[171] while another maintains that "force is the chief criterion of any relations under imperialism."[172] According to Soviet thinking, then, it is the economic interests of the monopolies which constitute the basis of the entire U.S. "policy of force" and which necessitate mutual dependence between the monopolies and the state. As mentioned earlier, Soviet analysts see "militarism" as an intrinsic part of this relationship. The state is used to maintain "international tension" so as to stimulate both domestic and foreign orders of military equipment from the military-industrial monopolies, which consequently reap enormous prcfits. In the words of M. Zakhmatov, "militarism and expansionist foreign economic policy . . . nurture each other" as they "exacerbate the international situation."[173] As the state strives to fulfill its functions of protection, this relationship between monopolies and state extends to other spheres of cooperation. Zakhmatov notes, for example, that the development of foreign sources of raw materials "is determined to a considerable degree by military-strategic considerations."[174] In satisfying its own requirements, the state conducts programs for the accumulation of strategic raw materials through import channels, thereby providing new opportunities for the monopolies to exploit. Thus, "military-political considerations exert a great influence on the export of capital."[175] In addition, Zakhmatov observes, these military-political imperatives are the primary determinant in the export of state capital (loans and subsidies), the main recipients of which are the "regimes that have linked themselves most closely to the militarily aggressive U.S. policy line."

I. Mosin has argued that an essential stipulation of the "American concept of economic 'aid' " is that all such assistance must lead to an increased demand for private American financing.[176] Thus, when granting "aid" to foreign countries, the state attempts to make the recipients encourage conditions that will stimulate monopoly investments. "Stringed loans" are another of the methods that characterize the U.S. government's policy of capital export. Such loans specify that the foreign borrower use the funds only for the purchase of American commodities—a stipulation that is said "to lead automatically to losses as high as 30 percent in foreign currency due to the high prices prevailing on the American market." So, while serving the direct economic interests of the monopolies, this policy of "aid," Mosin concludes, is "essentially a new form of political and economic bribery through which American imperialism tries to secure for itself military-strategic positions."

Soviet analysts portray the multinational corporations both "as a tool of imperialist foreign policy"[177] and as independent actors themselves. The former of these two roles is seen by the Soviets as exemplary of monopoly-state cooperation. Here, while pursuing their own economic interests, the multinationals add politico-strategic maneuvers to their repertoire. N. Turkatenko cites the "well-known subversive activity" of ITT and Kennecott Copper in Chile as an example—"activity aimed at preventing the accession to power in Chile of the government of Popular Unity headed by President Salvador Allende and then at creating conditions for a military putsch against this government."[178] The multinational corporations are also portrayed as exerting extensive efforts to serve American strategic imperatives by maintaining free access to Middle East oil. Turkatenko maintains that the attempt to use Israel as an "armed base" is one of the policies that illustrates the means by which America tries to fulfill these goals.

A final tool in imperialism's arsenal of general economic weapons is the policy of "economic blackmail"—a policy that the private monopolies or the state can carry out with equal effect. In 1975 R. Puchkov observed that ITT, "one of the biggest international monopolies, has stopped all financial support for its subsidiaries in Portugal," thus creating a situation in which "7,000 workers and employees of ITT's Portuguese enterprises may very soon find themselves unemployed."[179] Generalizing about the tactics used in such "campaigns of flagrant external pressure," Puchkov argued that:

> Initially, artificial difficulties are caused in the economy by pressing hidden springs and secret levers. Then in order to account for the proliferating acts of sabotage and boycott directed from outside, they [the monopolies] begin shouting at the tops of their voices about the "unstable situation" and the general "economic chaos" allegedly caused by "social experiments."

In Portugal and elsewhere, the purpose of such policies is, of course, "to prevent the development of the revolutionary process . . . and to sabotage the actions of those forces that are seeking to lead this country along the path of democracy." The state may perform similar acts of "economic blackmail," a favorite example being the alleged cancellation of U.S. loan commitments to India as a means of putting pressure on India during its war with Pakistan.[180] It is ironic that the Soviets can become so exercised at the withdrawal of the very forces that have been committing so much "parasitic exploitation," but Soviet propagandists are willing to employ any development that makes the imperialists look bad, even if they contradict the tenets of dialectical materialism in the process.

Scientific and Technical Means

As the Soviets see it, the use of science and technology by both the "monopolies" and the American "bourgeois state" constitutes "one of the principal spheres of [their] economic, social and political activity," and hence it is an important means of foreign policy.[181] To gain a proper understanding of this Soviet perception, it is necessary to recall the broader context in which Soviet analysts see both the "scientific-technical revolution" and the "contradictions" it produces in capitalist society. According to the traditional theory, the basic contradiction is that between the "revolutionary" properties of science and technology and the "reactionary" nature of bourgeois society. Private ownership, "selfish" interests, and the periodic "underemployment of productive capacities" of capitalism are all said to slow the pace (and prevent the full utilization) of scientific and technical progress, creating a contradiction between the "possibilities of the scientific and technical revolution and the obstacles capitalism places in its way." The traditionalist Soviet view is that these obstacles are "no accident," but simply the monopolists' efforts to preserve their socioeconomic system. As such, these "obstacles" imply that the monopolists realize (perhaps only subconsciously) that "in order to meet the needs of the scientific and technical revolution, a transition from capitalism to socialism must be made."[182] Soviet realists make a very different argument, concluding that the American bourgeoisie is, to some degree, successful in using science and technology to strengthen its position. The realist analysis, therefore, sees a greater bourgeois emphasis on using science and technology to ease as many contradictions as possible.

Both schools of Soviet analysis detect continuity and change in the American use of science and technology as a means of foreign policy but, in general, the traditionalists emphasize continuity while the realists diagnose and devote their attention to change. In some cases, members of both schools have identified elements of change, but their interpretations of its significance differ.

Soviet analysts have given particular emphasis to continuity in their discussions of the application of science and technology to politico-military strategy. Since, according to traditionalist theory, "force" has been the hallmark of all "capitalist relations," anything that aids the policy of force is considered an adjunct of that policy. Thus, Trofimenko discusses the development of military equipment under the conditions of the scientific-technical revolution, underscoring the fact that insofar as military force has been a primary means of American foreign policy, science and technology have been crucial in increasing the U.S. capability to use such means.[183] V. Zhurkin expands on this theme in his discussion of the capabilities of U.S. policy in international crises, pointing in particular to the role of the scientific-technical revolution in the development of "new, highly mobile means for transporting U.S. Armed Forces to international crisis zones."[184] The scientific-technical revolution has also been crucial to the creation of "an extremely refined system of information-processing and analysis," as well as "administrative centers equipped with the most modern means of communication and other technical innovations." Zhurkin also cites the importance of applying scientific methods to improve the actual policy-making process during international crisis situations. Such methods include the use of "the systems approach, decision-making theory, game theory, modeling (primarily in the form of experimental simulated political-military exercises), and various statistical methods of analysis (content analysis, communications analysis, and factor analysis)." Zhurkin pays special attention to the analytical techniques of "crisis simulation," highlighting such methodologies as: "PME—Political Military Exercise," an exercise in simulation of the decision-making of foreign countries; "INS—Inter-nation simulation," a crisis simulation technique using computers to quantify various qualitative phenomena; and "TEMPER—technological, economic, military, political evaluation routine," another computer-based methodology. He notes, however, that while "one must not overrate the influence exerted by new, and particularly simulated methods of analysis on U.S. policy in international crisis situations, particularly on the process of decision making, . . . the general 'climate' created by the development of such methods is undoubtedly making a definite impression on this process."[185] The development and utilization of such scientific methods are thus seen as occupying an important role in the policy of American administrations since the early 1960s, and it was this new "climate" to which Zhurkin attributes the Nixon administration's reconstruction of foreign policy decision-making, marked especially by the creation of the new organ of the National Security Council—the Washington Special Actions Group. While noting that this was the first time that a permanent body had been created for high-level decision-making during crises, Zhurkin declared that "the tendency to create such a narrow group [had] long existed in the United States."[186]

All of these developments contain a common denominator of continuity, no matter how new some of them may appear. The traditionalists detect such continuity in the persistent use of the "policy of force," otherwise known as the "from a position of strength" policy, and the use of scientific and technical methods as auxiliary means to expedite this policy. During the early 1970s, however, Soviet analysts—particularly the realists—began to note some changes in the general means and methods of American foreign policy, including those of the scientific and technical variety. It was during this period, it may be recalled, that the bulk of Soviet commentary diagnosed the major "shift in the correlation of forces in the world in favor of socialism." As noted above, this shift was a function not only of the rise in the power of the Soviet Union and all the "anti-imperialist movements" but also of the decline of American power, a process attributable to the exacerbation of the "crisis of capitalism" and its attendant "interimperialist contradictions." That many political circles in the United States were slow or reluctant to recognize these new world "realities" became a constant theme of Soviet analysis. The "refusal" to recognize these changes was seen as contributing to international tension, for it represented nothing more than the tenacious atavism of the "worn-out" and "rotten" mentality that U.S. policy must be conducted "from a position of strength." Nevertheless, since some Americans did acknowledge the changes in the world situation, Soviet analysts concluded that a debate was emerging among contending schools of thought.

First among these schools of thought, according to Anatoly Gromyko, is the " 'technological warfare' school of theoreticians." While paying lip service to the "new processes in international relations," these theoreticians allegedly "fight to continue the unrestrained arms race by using scientific and technical achievements in the military area."[187] Gromyko sees the policies of this school as expressed in such notions as: " 'Without superior technology, our [the United States'] strategy of deterrence is senseless.' . . . 'Without technological advantages we will never be able to fight and win small wars thousands of kilometers from our country or to prevent the occupation of Europe or Japan.' " He then declares that through repetition of these postulates, "the full array of decrepit dogmas of the 'position of strength' politicians is advanced by the advocates of 'technological warfare' as some kind of fundamentally 'new word' in the substantiation of a strategy called on to insure U.S. 'military superiority' over the USSR."

Those Americans who advocate "nonmilitary confrontation with the socialist countries" are said to constitute another school of thought. Gromyko notes that this group views the scientific-technical revolution as "a lever which the USA should use primarily to achieve an 'erosion' of the socialist community of states, to separate them from one another by a 'selective approach.' "[188] This school allegedly advocates "maneuvering, political pressure, blackmail, and creating crises," using trade and scientific-technical progress as the chief levers for carrying out such a policy. As Gromyko sees it, these people are the true "enemies of setting up truly mutually advantageous economic and scientific-technical links between the capitalist countries and the socialist countries. Without a 'demolition fuse' ["maneuvering, political pressure," etc.], these links simply do not interest them." This school, then, differs from the "technological warfare" school in that it recognizes, to a small degree, that the new correlation of forces renders the outright application of force impractical if not impossible. Nevertheless, it still clings to hopes of maintaining some kind of "position of strength."

A third school comprises those who promote the idea of "global convergence." As mentioned earlier, this theory predicts that the imperatives of new technological developments will lead to the political convergence of the capitalist and socialist systems under the guidance of a technocratic elite. Gromyko notes that the aggressive thrust of this theory is inherent in the idea that technology and the influence of scientific discoveries are the primary sources of national power and economic growth. It is alleged that this same idea leads to the conclusion that technology influences not only the social structures of states but also the structure of international relations. The imperative of convergence, it is said, will produce "universal integration," and thus the ultimate target of this school is "the international legal institution of state sovereignty."[189] Some Western commentators are portrayed as holding the blasphemous (to the Soviets) view that technological demands supersede all other political considerations, and that scientific-technical competition should therefore eclipse the significance of the struggle between capitalism and socialism. Whereas these theories totally ignore the "class content" of social processes (and thus merit the honor of being pronounced ideologically "bankrupt"), they are nonetheless regarded as one more step away from the "policy of force" mentality. Rather than calling for any sort of confrontation, such theories promote either a technological utopianism[109] or a disingenuous form of ideological subterfuge.

Soviet analysts see the growing debate among these three "schools," as symptomatic of a change in the atmosphere of American foreign policy. Even a relatively traditionalist analyst such as Gromyko, Jr. recognizes that while each line continues to serve the same old ends of American "imperialism," each represents a potentially different means toward those ends. The realist analysts modify this view only slightly when they say that each respective school represents one further step in the direction of "realism." Their real difference with Gromyko, however, is that whereas he sees such "realistic" groups as perennially dangerous, they see them as less so, and therefore view their emergence as more desirable from the Soviet point of view.

The upshot of this debate among the American policy-making groups was what Soviet analysts called the "New Technological Policy," which, in their view, was part and parcel of the entire shift of American foreign policy embodied in the Nixon Doctrine. America "was forced" to adapt its strategy to conform to the new correlation of forces in the world, reshaping it both in the general terms articulated in the Doctrine and in more specific ways, including the adoption of various new scientific and technical means. Gromyko concluded, therefore, that the emergence of the New Technological Policy was an expression of "the crisis of the USA's old global concepts which were based primarily on the policy of 'from a position of strength.' "[191] Also, as Arbatov noted, American ruling circles had to cope with the consequences of public reaction to the military aspect, which has allegedly been the primary focus of scientific and technical policy.[192] This reaction took the form of the "struggle against thermonuclear war" and objections to the "enormous economic costs of the modern arms race." The policy debate thus concluded with the at least partial defeat of the advocates of "technological warfare" and the rise of a new policy that stressed a "quest for opportunities" to make more active foreign-policy use of the scientific-technical revolution.[193]

At this point, one must ask what makes this New Technological Policy so new. Arbatov notes, after all, that throughout the postwar period American theoreticians and politicians often "spoke about the foreign policy opportunities afforded by scientific and technical supremacy."[194] In trying to explain what in fact distinguishes the new policy from previous positions, Arbatov argues that "it is in the seventies that the changes have taken place to transform these efforts into a *strategic policy direction*. This is linked with the obvious enhancement of the role of 'nonmilitary' means of struggle"[195] (my emphasis). To the Soviets, then, the New Technological Policy, represents an expansion and intensification of the various scientific and technical means of "struggle"—a process that coincides, as we shall see below, with the diminution of the direct use of force.

Among the methods of the New Technological Policy, the stimulation of scientific and technical progress within the United States itself is deemed the most important by Soviet realists. The object of this policy is said to be the transformation of science into a "direct production force" in order to "insure an uninterrupted stream of discoveries and innovations," thereby helping to maintain American political, economic, and military positions.[196] This goal is accomplished by "large-scale state appropriations for research and development, including nonmilitary fields" (even during periods of strict economy when funds for other programs are being cut), and by "encouraging the monopolies' efforts aimed at accelerating scientific and technical progress." The New Technological Policy is thus seen as a direct manifestation of mature "state-monopoly capitalism," a prime example of which is the American space program. Soviet analysis shares Gromyko's view that the scientific and technical research involved in this program is focused on realizing improvements in communications (with direct implications for the dissemination of "subversive" capitalist propaganda), meteorology, navigation, and transportation (with their military implications), as well as agriculture and education.[197]

The foreign dimension of the New Technological Policy is accorded equal significance by Soviet analysts. The characteristic method of this aspect of the policy is the creation of "a system of scientific and technical ties and cooperation" whereby the United States can penetrate and establish "exploitative" relations with foreign countries.[198] These efforts, Arbatov maintains, "are clothed in the appropriate phraseology designed to depict them as efforts according with 'the interests of all participants' and as being aimed at 'universal progress and prosperity.' "[199] The promotion of scientific exchanges among specialists is but one of the forms such ties may assume. G. Khozin refers to the establishment of "control over bases in one country or another, which, from the point of view of science and technology, are strategically important."[200] He maintains that such "control" can be achieved by the creation of joint research centers or laboratories—a process by which "the American organizational structure, American experience, American methods of control, and the American system of personnel training" are adopted as models. "All this," he concludes, "provides the Americans with completely definite advantages that are used in the sphere of foreign policy." Economic expansion abroad, especially through the offices of the multinational "monopolies," is another means of creating such "ties." Soviet analysts portray the United States as trading in the science and technology business, and doing so in typically "imperialist" fashion. While trying to reduce the cost of acquiring foreign scientific-technical knowledge, Gromyko argues, the United States is "endeavoring to 'concede' its own achievements in the area of science and technology to others at a higher price."[201] It is also alleged that such ties are useful for avoiding costly duplication of research efforts, using the talents of foreign scientists to serve the interests of the United States,[202] and shifting the burden of expenses onto the shoulders of other countries.[203] Furthermore, the extensive sale of American technology is meant to create a situation of even closer links: a relationship of constant dependence on the United States, its experts, and its spare parts[204] which Arbatov describes as a new form of the " 'traditional' relations of domination and subordination."[205] According to Khozin the supply of technical aid has a similar effect: it forces other states "to follow a political or scientific-technical course predetermined by the United States."[206]

Although they view the New Technological Policy as a significant shift in the *means* of American foreign policy, the Soviets give it no prospect for success. For traditionalist Soviet analysts like Gromyko, it is merely a "new means toward old ends."[207] The fundamentally "imperialist" nature of U.S. capitalism has not changed, and no matter what new means are employed, the "contradictions" of capitalism will persist. As for the New Technological Policy itself, it is said to be "unquestionably doomed to failure," because it "contradicts the national interests of other states." As Gromyko declares, this policy "is in no way altruistic": rooted in "exploiter relations," it can only meet the "resolute rebuffs" of all the anti-imperialist movements.[208] Furthermore, as Arbatov notes, "U.S. hopes of effectively utilizing in foreign policy the achievements of the scientific-technical revolution have not justified themselves," at least in part because "the United States has not managed to establish and retain a monopoly on these achievements."[209] The United States is confronted with resolute competition from the socialist community of states, and this competition limits U.S. freedom to pursue its scientific and technical policies, be they military or economic.

As we can see, Arbatov, the realist, shares some of the views of a traditionalist like Gromyko. The major difference lies in their assessments of the significance of the change in U.S. policy. Whereas Gromyko says that, essentially, the new means of U.S. foreign policy make no difference, Arbatov is willing to draw more positive conclusions, observing that the change in U.S. policy is a sign of greater "realism." He admits that those who "see things more realistically . . . are by no means engaging in philanthropy but are primarily considering American interests," but goes on to issue an important caveat: "They [the American realists] perceive those interests differently from the open or covert supporters of the cold war and they proceed above all from a recognition of the truth that in the nuclear age there is no acceptable alternative to a policy based on the principle of peaceful coexistence."[210] Of course, since peaceful coexistence is the Soviets' preferred form of struggle, the change in U.S. policy is, to the realists, a propitious development.

Military Means

As was noted above, the traditionalists among Soviet analysts view "force" as the hallmark of all capitalist relations." In other words, whatever the capitalists do, their actions are invariably accompanied by the use or the threat of force. To the traditionalist, then, force (the military means) is the real basis of American foreign policy, without which other means could not possibly succeed. In addition, these analysts insist that, like all other elements of U.S. foreign policy, force is a "class means." Writing in *Krasnaia zvezda*, K. Vorob'ev notes that bourgeois ideologists have been trying to deny this fact by arguing that the American army is politically neutral, a "supra-class" element in society. Vorob'ev holds that such "arbitrary constructions ... collapse into dust as soon as they come into contact with objective reality"—the reality being that the army is "part of the political superstructure of society" and is therefore "used by the dominant classes to achieve their own fundamental objectives."[211] V. Berezin makes the same point when he argues that after the American War of Independence, the U.S. armed forces "did not become a people's army" but instead, "throughout their existence, ... have served not the working people but their main enemy—the bourgeoisie."[212] Berezin's comments, incidentally, introduce a review of the Soviet book, *The USA: 200 Years—200 Wars,* in which the author is said to show that immediately after achieving independence, the United States "embarked on the path of aggression, and traveled along this inglorious path for two centuries, right up to the present."

The class nature of the U.S. armed forces is manifest in the close link between the army and the monopolies, a connection that is graphically expressed by the influence of the "sinister" "military-industrial complex." In his 1976 article, Vorob'ev alleged that this complex "is increasingly becoming the actual ruler of the state and determines the state's domestic and foreign policy."[213] Determined to secure this link and thereby fashion the army into a "more reliable instrument of antipopular policy," the ruling circles "strive to wrench it away from the people and educate it in an elitist spirit," choosing the high command from their own milieu and creating a career system of staffing in order to "alienate the army from the people." Indeed, Vorob'ev even claims that the ruling circles are trying to create an army that will perform as a mercenary force: "to train the kind of professionals, who, in return for money, will, for the sake of monopoly capital's interests, shoot not only at the soldiers of another army, but also at the workers and peasants of their own country who are struggling for social liberation." Having proved that the army is an instrument of the monopolies, Vorob'ev can argue that it is used to expedite their plundering ways: "Everywhere the soldiers of capitalist countries appear, their arrival brings a toughening of the exploitation of the working people, the crushing of the progressive movement, and the assertion of the power of the monopolies." The same tactics are used in dealing with domestic situations, for as Vorob'ev notes, American troops "have repeatedly participated in breaking up workers' demonstrations, actions by young people (and especially students), and in putting down Negro disturbances."

In general, when referring to U.S. policy pursued with the use of the military, Soviet analysts speak of the "policy of force" or, in some cases, the policy "from a position of strength." Under this general rubric they include not only the threat and the use of force by the United States, but also U.S. "maneuvers" to coax allies to use force so as "to serve the interests of the monopolies." The policy may thus take many forms and be motivated by both domestic and foreign factors. According to the traditionalists, the domestic determinants are embodied in the phenomenon of "militarism," whereby the military-industrial complex seeks to augment its profits by building a "colossal military machine" that will lead, in effect, to the "militarization of the economy."[214] Militarism has its foreign aspects as well, including: "barefaced anti-Sovietism"; the stimulation of the arms race with the socialist community of states; the "provocation of major international conflicts" and local tensions that will engender regional arms races; "wars";

the "blatant flouting of international agreements and the sovereignty of other countries"; the pursuit of international relations that are based on "supremacy and subordination," the "oppression of the weak by the strong," "diktats, threats, force, and tyranny"; and the use of aggression "as a natural means of solving international questions."[215] All these aspects of militarism have one common denominator: the creation of a foreign market for the arms-manufacturing monopolies. In short, Soviet analysts argue that the more wars, the more arms races, the more tension, the more oppression —the greater the profits reaped by the militarists. Militarism is also designed to cope with any perceived threat to its own basis of existence, the capitalist system, and any threat to its economic well-being from other imperialist "predators." These two types of threats constitute the external determinants of the "policy of force." As perceived by the U.S. militarists, the first type of course stems from the rising power of the socialist community of states, the "national liberation movement," and the "international workers movement." In responding to threats of this type, militarism is used as a weapon in the "struggle between the two social systems." The second type of threat prompts militarism to join in the struggle that is dividing the capitalist world among the "imperialist vultures," thus creating "interimperialist contradictions" and exacerbating the "crisis of capitalism."[216]

Soviet analysts see the "arms race" as the chief means by which the United States realizes the imperatives of "militarism." Directed primarily against the Soviet Union and the socialist community of states, this policy is seen by the traditionalist Soviets as one of the principal U.S. weapons in the struggle between the two social systems. Besides being constant "preparation for new aggression,"[217] the arms race is said to intensify the competition between the United States and the Soviet Union in the economic and the scientific-technical, as well as the military spheres. Iu. Katasonov notes, for example, the American attempt "to draw the socialist countries as deeply as possible into this race in order to exhaust their economies, undermine the economic foundations of their sociopolitical development, and strengthen its own positions in the economic competition with socialism."[218] Katasonov argues that the imperialists base their hopes for the success of this policy "on the opposition between the basic social natures and aims of the two systems."

He maintains that whereas "the militarization of the economy" is "a natural means" by which capitalism tries to achieve "the political and economic goals inherent in its nature," socialism's utilization of "any resources for military purposes" is forced upon it by external circumstances, that is, "results not from its own requirements but exclusively from the existence of an external threat." In addition, American ruling circles rely on the fact that the gross national product of the socialist countries is "still inferior" to that to bear a proportionately heavier burden if both sides devote equal resources to military purposes.[219]

The arms race has a concomitant impact on scientific and technical progress which in turn affects the economy and the scientific-technical struggle against socialism. Discussing this aspect of the arms race, G. Mukhanova notes the phenomenon of "spin-off"—"the transmission of scientific and technical achievements from the military and space fields to civilian sectors of the national economy,"—and claims that it serves as a useful ploy for domestic propaganda: the ruling circles "try to depict expenditures on the war and on military research as beneficial in the final analysis to the country's economy."[220] The arms race thus serves several aspects of the struggle against socialism, but no matter what its focus, it is characterized, at least in Soviet thinking, by the incessant desire for "superiority" in the general balance of forces.

Like the other military means of American foreign policy, the arms race is accompanied by various forms of the threat or the actual use of force, designed ultimately "for the purpose of territorial annexation, the establishment of political domination, or simply for blackmail."[221] The use of force takes various forms, among which Soviet analysts list: murders; assassinations of disagreeable leaders; military coups d'etat; "police operations"; "big stick" diplomacy; "armed provocations"; kindling of national and tribal dissension and separatist movements to provoke civil wars and revolts for the purpose of "overthrowing governments that the imperialists find objectionable"; blatant acts of military "aggression"; the support of counterrevolutionary forces and the "export of counterrevolution"; the related policy of "counterinsurgency"; the creation and control of "crises" (the overwhelming majority of which, since World War II, are said to have been initiated by the United States and its allies); and "the unleashing of local wars through inciting small states, which are dependent on imperialism, to aggression against neighboring countries that have selected a progressive path of development."[222] Wars are also seen as useful for testing the weapons and tactics that will be used in future wars.[223]

To aid in the perpetration of such acts, the United States is said to follow a "military base strategy." R. Simonian declares, for example, that the United States has more than 2,000 bases* in thirty countries which are used to "pursue a policy of neocolonialism," "pressure junior partners in military blocs," "render support to antipopular regimes," and, needless to say, "wage war."[224] Thus, according to Iu. Gavrilov, the United States suffers from "base mania," allegedly "the incurable ill of the U.S. military."[225] Simonian writes that these bases have been created by the imperialists "on the basis of so-called bilateral 'treaties.' "[226] He does not explain why he chooses to ridicule these treaties with the use of "so-called" and quotation marks. It may be inferred, however, that by doing so he may be questioning the legitimacy of the governments that are party to them—especially since any government that would permit the United States to maintain a "base for aggression" must surely be "antipopular" and therefore illegitimate. Alternatively, Simonian may be highlighting the asymmetry in any putatively "bilateral" agreement between the imperialist United States and its weaker partner-victims. Whichever of these speculations comes closer to the mark, they both illustrate the remarkable depth and attention to detail of contemporary Soviet, Marxist-Leninist analysis.

In addition to the actual use of force, the American "imperialists" are said to employ the threat of force or the "constant threat of war" as a principal instrument of policy. Among the many forms that such threats may assume are "gunboat diplomacy" and the use of military maneuvers, considered by Soviet analysts to be a form of gunboat diplomacy. Such maneuvers are often said to have "political as well as military aims."[227] In reference to some 1975 NATO maneuvers in the Mediterranean, for example, V. Mayevskii notes that they were "a means of exerting pressure on the sovereign states of the eastern Mediterranean, primarily Greece and Cyp-

*Evidently, Mr. Simonian considers an installation such as a radar station operated by half a dozen men a "base."

rus."[228] NATO warplanes allegedly flew over Cyprus' airspace, thereby "violating its sovereignty" and committing "provocations" and "air sabotage"—all for the purpose of securing the island "not only as an 'unsinkable aircraft carrier' in the Mediterranean but also as an imperialist military base." A different purpose was ascribed to another series of NATO maneuvers. According to Iu. Kharlanov, the NATO generals were "artificially fanning the 'threat' myth, which the NATO politicians then [used] to justify new appropriations for the arms race." These maneuvers were characterized as "another attempt to put pressure on the countries of NATO's northern flank in order to involve them in a new round of the expansion of the arms race and lash them more tightly to the Atlantic war chariot."[229]

Soviet analysts maintain that this persistent threat to use force is a policy that constitutes much of the basis for American military strategy. A. Bovin diagnoses threat as the general principle underlying the "approach to international affairs which aims to stabilize the situation at the level of the 'balance of fear.' "[230] With specific reference to nuclear strategy, he observes that "the desire of imperialist politicians to base security on growing arsenals of nuclear missiles essentially means the perpetuation of the threat of war." These principles are embodied in what the Soviets term the policy of "controlled tension," a policy whereby the level of threat is kept as high as possible without causing a shift into a situation of direct confrontation.[231] In a similar vein, G. Trofimenko argues that these principles form the basis of an American foreign policy in which "peace" has come to resemble a form of war:

> War continues to remain policy's servant, but at the same time it is penetrating increasingly deeply into imperialism's "peace" policy, blurring the line between purely political and purely military decisions and actions. U.S. foreign policy in peacetime becomes war to a certain extent—the cold war, in which the country's colossal military potential is utilized for the purpose of exerting political and psychological pressure in the international arena.[232]

In short, Trofimenko sees the policy of threat as a means by which the American imperialists attempt to use military force indirectly, a policy that is preferable when one wishes to retain force as an instrument of policy but finds that, for whatever reason, the use of direct force is either impossible, too risky, or too costly.

Soviet commentators, especially the realists, analyze intensively the factors that prevent the United States from using force directly, for such factors have a direct bearing on the Soviet assessment of the correlation of forces in the world as a whole and in specific regions. In the view of both schools of Soviet analysis, the more the correlation of forces favors socialism, the "national liberation movement," or the "international workers movement," the greater the constraints on the direct use of force by U.S. "imperialism." As we have seen, the Soviets believe that the "correlation of forces" shifted in favor of both socialism and the "national liberation movement" at a constantly accelerating rate during the 1960s, culminating in the new correlation that was formalized in 1972. The result was a corresponding decline in the applicability of American military force. In explaining this change, Soviet analysts stress the catalytic role of three developments: the rise of Soviet strategic power, the victory of the Vietnamese "liberation struggle," and the emergence of "realism" and the "realist" faction of the American ruling class.

The Soviets see the increase in their country's strategic power as the single most influential factor "restraining" the United States from the direct use of force. In his 1976 article, Kuznetsov repeated the familiar Soviet refrain that the U.S. attempt "to retain and preserve a monopoly on the most powerful types of military strength, and above all, nuclear weapons, has not been successful."[233] Soviet realists argue that, increasingly, this situation obviates the possibility of the direct use of nuclear weapons, because it guarantees that there will be suicidal consequences for the country that strikes first. Consequently, then, the United States' very development of these most destructive means has led to their "distinctive devaluation," "to a shrinking of the sphere where military force can be used for the rational objectives of policy."[234] Soviet realists hold that American strategists and politicians are fully conscious of these limits.

This line of argument is particularly interesting because it marks one of the few points at which the realists diverge from the traditionalists on military issues. While the traditionalists do point out that the United States no longer enjoys a monopoly on advanced weaponry, they are reluctant to say that nuclear weapons "shrink the sphere where military force can be used," for such an admission would apply to the Soviets as well. These more recent disputes echo an old debate, one that flourished during the Stalin succession struggle and reappeared in the mid-1960s when N. Talenskii, Ye. Rybkin, and I. A. Grudinin argued the possibility of victory and the relationship between war and politics in the nuclear age.[235] The appearance in the early 1970s of a more sophisticated analysis of the United States and its foreign and defense policies sparked a new round of the debate. The traditionalists continue to assert that nuclear weapons may serve as an instrument of politics, while the realists continue to accept the idea of mutual deterrence. We shall find intimations of this disagreement in Soviet analyses of American strategy.

Soviet analysts point to the American defeat in Vietnam as the second major reason why the policy of direct force "can no longer justify itself." The American "aggression" in Vietnam is regarded as the quintessential illustration of the use of direct force by U.S. "imperialism." Trofimenko asserts that, in launching this intervention, the United States undertook not "a purely local task," but an effort "to demonstrate [its] power as an international policeman and to 'turn back the tide' of the people's national liberation movement."[236] He enumerates three reasons why victory proved unattainable: (1) "the Vietnamese people's heroic resistance"; (2) "the powerful material and moral aid and support that was rendered to fighting Vietnam by the Soviet Union, the other socialist countries, and the progressive forces of the whole world"; and (3) "the objectively existing correlation of forces between socialism and imperialism on a global scale," which "set a limit to the military escalation that the United States carried out in Vietnam. The U.S. armed forces' transition to the next step of the 'ladder of escalation,' as Washington well understood, could return the world to a general war fraught with the most catastrophic consequences for the United States itself." Within the framework of what was "permitted," then, the "imperialists" could not win a military victory.[237] In Trofimenko's view, American strategists "underestimated the vital force of the national liberation movement, its profoundly popular nature, and consequently, its invincibility." This "invincibility," an expression of the inexorable march of the "progressive" historical forces, would hereafter impress upon imperialism the ultimate futility of the direct use of armed force. As Khmara emphasizes, "the imperialists can no longer interfere unimpeded in the affairs of other countries and count on their military adventures going unpunished."[238] And given this situation, Soviet analysts argue that the United States had no "realistic" choice but to "adopt the Leninist principle of peaceful coexistence."[239]

These statements introduce an element that complicates our view of which Soviet school of analysis propounds which line. It is clear that a number of traditionalist analysts agree that U.S. ruling circles were "forced" to become "realistic" by the victorious national liberation movement in Vietnam. Many of these same commentators also acknowledge the role of Soviet might in limiting the imperialists' freedom to employ force. However, they do not share their realist colleagues' view that a large faction of the U.S. ruling class has concluded that militarism is incompatible with its class interests. Thus, although both schools acknowledge a new American "realism" and agree on certain of its causes, they are not in complete accord as to the relative influence of its various components.

Both schools agree, however, that these impulses toward "realism" in no way indicated the wholesale conversion of the American ruling classes. Indeed, a total commitment to "realism" would have involved their joining the choir of "progressive" voices in the world struggle for socialism, but instead, the imperialists merely proceeded to change the means of their foreign policy. This change, the general sense of which was embodied by the "Nixon Doctrine," found its more specific, military expression in the "Strategy of Realistic Deterrence" and subsequent developments in military doctrine.

The Strategy of Realistic Deterrence is viewed as the American response not only to the failings of nuclear and conventional strategies taken individually, but also to the shortcomings of the policy of "flexible response," which attempted to join the two strategies in a coherent union. Although it was in fact the major strategic statement of the Nixon administration, the Strategy of Realistic Deterrence was seen as having failed to resolve some key questions, especially in the area of nuclear weapons. Thus, Soviet analysts saw the strategy as a step in an evolution of strategic thinking whose uncertainties diminished during the 1970s.

159

In the realm of nuclear strategy, the Strategy of Realistic Deterence amounts, in the eyes of Soviet realists, to a formalization of the ideas of its predecessor—the strategy of "flexible response"—which "already virtually admitted the impossibility of using a big war as a means of policy."[240] It is argued that the Americans reached this conclusion because the rising strategic power of the Soviet Union was making nuclear war increasingly impractical if not impossible.[241] Thus, realists like Trofimenko argued that strategists believed "the Kennedy-Johnson line, as far as nuclear war is concerned, was completely realistic."[242] This being the case, the new doctrine freed U.S. policy makers from having to make any significant changes in their policy of building new nuclear forces. The realists thus argue that "Realistic Deterrence" merely codifies the deterrent element of the strategy of flexible response by adding the word "deterrence" to the title of the new strategy. As Trofimenko puts it, the strategy, henceforth officially, "proceeds from U.S. reluctance to be the initiator of such a [nuclear] conflict and stipulates only the U.S. right and resolve to inflict a counterstrike in the event of an attack on itself." Thus, Trofimenko obliquely accepts the idea of mutual deterrence, while noting that American policy unabashedly admits to the "realistic" policy of recognizing the invincible power of the Soviet military.

Insofar as it adds anything new, the strategy of Realistic Deterrence is said to incorporate a psychological element, manifested in its authors' hope "to raise the effectiveness of this [the American nuclear] arsenal not by direct means but with the help of politico-psychological pressure."[243] Indeed, Trofimenko maintains that " 'deterrence' is, in its very essence, a concept of exerting psychological influence on the opponent."[244] It is in this sense, he argues, that "deterrence" embodies U.S. policy makers' hopes for "favorable possibilities" to pursue their "imperialists interests."

The element of uncertainty engendered by the introduction of the concept of "strategic sufficiency" was one form of "psychological influence" which some Soviets saw as a product of the Strategy of Realistic Deterrence. According to a 1976 article by Simonian, this concept was the most recent "principal criterion" by which U.S. policy makers determined the level of strategic armament.[245] In fact, Soviet analysts have regarded the concept of sufficiency as a major criterion of U.S. strategic policy ever since the McNamara era, but traditionalist Soviets have detected an evolution in the concept—an evolution away from their own preferred interpretation. In the traditionalist's opinion, the McNamara concept, although not officially termed "sufficiency," nonetheless sought to achieve the "optimal correlation between the number of strategic strike devices and the number of targets selected for destruction."[246] The criteria used in assessing this correlation were seen as strictly quantitative, including the measurement of cost-effectiveness and the establishment of "rational levels" of armament (i.e., the level beyond which increments of destructive power yield declining returns in combat effectiveness). Even though this concept of "sufficiency" was part of a policy that sought to maintain American "superiority," traditionalist analysts implied that its very straightforwardness made it preferable to its successor. Given its quantitative criteria, the McNamara concept included at least one redeeming element of restraint: the Pentagon was bound to weigh the "unprofitability" of further unnecessary stockpiling of nuclear weapons.[247]

For these same traditionalists, the concept of "strategic sufficiency" enunciated by the Nixon administration marked a devious turn in American strategic policy. V. Larionov argued that with this new concept "the only objective in maintaining the American armed forces at a certain level of 'sufficiency' is proclaimed to be deterrence and preventing a nuclear war," and that goal of deterrence is qualified only by the necessity of maintaining a survivable deterrent.[248] Larionov alleged that these policy prescriptions were dangerously open-ended, qualified only by this caveat quoted from a presidential report to Congress: " 'It would be incompatible with the political meaning of sufficiency to base planning of our forces exclusively on some *ultimate—and theoretical—ability to inflict losses that would be unacceptable to the other side*' " (Larionov's emphasis).[249] "Therefore," Larionov observed, "the limits of sufficiency are not established with the aid of some definite quantitative criterion, as McNamara, for example, attempted to do." Then, noting the Nixon statement that " 'sufficiency,' in itself, becomes the 'absolute criterion' " of strategic policy, Larionov concluded that the new concept "can be so variable and dependent on subjective appraisals that it is difficult even to imagine the possible level of U.S. strategic forces in the long term." As Simonian noted, the new concept "is marked by vagueness and changeability."[250] Similarly, Larionov stressed that there is considerable "scope for arbitrary decisions given the fact that this 'absolute level' [of necessary nuclear forces] can rise *ad infinitum* according to a subjective appraisal of the level of threat on the basis of 'worst-case' analysis." Worst-case analysis, said to be the basis "on which strategic planning in the Pentagon is conducted and military programs formulated," is in turn ascribed its own insidious character. Describing it as "the deliberate presupposition that the enemy is much stronger than the United States," Larionov adds, that "here the enemy is ascribed intentions so irrational that they would seem insane to its military-political leadership."[251] In addition, worst-case calculations are said to be based on "the traditional and completely groundless military-philosophical premise that there is no such thing as excess in war and that it is impossible to overrate a threat and dangerous to underrate it."[252]

These comments again provide evidence that there are two conflicting Soviet views of American defense policy. On the one hand, the traditionalists hold that everything the United States does is just as insidious and imperialist as ever. As Simonian says in a 1976 article, the difference between the concepts of "achieving superiority" and "strategic sufficiency" is "practically indiscernible,"[253] and the main means of the policy guided by these concepts, the arms race, continues unabated. The only distinction between "strategic sufficiency" and the earlier policies is that "this race is now being carried out not so much through a quantitative build-up as through the qualitative improvement of strategic arms." For Simonian and other traditionalists, then, "sufficiency" is simply a more "diplomatic" formula than the expression "achieving superiority." Consequently, the new concept is said "to satisfy completely the supporters of the 'from a position of strength' policy and also the claims of the representatives of the military-industrial complex."[254]

On the other hand, the realists perceive a real change in U.S. strategic policy. As Trofimenko noted in 1970, the United States had always striven "to utilize an unrestricted arms race" to create a position of "absolute strength."[255] With the new correlation of forces and a new conceptual framework, however, the U.S. leaders are portrayed as "realizing to a certain degree the endlessness and consequently the hopelessness of the nuclear arms race."[256] Soviet realists argue that this awareness has forced the United States to recognize, officially now, the impossibility of using a big war as means of policy, to agree to the need for setting a ceiling on strategic arms through SALT, and even to modify its language by replacing the "provocative concept" of U.S. "strategic superiority" with the less provocative "sufficiency."[257] Moreover, these changes have been realized despite U.S. efforts to retain war as means of policy—a perennial problem over which "U.S. political and strategic thought has been persistently toiling."[258] Trofimenko's realist analysis amounts, then, to a corroboration of what Arbatov has claimed to be both possible and desirable (see above, p. 101), namely, that the United States can be forced to adapt its policy. Trofimenko made the point explicitly in an indirect criticism of his traditionalist colleagues: "To say that nothing new has appeared in the U.S. strategy means failing to take into account imperialism's attempts to adapt itself to the new situation in the world."[259]

The Strategy of Realistic Deterrence, having presented skeptical Soviet traditionalists with the ambiguities of "sufficiency," left one of their most urgent questions unanswered: How would the United States resolve its problem of retaining war as an instrument of policy? As mentioned above, the traditionalists believe this strategy to be so flexible that it can allow room for a continuation of the "arms race" and the maintenance of a "position of strength." But is that all? Would it merely involve more of the same policies that the new correlation of forces had shown to be "bankrupt" and "suicidal"? Still another related question gnawed at Soviet analysts. In 1971, in an analysis of the original "Realistic Deterrence" strategy, Trofimenko noted that under the old strategy of "flexible response," American policy had observed the principle of the "measuring out of the use of force"—a principle that consisted of "the fundamental and qualitative separation of nuclear and non-nuclear warfare."[260] Trofimenko furthermore asserted that, working with this principle, the U.S. government "determined the parameters of the U.S. use of military force and admitted that in a new strategic situation, they could make up their minds to use their nuclear force only in exceptional and specific cases—basically only in the event of retaliatory defense against an inconceivable direct nuclear attack by the Soviet Union on the United States or on their main allies in

Europe." He concluded that "this and nothing else" was "the essence of the Kennedy-Johnson principle of the 'measured out use of force.'" Then, when analyzing the Strategy of Realistic Deterrence, Trofimenko asked a question that has provoked another controversy between the two Soviet schools of thought: "Does not the Republican administration in fact intend to observe this basic principle of 'measuring'?"

Trofimenko himself notes that "when you start to look for a clear answer to this question in the utterances of the U.S. leaders, you discover that an unambiguous answer is not given."[261] He then diagnoses a duality in the American position, arguing that President Nixon's statements make a precise distinction between nuclear and non-nuclear wars, whereas the statements of Defense Secretary Melvin Laird treat the question of the use of nuclear weapons with "boastful courage": "He [Laird] says that the division of weapons into nuclear and non-nuclear [categories] has no fundamental significance—the United States will use the weapons best suited to the situation."* Trofimenko concludes that the duality of the American position simply reflects the basic contradiction of American strategy: "the contradiction between the desire to preserve war as a political means and imperialism's ever narrowing opportunities for waging a successful war that brings results." He observes that this contradiction can take various forms:

> as in the contradiction between the violence of threats and a certain restraint of actions; as in the contradiction between the instinctive dislike of accepting any restrictions on U.S. force and the enforced necessity of taking into account the power of enemies and showing caution in the practical use of force; or as in the contradiction between the desire to achieve a position of absolute strength and the rational recognition of the inaccessibility of such a position given the conditions of today's world.

The result of these contradictions is what Trofimenko terms a dual policy: while "striving to demonstrate the hardening of the

---

*It is interesting to speculate that by ridiculing Laird's "boastful courage" on this score, Trofimenko may be criticizing his own traditionalist comrades who also vehemently assert that there is no difference between nuclear and conventional arms.

U.S. position and the United States' great readiness for the decisive use of military force," the American leaders are also obliged to acknowledge the new correlation of forces and restrain their behavior. In short, the various efforts to show that war remains a means of U.S. policy are, to a large extent, bravado that is belied by American actions.

Realist analysts argue that U.S. attempts to introduce the concept of "limited strategic war" represent precisely this kind of bravado. Washington's initial effort in this regard was the attempt to introduce some "rules of the game," that is, "some rules of 'conduct' in conflict which would create certain guarantees that the United States would succeed (through various types of previously agreed limitations) in avoiding suicidal consequences for the United States should it unleash a major armed adventure."[262] Trofimenko notes that U.S. policy makers hoped that these "rules" "would make it possible to reveal the 'victor' on the basis of limited 'tests of strength'—without the utilization of the entire nuclear missile arsenal."[263] Here, then, were the first intimations of the American desire to use the concept of limited war as a means to preserve the usability of the American arsenal as a means of policy. When the Soviets scorned these "rules," however, American strategists had to try other tactics, soon producing variations on the theory of limited war—all of which were seen as attempting to blur the distinction between nuclear and non-nuclear conflict. Though Soviet realists saw all these efforts as malevolent and therefore as a "demonstration" of the American hard line, they nonetheless concluded that the new correlation of forces had obliged the United States to behave more "realistically."

The traditionalist analysts, in contrast, saw such malevolent noises about rules and limitations as having been translated into malevolent policy. When considering the American concept of the measured use of force, they give particular attention to the "Schlesinger Doctrine" and its ideas on limited war. This doctrine is said to be based on a strategy of "selective targeting," which, according to Simonian, "envisages many scenarios for the use of the strategic offensive forces of the United States and its NATO allies."[264] The Soviets recall that the United States previously relied primarily on total war ("strategic nuclear war") as the scenario for nuclear conflict—a strategy that prescribed the targeting of the enemy's armed

165

forces, military targets, and industrial, administrative, and civilian centers. "According to the Pentagon's calculations," Simonian notes, it was precisely the strikes against these latter centers which "were to result in the 'guaranteed annihilation of the enemy state as a viable society.' " As the Soviet traditionalists constantly repeat, this amounts to a program of "assured destruction." It is significant that, while distinguishing between the American strategies of "massive retaliation" and "flexible response," these analysts rarely, if ever, discriminate between their results, that is, they do not distinguish "assured destruction" from "*mutual* assured destruction." For the traditionalists to grant that the word "mutual" figured in American strategic thinking would be, essentially, to suggest that states other than the United States and its imperialist allies were capable of "aggression." Such a concession would also ascribe a certain generosity to the Americans, implying that Washington saw Soviet retaliation as eminently justified should the United States act as a nuclear aggressor. In short, the traditionalist analysts do not want to convey any message that could possibly be construed as an acceptance of mutual deterrence.

But, since changing circumstances were making "assured destruction" an increasingly untenable scenario, the United States, the traditionalists argue, was compelled to look for alternatives. Thus there emerged the concept of "selective targeting" with its scenario of "limited war" which, according to Simonian, "envisages the delivery by strategic offensive forces of a sudden massive strike against the Soviet Union's military targets alone."[265] These targets are said to include: "strategic missile launching silos, strategic aircraft on airfields, nuclear weapons dumps, the command posts of the supreme state and military authorities, large troop concentrations, and other important military targets." The strike is restricted to such targets to avoid extensive secondary destruction to civilian centers—a policy designed, Simonian argues, in the hope that it gives the United States "the opportunity, in the event of an outbreak of nuclear war, to 'force the enemy' not to attack the cities of the United States and its allies." "In other words," Simonian declares, "the strategists across the ocean are hoping not only to convince the potential enemy of the acceptability of a 'limited' nuclear war, but also to make him wage it on terms advantageous to the United States." Thus, as the traditionalist Soviets see it, the tradi-

tion of attempting to establish "rules of the game" continues unabated in American strategic thinking.

Arguing that "it would be naive to believe that the Pentagon
leaders are concerned with 'limiting the damage' equally 'on both
sides,' " Simonian says that they aim "to place the 'potential enemy'
in a position where he would be deprived of the possibility of de-
livering a crushing retaliatory strike against U.S. territory or at
least to weaken the strength of this strike as much as possible."[266]
As a result, the limited war scenario is said "to copy totally" the
main theses of the "counterforce strategy," a strategy whose essence
is described as "creating the kind of strategic nuclear forces and
maintaining them at the degree of combat readiness which would
enable the United States to deliver a preemptive nuclear strike and
achieve victory on this basis." This strategy is allegedly pursued
through the qualitative improvement of the strategic forces—"the
creation of 'surgically accurate' weapons with a more powerful nuclear charge."[267] Such weapons could give the United States greater
flexibility, enabling it to choose all-out nuclear or limited war—
"assured destruction" or counterforce—in each "contingency" that
arises. A traditionalist commentator brands this kind of "flexibility"
as "flexibility in dealing with the fundamental question—the question of the basic inadmissibility of nuclear war," [268] while another
traditionalist notes that this flexible posture is being achieved by
the "erosion of the differences between conventional and nuclear
wars."[269] Thus, in contrast to Trofimenko's realist analysis, the traditionalists believe that the United States has rejected not just in
word but in fact the principle of the "measured use of force," a
principle that distinguished between nuclear and conventional wars.
Furthermore, they see in this U.S. strategy a "correction" of the
failure to link the two types of warfare coherently through the concept of "flexible response."

Traditionalist analysts point to two more justifications for the
adoption of a limited war option: (1) the tendency to ascribe similar strategic concepts to the Soviet Union while stressing the vul-
nerability of American military targets,[270] and (2) the so-called
theory of the lesser evil, according to which American "ideologists"
maintain that a limited war is less evil than an all-out nuclear
war.[271] A. Karenin argues, however, that this theory "conceals
within itself an extremely great evil and tremendous peril": it pro-

pounds as fact the notion that it is possible to limit war in the first place, and, given this premise, it actually works to lower the threshold of nuclear war.[272] The premise that nuclear war can be limited is, in Simonian's view, "totally untenable," a fact that he insists is "clear to every sober-minded person."[273] He adds that "it is unlikely that the strategists across the ocean do not know this." Nevertheless, in the traditionalist view, since the United States persists in entertaining such concepts, it only reveals its "aggressive essence," poses a threat to world "peace," and further fuels the arms race.

In the realm of conventional strategy, Soviet analysts, both realist and traditionalist, are in substantial agreement that the strategy of "realistic deterrence" has led to more substantial changes in the American stance; indeed, that the term itself represents an admission that the previous course was "unrealistic and impractical."[274] Trofimenko, for one, finds comfort in the apparent coincidence of the Soviet and American conceptions of "realism," explaining that "one can fully agree with this the more so since, as the U.S.–Vietnam fiasco has shown, the former U.S. strategic course really did not take into account many objective factors of the international situation; this is where its unrealistic nature showed through."[275] Scrutinizing Washington's view of the shortcomings of its former strategy, Trofimenko is able to show where the two strategies diverge. He first cites Secretary of Defense Laird's dissatisfaction with the unrealistic quality of "flexible response," quoting him to the effect that this strategy " 'did not prevent us from getting involved in the most prolonged conflict in our history.' " Trofimenko then observes:

> Laird is distressed not because of the very fact of involvement as such (it would at the very least be strange for the leader of the U.S. Defense Department to be distressed on such an account); he is troubled by the duration of the conflict, or, more precisely, by the lack of success of the overseas military operation undertaken by the United States in the hope of rapid success.

The strategy of realistic deterrence, Trofimenko and other Soviet analysts argue, was designed to overcome this basic shortcoming.

The main feature of the new strategy is said to be not the "truly realistic" course of excluding war altogether, but rather the "reduction of the chances of the direct participation of U.S. manpower in conflicts."[276] One means of accomplishing this goal, according to G. Sviatov, is by reducing the level of preparedness from "two and one-half wars" to "one and one-half wars."[277] This switch in preparedness doctrine is said to express the general American reluctance to maintain the same levels of military expenditures as had been sustained in the past. For Soviet analysis, the "unrealistic" nature of former obligations is epitomized by the famous Kennedy statement, "We shall pay any price, bear any burden, meet any hardship, support any friend, oppose any foe to assure the survival and success of liberty." They argue that the United States subsequently found the "price" too high—especially the price of the "Vietnam adventure," and the result has been a reduction in the level of military preparedness.[278]

This reduction, however, is seen as ancillary to the fundamental thrust of the new strategy, which is to shift the responsibility of supplying manpower for local conflicts from the United States to its allies and "junior partners." Such a shift is implied both by the "partnership" component of the Nixon Doctrine and the "combined force" concept of the strategy of realistic deterrence. As Trofimenko observes, "Washington is trying increasingly to regard the armed forces of U.S. partners and allies as a direct extension of the United States' own 'military arm.' "[279] Such military partnerships are said to serve the purpose (conceptually related to the nuclear aspect of the strategy) of permitting a shift in emphasis from quantitative to qualitative improvement in conventional forces. In Trofimenko's words, "the quantitative aspect of military preparations in the field of conventional forces is ... now regarded by Washington as primarily a matter for U.S. partners and allies in various military blocs." Washington, meanwhile, sees its basic task as the qualitative modernization of its conventional forces "on the basis of new equipment." Like the new nuclear strategy, the conventional aspect of "realistic deterrence" is also said to have increased flexibility as a chief goal. By expanding military "partnership" and increasingly relying on allies to supply manpower, American leaders are "trying to create freedom of action for themselves in critical situations, having to some extent freed themselves from the rigid obligations and concepts that required the indispensable military participation of the U.S. armed forces in any conflicts that threatened to change the social status quo to the advantage of the progressive, democratic, anti-imperialist forces."[280]

Larionov has argued that, in addition, such freedom of action would "let the United States keep the right to decide for itself at what stage and with what forces to engage in [any] conflict."[281] The main strategic corollary to this quest for flexibility is the increased reliance on a "blue-water" or "ocean" strategy, accompanied by a growing adherence to "the spirit of Mahan," which is said to emphasize control over that "no-man's land," the world ocean.[282] Trofimenko claims that American strategists believe that "having increased the emphasis upon naval forces, which are more autonomous, the United States will be able to act somewhat more flexibly, more independently of its allies, and at the same time to provide the latter with tactical support."[283]

Soviet analysts maintain that certain changes in American "crisis policy" have accompanied the new strategy. ("Crisis policy" is a favorite focal point of Soviet analysis because, according to V. Zhurkin, "every international crisis reflects in concentrated form the characteristic features of the foreign policy course of the state involved in it."[284]) While claiming that "force" is still "at the basis of every 'crisis policy' of the United States," Zhurkin sees the new policy as reflecting a desire to avoid the negative consequences incurred in Vietnam.[285] U.S. "ruling circles" are said to have become more clearly aware that "any major international crisis can, under certain conditions, get out of control and evolve into a conflict in which the very existence of the United States would be called into question."[286] Given this awareness, the Americans hope to eliminate "prolonged combat actions" from their crisis-policy repertoire, while "intensifying the element of flexibility" and improving two other types of crisis policy: "brief operations" with the "active use of armed forces," and "demonstrations of force in order to frighten, to intimidate, to blackmail, and sometimes also to bluff."[287] As was mentioned earlier, the Soviets believe that the mechanisms for decision making have been improved, especially with the aid of new scientific techniques. They also ascribe considerable significance to the improvement of the military mechanism for application in crisis situations,[288] and particularly to the development of relatively small but highly mobile forces for use in brief "aggressive adventures."[289] Zhurkin adds that such forces are instrumental in carrying out a tactic of increasing importance, the "policy of the *fait accompli*," the essence of which is "the rapid inflicting of blows and immediate withdrawal to initial positions in order to present the U.S. public and the entire world with a *fait accompli*, in an attempt to weaken those numerous negative domestic and foreign consequences that follow prolonged wars of the type of the intervention in Vietnam."[290] In addition, this policy of "brief strikes" is said to be a reaction to the failure of the "policy of gradual escalation."

The psychological aspect of the new U.S. strategy also attracts the attention of Soviet analysts. This aspect is especially evident in America's alleged reliance on the use of deception, including such tactics as: "misinforming the enemy," "remaining silent about certain decisions," and "excessively publicizing other decisions in order to improve its own strategic position through such 'psychological games.' "[291] In this regard Melvin Laird is cited as quoting the ancient Chinese sage Sun-tsu to the effect that " 'all military art is based on deception.' "[292] Related to the psychological aspect of this new strategy is the desire to use the American arsenal, and especially nuclear weapons, in an indirect way—"politically and psychologically."[293] Trofimenko has called this method the "strategy of initiative," a strategy that relies increasingly on "intimidation," and is based on a rejection of the idea of "reacting" which was an explicit element of "flexible response." Under this old strategy, according to Larionov's 1971 article, the United States

> merely "adjusted" to what was happening and suffered from the illusion that it was capable of changing the course of events in its own favor through resolute interference in a conflict that had already arisen. At the same time, no energetic actions were undertaken to avert conflict, in order to avoid encountering the *fait accompli* of an undermining of political prestige or a deterioration in the military-strategic situation. As a result, the United States lost the initiative in the psychological plane.[294]

With its new strategy, however, the United States seeks to "regain this initiative by 'intimidating' potential enemies." In other words, "without waiting for the moment of decisive skirmish with the enemy, the United States must attempt to sow the illusion that the enemy is unable and unprepared to carry out a threat."[295] It is thus alleged that intimidation is carried out "for purposes of 'show,' " and that it is a significant aspect of the process of "refining" the methods of military force.[296] Larionov argues that the United States uses intimidation in an attempt to reduce the degree of involvement in local conflicts.[297] At the same time, it employs "initiative," seeking to demonstrate "strategic resoluteness" and thereby "to conceal its own local provocations, its own local military actions."[298]

As was mentioned above, Soviet analysts see the definition and allocation of responsibilities among the various components of America's overall defense posture as the heart of the new American strategy. The new emphasis on basing military construction and force planning on the degree of "threat" is one important component of this process. The Soviets argue that the new strategy was designed to be flexible enough to deal with any potential threat. The essence of the new "flexibility" is that it provides room for interpreting what constitutes a threat, assessing what are its dimensions, and, in the end, evaluating the extent of U.S. responsibility. The former strategy relied for its development programs on a ratio of targets to the weapons necessary to destroy them, while ignoring the effects of a possible change in the correlation of forces. The new strategy, in contrast, is designed to cope with any level of threat (including one that arises from changes in the worldwide correlation of forces) and to make use of any means of warfare for either deterrence or war-fighting purposes.[299] It is in this flexibility and responsiveness to any kind of threat that the new strategy is seen as attempting to provide a coherent link between conventional and nuclear strategy.

The other component of the definition and allocation of defense responsibilities is international, pertaining to the division of responsibility between the United States and its allies. In articulating the policy of "global responsibility," the United States is said to have recognized that it "assumed a burden of military pledges which was beyond its powers, pledges that did not correspond to the true interests of 'national security.' "[300] The policy of "shared responsibility" was the direct result of this situation.[301] In trying to determine relative shares of responsibility, the United States has allegedly developed a "technique" of classifying wars, devising a precise continuum that extends from full-scale strategic nuclear war, through various theater wars, to local wars.[302] Simonian argues that these classifications, and the "desire to 'detail' them to a greater degree," have a "significant political aim": "While maintaining its predominant role in NATO and other imperialist blocs [the United States seeks] to shift a considerable share of the burden and responsibility of preparing and waging certain types of wars onto its allies."[303]

In order to expedite such a shift and insure its efficacy, the United States increases its military assistance and arms sales to its allies, enabling these "junior partners" to bear a greater part of the military burden. Soviet analysts, however, are quick to point out that such arms transfers "not accidentally" have effects other than those that are officially acknowledged. They remark upon "the growth of tension in the regions that receive weapons, the development of conflict situations there, and the involvement of the recipient countries in an expensive arms race." At the same time, these arms deliveries are said to "defend the interests of America's monopoly capital and to insure the constant presence of American armed forces abroad."[304] They "strengthen American positions" in the recipient countries,[305] and thus ultimately serve what is alleged to be an "expansionist aim."[306] In short, Soviet analysts conclude that the policy of "shared responsibility" is a "realistic" way of carrying out the traditional "aggressive course."

In light of all the American talk about "realism," Soviet realists such as Trofimenko ask, "How real is Washington's hope of waging local wars by foreign hands?"[307] In general the answer is that the strategy will not work, except perhaps in those areas where the interests of the United States coincide with those of its "partners in local aggression." In such cases, Trofimenko notes, "there can be some grounds for such hope." For Soviet analysts, the "classic example" of such a coincidence is the common American and Israeli interest in imperialism, but, Trofimenko cautions that such situations are rare, that the dovetailing of interests is strictly the exception rather than the rule. Trofimenko regards this as the only explanation for the continued presence of American forces in Europe—forces that remain despite the increased allied contributions upon which the United States has insisted. Since the "actual forces

173

and opportunities for implementing" the partnership doctrine do not exist in Europe to the desired degree, the new strategy remains "arbitrary,"[308] "extremely unsubstantiated, and unrealistic."[309]

Soviet realists find other "contradictions" that militate against the "realism" (in the American sense) of the new strategy. Outstanding among these is the contradiction between the desire to preserve war as a political means and the ever-narrowing opportunities for waging one successfully. Whereas the United States is seen as trying to demonstrate a new readiness to use decisive force to meet whatever threat (in lieu of "measuring out the use of force"), the opportunities for employing such force effectively are decreasing no matter what policy the U.S. pursues. This situation results from the change in the worldwide correlation of forces, a change that "is forcing the U.S. leadership toward not a lesser, but a greater 'measuring' of force."[310] For instance, Trofimenko explains, "the U.S. leadership is now obliged to discuss the question of the 'price' (for the United States) of a conventional 'local' conflict and not only of a global nuclear missile conflict." Thus, whether or not the United States rejects "measuring," and whether or not it "shares" its "responsibilities," the success of any "military adventurism" will be constrained by the new correlation of forces. Added to these constraints are the aggravations of "internal contradictions"—the "complications in the domestic situation in America," characterized by "growing dissatisfaction with foreign policy adventures, burdensome pledges and U.S. participation in aggressive wars." Under such conditions, the American administration is said to "experience a noticeable nervousness" because other powers recognize these "contradictions" and see that they are "limiting the freedom of Washington's hands."[311] Arbatov has argued that such nervousness tends to push the American leadership into "adventuristic actions" in order to "prove that the U.S. government continues to have at its disposal complete freedom of action, and, if need be, is ready for any aggravation of the situation, and can 'go all the way,' as they say."[312] All of this amounts, then, to what a realist like Arbatov sees as the increasing "inferiority complex" of American foreign policy—a complex that is said to "evolve from striving to appear 'stronger' and 'more resolute' even as the objective situation [i.e., the change in the world correlation of forces] becomes less and less favorable to the former [policy of] power play and dangerous adventures."

The traditionalist analysts reach a different conclusion, preferring to issue warnings rather than make such a direct diagnosis of the prospects for American success or failure. Sviatov, for example, has argued that U.S. ruling circles continue to resort to the only policy they know well, the policy of force, in spite of its "contradictory" aspects. As evidence, the traditionalists cite the continuation of "record increases" in the U.S. military budget, as well as the "gradual buildup of U.S. military potential," the "preparation for wars on different scales," and the "unprecedented NATO militarist dress rehearsals."[313] Despite changes in official policy, U.S. leaders continue to find justifications for continuing the use of force and the arms race. When the policy is that of cold war, the use of force and the arms race are justified by the invocation of the "Soviet threat." If the policy is one of "detente," the imperialists still find ways to justify the use of force and the arms race. Karenin cites an American theory "according to which the arms race not only does not hinder detente but even allegedly assists it."[314] According to V. Soldatov, the exponents of this theory reason as follows: "In order to get further progress in detente we need to strengthen the West's military might since otherwise the Soviet Union would not be prompted to strive for this aim. This element of force, which, they say, is often ignored, is a most important element of detente."[315]

In sum, traditionalist Soviet analysis characterizes the new policy as "dangerous." In the first place, it combines the old policy of force with the new "strategy of initiative," the use of intimidation, and a policy of the *"fait accompli,"* thus creating "in the heads of its authors the illusion of the 'effectiveness' of such manipulations of military force, as well as the illusion of the impunity of this policy."[316] Such illusions are said to foster the idea that American "aggression" can go further and further without resistance—an idea that is in fact just another illusion, given the posture of the Soviet Union and its "progressive" allies, who stand ready to deal a "resolute rebuff" to "imperialist aggression." At the same time, the new policy is said to spawn in its perpetrators a dangerous "tendency not to yield" in the event of complex situations. Zhurkin maintains that the repetition of these "refined" methods of the use

175

of force leads to the ossification of that tendency, and "the authors of that policy become accustomed to that tendency, and that fact creates, overall, an extremely dangerous type of 'crisis policy'— 'crisis reaction.' "[317] In Zhurkin's view, this mentality increases the likelihood of confrontation with the Soviet Union: earlier American crisis policy "always included one major element—the attempt to avoid direct confrontation with the Soviet Union," but this element "is to a certain degree lessened" under the new policy. In discussing such confrontations, Zhurkin explains that he is thinking not so much of another Cuban missile crisis, as of some other type of crisis deriving from a "logic of events in favor of the type of U.S. behavior that develops in international conflicts." In other words, Zhurkin interprets the new crisis policy and mentality of the United States as simply more amenable to the "logic of events" which arises in crisis situations.

This discussion shows that there are two distinct Soviet views of the military means of American foreign policy. One view, the traditionalist, asserts that the United States has not abandoned the imperialist policies of force and the arms race. The second, realist view counters by arguing that the United States has indeed retreated from these exclusively aggressive policies as a result of its recognition of the new realities of the new correlation of forces. Although these views appear to be mutually exclusive—and in essence they surely are—they overlap in certain crucial areas.

For example, no matter how much Trofimenko stresses the elements of change in U.S. strategy, he issues a caveat that shows his views to be based on the same quasi-religious beliefs that his traditionalist colleagues espouse. Noting that the new U.S. strategy has been devised by the ruling class, he asserts that this strategy "maintains, regardless of its specific formulations, the continuity of the fundamental aims and purposes of this class, which have been worked out over the decades, and the immutability of the general approach to the methods of achieving these aims."[318] In addition, he emphasizes a combination of factors which further reduces the possibility of rapid and radical changes in strategy: the "enormous cost of the basic nucleus of the armed forces of larger states" combined with the lead times between the "conception of an idea" and "the combat deployment of a system." As a result, American strategy is embodied not only in existing force structures, but also in those that have been recently ordered and will not actually be deployed for several years.

The traditionalist commentators, while refusing to acknowledge many of the changes in U.S. policy discerned by their realist colleagues, are willing, however hesitantly, to admit that some of the positive changes in the world correlation of forces have, to an extent, influenced U.S. policy. Larionov, for example, has cited the American renunciation of "automatic involvement" in crisis situations and the "reduced political and military opportunities" for the United States throughout the world as evidence of a decline in American power.[319] Of course, to admit such changes is perfectly consistent with the optimism that orthodox Marxist-Leninists are obliged to entertain. In Gromyko's words, the evolution of American foreign policy "will be determined by the further weakening of Washington's international positions."[320] Nevertheless, it is likely that such assessments, especially when held by the realist school as well, are in fact genuine and not merely the expression of a ritualized optimism. For the realists, as we have seen, combine such optimistic views with some elements of pessimism which cut against the grain of traditionalist Soviet analysis, both in terms of their credibility and in their departure from established rituals. On balance, however, the optimism of the realists surpasses their pessimism with respect to American military strategy. Thus, their analysis forms a credible image of a United States forced to retreat by the realities of the changed correlation of forces.

Diplomatic Means

According to Arbatov, there have been two primary tactical lines in American foreign policy. One is characterized by the policy of force, which, in its most aggressive modes, employs "frontal attacks." The second features a shift to the use of "maneuvers, concessions, and compromises" combined with less direct forms of "pressure."[321] This second tactical line embraces the diplomatic means of American foreign policy as understood by the Soviets. Soviet analysts do not see the use of the various diplomatic means as signifying an abandonment of the "fundamentally aggressive nature" of American foreign policy. Instead, their use represents, at least to some analysts, a tactic subordinate to the main "policy of force," while others think that the use of such means indicates a more defensive posture—one that reflects the relative weakness of the United States resulting from the shift in the world correlation of forces. It must be noted that the Soviets rarely use the word "defensive" to characterize American foreign policy. Such usage would imply a defense against some kind of offensive—one presumably mounted by the opposing social system—and it would thus contradict the Soviet determination to avoid appearing as an "offensive" "exporter of revolution." Since, in the Soviet view, revolution is a "law-governed process" of internal socioeconomic development which cannot be "exported" but only "aided," Soviet foreign policy is merely an agent of this inexorable historical process and does not constitute an "offensive." Insofar as the policy of the United States has become *more defensive*, then, it has done so in response to the "resolute rebuffs" dealt it by these "forces of historical progress" as they retaliate to fend off the "blows of imperialist aggression." Finding itself comparatively weaker than before, and no longer able to count on the unimpeded success of its aggressive demarches, the United States is forced to resort to the more subtle and indirect maneuvering of diplomatic means.

Among these diplomatic means is the policy of the "status quo." For the traditionalist analysts this policy and its corollaries are simply another form of American imperialist aggression, clear evidence of the immutability of American foreign policy. The realists, in contrast, tend to see it as a policy to which the United States was forced to resort when it discovered that it was increasingly unsuccessful in obtaining beneficial results from its policy of force. The realists argue that since the changing correlation of forces compelled the United States to abandon the "bankrupt" policy of "liberation" (the Dulles slogan for liberation of the Soviet satellite nations), and since its policy of "exporting counterrevolution" failed by and large, it was forced to devise a new policy with which it could cling to the remnants of its "imperialist hegemony." It is important to note, however, that both schools of Soviet analysis agree on the fundamental nature of the policy of the status quo and other diplomatic means; their main difference is in their evaluation of the significance of these policies.

According to representatives of both schools, the gist of the policy of the status quo lies in the calls for "world order," "world stability," and "equilibrium," as well as in the actions that would institute such "order." When discussing the policies with which the United States pursues these goals, Soviet analysts generally speak in terms of "hegemonism" or the attempt to establish "spheres of influence." The concept of "spheres of influence" is termed a tenacious atavism from the days of colonial imperialism, when "great powers" divided regions among themselves for profit and plunder.[322] American ruling circles allegedly view the world through the prism of this concept, for, according to Soviet analysts, such a view is the only possible explanation for the "bourgeois" interpretation of the principle of "peaceful coexistence"—an interpretation that calls for peaceful coexistence of ideologies and the maintenance of the social status quo, or, in other words, for abandoning the "just struggles" of "national liberation."[323] The American version of "peaceful coexistence" in fact seeks to divide the world into spheres of influence with the Soviet Union and other great powers and demands tacit recognition of the inviolability of those spheres. The great power's hegemony in such a sphere of influence is maintained, the Soviets argue, through the support of "reactionary" regimes, support that can take such forms as: economic, scientific-technical, and military assistance or even the installation of imperialist "puppets" in the subject countries.[324] The Soviet view holds that these puppets must, of course, be dictators, for, in the words of V. Saprykov, "Dictators insure the best conditions for enriching U.S. monopolies."[325]

The Soviets see the creation of military blocs as another method by which the United States maintains regional hegemony. Such "aggressive blocs" are said to have been "knocked together" under the cover of the concept of "collective security," whose meaning the imperialists have allegedly twisted to coat their "antipopular" policies with a "peace-loving" gloss.[326] As this bloc policy has grown increasingly unable to guarantee success, however, its authors have attempted a number of variations on the theme, including the exploitation of Asian "regionalism," that is, "the aspirations of the Asian countries for cooperation."[327] This policy is carried out not only through the aforementioned military blocs, but also by facilitating the creation of other regional organizations in which the United States is not formally involved, but which it can use to serve its imperialist purposes. Among the examples of such organizations cited by Volskii are the Association of Southeast Asian Nations (ASEAN), the Bank of Asia, and the Asian and Pacific

Council (ASPAC).[328] Soviet analysts also allege that the United States has attempted to create a "wide-ranging political system" that would allow it to exert a primary influence on large countries, and through them, on their smaller neighbors. Once again, Asia is used to illustrate the Soviet argument, which holds that—largely because of the American failure in Vietnam—India, Pakistan, and Indonesia are "large countries" that fit into imperialism's "aggressive plans."[329] Washington is said to believe that various forms of assistance may prove more attractive to these countries than the bilateral security treaties with which the United States "enmeshed" them during the cold war.[330]

It is also argued that Washington seeks to insure the continuation of the status quo through the policy of "controlling conflicts," especially those in the Third World. In elaborating on this diplomatic means, Soviet analysts note both bourgeois speculations that Third World conflicts could lead to international crises that have the potential to spark nuclear war and bourgeois recommendations that so-called international mechanisms be used to control these conflicts. Thus, in a 1969 article, D. Kraminov referred to Washington's "hints ... at the Soviet Union's possible participation in 'international actions' insofar as it is also interested in insuring the stability of world order."[331] He noted that "Nixon declared that the more the United States and the Soviet Union can carry out their policy in such a way as to solve conflicts in the 'Third World' with the help of the United Nations or another international organization, 'the more chances we have of averting the opposition that ... both powers would like to avoid.' " Kraminov went on, however, to interpret the Nixon statement as an example of the way in which the United States uses the policy of "controlling conflicts" to guarantee the status quo:

This statement, even if dictated by an urge to reduce tension in relations between the USSR and the United States, is an example of "peace-loving" phraseology concealing the essence of the question. Indeed, the term "conflicts in the Third World" can designate completely opposite things: they could be both revolutionary changes of existing orders in various states of the "Third World" dictated by the will of the people and hence in full agreement with the clauses of the U.N. Charter, and also relapses of the colonial or racist policy contradicting the charter. . . . The essence of the matter lies in the fact that the U.S. leaders are hoping to send "international forces" into remote regions in accordance with their political aims and concepts of insuring a "stable world order."

U.S. efforts at "peacemaking" without the use of international mechanisms are said to serve similar purposes. Since the American bourgeoisie ignores the "class nature" of war and therefore cannot comprehend its "true causes," any American peacemaking attempts are aimed at maintaining the social status quo and preventing the victory of the "progressive forces" in any war. V. Kudriavtsev argued, for example, that in the Indo-Pakistan war the imperialists used peacemaking "as a cover for their malicious plans."[332] He maintained that while advocating the cessation of the conflict the United States not only ignored the real reasons for its existence but also tried "to profiteer from the people's desire for peace."

The idea that the "superpowers assume the role of custodians of equilibrium" is another of the diplomatic means by which Washington seeks to maintain the status quo.[333] The very term "superpower" is anathema to Soviet analysts, who work strenuously to disavow such status for the USSR, especially when it is attributed to them by the Chinese.[334] The Soviets argue that the very idea of a "superpower" expresses an ignorance of the fundamental "class nature" of international politics and, accordingly, they disdain any talk of the maintenance of international equilibrium by these so-called superpowers. In his 1970 article, S. I. Beglov cited Henry Kissinger's formulation of the main aspirations of a superpower that has assumed an equilibrating role: " 'to maintain its dominant position among its own allies, to intensify its influence in the nonaligned world, and to consolidate its security in the face of an opponent.' " Beglov concluded from this set of aims that "the American leaders are actually more concerned about how to keep their allies on a common leash and limit the sphere of their independent political initiative in the face of new demands for detente."[335] Once again, the emphasis is on the maintenance of the status quo.

Another of the main means of U.S. diplomacy, also related to the policy of the status quo, is the traditional American policy of the "balance of power." On account of a "careless juxtaposition of words by bourgeois theoreticians," "balance of power" is said to have a dual meaning. On the one hand, it represents "the uncomplicated policy of maintaining a mutual balance of forces effected by two states in a state of direct confrontation with each other." On the other hand, the "imperialist" balance-of-power policy "in the genuine sense of the word" is described as "a state's treacherous conduct in the international arena aimed at setting other countries against each other for the purpose of securing for itself the advantageous position of arbiter."[336] This task of "setting other countries against each other" amounts to "preserving and exacerbating friction," "mutual suspicion," and the "whipping up of tension" among other countries.[337] This policy is further characterized as having "expansionist aims" whereby "a state pursuing such a policy frequently regards a war between its rivals as a boon for its own interests."[338] The particular "class nature" of this policy lies in the fact that it is aimed at "hindering the strengthening of socialism's positions, preventing the growth of the revolutionary and national liberation movements, and thereby preventing the further change in the correlation of forces in favor of peace, progress, and democracy."[339] Of course, given the "contradictory" nature of capitalism, the U.S. balance-of-power policy also has its self-defeating aspects: it involves a "striving to crowd out its chief imperialist competitors" in order to gain greater hegemony in the regions of American expansionism.[340]

According to A. Topornin, the balance-of-power policy is heir to the tradition of American isolationism, a policy by which the U.S. bourgeoisie "utilized the contradictions among the European powers for its own enrichment."[341] During the period of American continental expansion and the Monroe Doctrine, considerations of the balance of power were "not only *not* alien to, but even loosely intertwined with the U.S. 'isolationist' doctrine" (my emphasis). During this period, the balance-of-power policy was already operational, but in its "less active forms," for "interventionism" had not yet begun to be utilized as an integral part of the policy. Toward the beginning of the twentieth century, however, the policy was transformed "from a convenient instrument of profit and a unique sort of shield for U.S. territorial expansion in the new world into one of the most important instruments of policy aimed at securing the U.S. ruling circles' global claims."[342] Topornin argues that the balance-of-power policy is continuing "to protect the United States from direct involvement in expensive and bloody armed conflicts while ensuring its expansionist interest in the world arena."[343]

The traditionalists in particular see this last aspect of the balance-of-power policy as an important adjunct to the Nixon Doctrine. They argue that as the direct struggle with the Soviet Union, the socialist community of states, and the worldwide national liberation movement became too costly and dangerous, Washington began to attach great significance to breaking out of this rigid bipolar confrontation in order to return to a true balance-of-power policy. An effort was made to "split the Old World into at least two approximately equal centers of strength," in an attempt to find both a "counterbalance" to the Soviet Union and forces that could be enlisted to defend America's "expansionist aims."[344] Soviet analysts such as Topornin see two alternative systems as having emerged from the "calculations" of the "bourgeois theoreticians": a "triangular scheme" and a "pentagonal system."

The "triangular scheme" is based on the "intensification of anti-Soviet tendencies in Peking's policy," which American strategists saw as a starting point for "political intrigues" against the USSR and the other socialist countries.[345] By exploiting this exacerbation of Sino-Soviet relations the United States was attempting to make China the "counterbalance." These political maneuvers are supplemented by economic considerations, for in its attempt to expand its political relationship with the PRC, the United States and its business circles "cannot afford light-heartedly to hand over to their main trading rivals (and primarily Japan) the potentially extremely big China market."[346] Despite the hopes of the imperialists, Soviet analysts have seen that the untrammeled success of the triangular policy would involve certain costs, primarily in regard to America's relations with some of its allies, especially Japan. As Lukin observed in 1973, "Washington is having to 'pay' for its policy of rapprochement with Peking with the deterioration in its relations with Japan."[347] The root of this problem, of course, is said to be the interimperialist contradiction arising from the struggle for regional political and economic influence.

The "pentagonal system" is depicted as operating in a similar fashion, even though it involves the interaction of a larger number of states. In this case the American "balancing" scheme includes the United States, the USSR, the PRC, Japan, and Western Europe, the latter preferably as an integrated capitalist entity containing a remilitarized Germany.[348] Karenin argues˘ that the authors of this plan hope to follow the classical balance-of-power policy of "carrying out within the framework of the 'pentagon' the kind of diplomatic maneuvers which would assure a position of predominance for the United States—the role of an 'arbiter,' capable of deriving direct benefit from the relations that have taken shape among the system's four other members."[349]

A final tactic which the imperialists use to apply principles of the balance of power to the Nixon Doctrine is enlisting others to assume the United States' military burdens. Arguing that the balance-of-power policy was designed to protect the United States from direct military involvement, the Soviets view policies such as "Vietnamization" and the increased "Europeanization" of the NATO burden as aspects of Washington's general "balancing" act. However, as Topornin observes, "the people of the world do not wish to play the role of puppets of the State Department or the Pentagon."[350] Thus, when the United States encounters situations that threaten imperialism's interests and cannot find others to be its "cannon fodder," it will allegedly undertake "direct military adventures"—an indication that the tasks of political balancing "have had to be relegated to second place."[351] For the Soviet traditionalists, then, the balance-of-power policy in all its forms remains "a variety of the foreign policy line that is based on the notorious 'position of strength' and that pursues the aim of liquidating socialism and struggling for world domination"—a policy that is "groundless," "illusory," and "dangerous."[352]

A related policy, which some commentators say is the basis for the balance-of-power policy, is the general American strategy of "divide and rule," yet another heir to the classic strategy of colonial imperialism and a basic element of the American diplomatic arsenal.[353] Similar to the balance-of-power policy, "divide and rule" tactics allegedly seek to perpetuate and intensify differences between countries, although they place special emphasis on the enemy— "the zones, countries, and organizations that are fighting for national and social liberation."[354] In the words of E. Zhukov, "the method of splitting and disintegrating the forces of the enemy is the general strategy of imperialism."[355] V. Kudriavtsev has cited the alleged imperialist attempt to "split the national liberation movement in Angola" as an example of this general policy—a policy that aims "to drive a wedge between the national liberation movement and the Soviet Union."[356] In such cases, the United States is described as striving "to deprive the developing countries of their loyal friend and reliable ally and to isolate the peoples who are struggling for their freedom." Kudriavtsev goes on to argue that the American imperialists are being aided by the Chinese, who have developed a theory that divides the world into rich and poor countries, assigning the Soviet Union to the first category and thereby classifying it as an imperialist power. Kudriavtsev maintains that the Chinese theory was designed to discredit the USSR in the eyes of the Asian and African peoples and observes that the United States quickly adopted a similar concept—the notion of a "North-South" dichotomy—for similar purposes. Indeed, he described Washington's concept as "a geographical variation of the same Maoist slogan." The United States tries to further the disunity of "progressive" forces on a regional scale through the construction of military blocs. To this end, the United States allegedly strives to exploit any existing "contradictions" between countries. Kudriavtsev cites U.S. policy in the Middle East as a perfect example of this strategy: by "disuniting the Arab States" and setting them at odds with each other, Washington may "force them to conclude separate agreements with the Israeli aggressors," a situation that "will cause an upsurge of narrow-minded nationalism in the Arab countries which will promote the isolation, and in the final analysis, the liquidation of the Palestinian resistance movement."

Soviet analysts discern another variation of the "divide and rule" policy which one commentator terms the "differentiated approach."[357] With this approach the United States allegedly seeks to maintain good relations with some of the states in a given region by offering economic aid and reducing trade barriers—all in exchange for an accommodating attitude toward American policy. Simultaneously, however, Washington exerts political and economic pressure on those states in the region which do not cooperate with imperialism's malicious plans. The object, as usual, is to divide these countries so as to shift the regional balance in favor of imperialism.[358] V. Levin terms this tactic the "individual approach."[359] Using American policy toward Latin America as an example, he describes this approach as beginning with the discarding of the collective methods of the Alliance for Progress and its aid programs, which had been merely "a propaganda cover for neocolonialism." In their place Washington initiated a policy of building relations with Latin American countries on an individual basis, to "strengthen the positions of U.S. monopoly capital" and "to prevent the kinds of changes which correspond to the interests of the Latin American people."

It is interesting to note that most of the discussion of the variations on the policy of the status quo occurred before 1971; after that year there was comparatively little analysis of this subject. This pattern of analysis suggests that during the period before 1971 both traditionalist and realist analysts could concur on many of the fundamental features of U.S. foreign policy. After 1971, however, the realists tended to see less danger in the policies of the status quo, concluding from their new assessment of the correlation of forces that such a policy was the mark of greater weakness. Furthermore, Soviet realists were by then beginning to focus their analyses on the evolution of a new American policy.

This new policy, the last of the major diplomatic means that we shall catalogue, can be generally subsumed under the rubric of "negotiation"—one of the essential "pillars" of the Nixon Doctrine. As defined by Soviet analysts, this policy includes not only actual negotiations, but also the spirit, intentions, and policies that underlie them. Epitomized by the Nixon expression "from an era of confrontation to an era of negotiation," this policy is the basis of the Soviet conception of the *American* policy of "detente." In the Soviet view, this new policy was inaugurated by the SALT talks and the complement of agreements on various problems of mutual interest which were signed in Moscow in May 1972. For the Soviets, the most significant of these accords was that on "Basic Principles of Relations" between the two great powers. As mentioned earlier, this agreement is seen as having officially codified the "Leninist principle of peaceful coexistence." Somewhat later in this "period of negotiation," the Soviets attached great significance to the 1975 Helsinki accords on "Security and Cooperation in Europe," which, among other things, officially recognized the European borders established at the conclusion of World War II.

But how do Soviet analysts interpret these negotiations and the policy of detente? According to the realist school, they represent a "recognition of reality" by the United States, whereas the traditionalist school holds that they are simply a more refined avenue for the attainment of imperialist goals. As Soviet realists constantly repeat, the United States was "forced" to recognize various "realities" by the change in the worldwide correlation of forces. One of these "realities" is the "fact" that "there is no alternative to peaceful coexistence." When Richard Nixon signed an agreement to this effect and Henry Kissinger adopted this very Soviet vocabulary in a June 1972 address to Congress, the Soviets were very gratified. Arbatov claims that another such "reality" is the futility of attempting to seek "unilateral advantages" in the military and economic spheres.[360] In acknowledging this futility, the United States is said to have recognized the "principle of equal security"[361] and the related principles that constitute the "modern concept of international security," including those of "sovereignty, equality, noninterference in internal affairs, mutual advantage, the inviolability of borders, territorial integrity," and the fact that "differences in ideology and social systems are not an obstacle to the development of normal relations."[362] The recognition of this reality is based, of course, on the attendant fact of Soviet military power, now apparently unsurpassable. In the Helsinki agreement, which Brezhnev described as a "victory for reason," and which Z. Mirskii called one of those events which amount to a "conquering of key frontiers" and a "consolidation of what has been achieved" by the progressive forces, the United States is said to have recognized the reality of the progressive "restructuring of international relations" on the basis of "collective security," "peaceful coexistence," and the "relaxation of tension."[363] Furthermore, in the wake of these accords, many Soviet analysts referred to the "healthy recognition" in much of the capitalist world that "peaceful coexistence does not and cannot signify a social status quo."[364]

Probably not since Roosevelt recognized the Soviet Union have any American actions provoked such open manifestations of deep Soviet satisfaction. Their barely restrained joy is the measure of their conviction that these events constitute the most significant legitimation ever accorded the USSR, its policies, and its historical faits accomplis. Furthermore, the Soviets see this conferral of legitimacy as corroborated by the projection of their image as the rising world power—an image notarized by a weakening United

States. One must note here that the Soviet analysts never use the word "legitimacy," or speak of its conferral as such, for to do so would admit the possibility of an earlier illegitimacy. Nevertheless, the idea is, if you will, explicitly implied, and can be gleaned by examining the connotations of certain Soviet terms. As we have observed, many Soviet expressions have normative connotations that combine with a face-value quality that means something entirely different to noncommunists, for example: "peaceful coexistence," "collective security," "security," "peace," "progress," "independence," "normalization of relations," "ideological struggle," "imperialism," and so on. "Reality" (or "realism") is another word of this sort. "Reality" connotes "objective truth" and "reason" in the Soviet lexicon, and thus anyone who is "unrealistic" and does not recognize "reality" is challenging the "truth" (*pravda*) with distortions and lies. That truth, of course, constitutes only what communist doctrine says it is. As Iu. Oleshchuk has put it, "On the whole, *realistic* foreign policy in American society has seriously crowded out *bias,* and recognition of the impossibility of a policy based on opposition to the USSR is becoming more widespread" (my emphasis).[365] In other words, the more "realistic" one becomes, the more one admits to the legitimacy of the ideas and policies that constitute and derive from the "truth." That U.S. "realism" signifies a conferral of legitimacy on Soviet policy was made explicit, in Soviet eyes, by the international, legal recognition at Helsinki of the borders that divide Europe—borders drawn by Soviet conquest.

The Soviets do not speak loudly of the "weakness" of the United States either. To do so, of course, would surely risk alarming those Americans concerned with the dangers of being perceived as weak —alarm that might translate itself into an undesirable increase in tension and an acceleration of the arms race. However, repeated observations that the United States was "forced" to recognize reality and sign various agreements (when such "forcing" had not been seen as possible previously), leaves no doubt that the Soviets have perceived a comparative weakness on the part of the United States. Similarly, the more "realistic" the United States becomes, the more illegitimate, groundless, and therefore weak become its imperialist ideas, policies, and positions.

This image of a weaker United States, forced to recognize reality, is not the sole Soviet interpretation of the American policy of "negotiation" and "detente." Traditionalist analysts see that such a view could engender complacency among the struggling cadres both in the USSR and throughout the world. As a result, traditionalist analysis is more cautious, portraying a still dangerous and crafty United States that has simply shifted to more subtle methods of policy. Much of the analysis of this sort (which is done by some realists as well) seeks to focus attention on the so-called opponents of detente, reactionary forces that are seen as having a sizable influence on American policy. This influence manifests itself in several ways, among which is the advocacy of a policy of "linkage." The Soviets see "linkage" as the process of joining easier to more complicated problems in a negotiating process.[366] As Arbatov explains, when a problem is complicated and it is difficult to come to an agreement, the Americans often put forth the slogan, which "everyone knows" anyway, that "in such cases it is difficult to find a rapid path to settlement." However, in those situations when it is easier to find agreement, "the American leaders do not want to engage in negotiations, at least not 'for free.' " Washington therefore acts to hinder negotiations or "pose preliminary terms that, in essence, require a concession in other [more complicated] questions."[367] The Americans, then, would have the Soviets "pay" for detente and agreements.[368]

Closely related to the policy of "linkage" is the concept of "limited detente," which is strongly advocated by the "opponents of detente." As defined by Oleshchuk, this concept calls for the "normalization of relations" between the United States and the USSR "not on the basis of equal rights and mutual benefit, but on concessions on the part of the Soviet Union alone."[369] This "contradictory and essentially frail surrogate of peaceful coexistence" further posits that the Soviet Union "should not go halfway to meet the United States, but cover a considerably longer distance," and concludes that "only if the USSR agrees to act in this manner is it expedient for the United States to agree to develop constructive ties with our country." Oleshchuk refers to U.S. arguments that call for " 'testing the sincerity of the peace-loving intentions' " of the Soviet Union, as well as those that refer to "imaginary economic difficulties of the USSR" and "strive to create the impression that our country is in a situation where one can pressure it and obtain the required concessions." Furthermore, these proponents of "limited detente" are said to "go so far as to attempt intervention in our domestic affairs."

It is interesting to note the one-sided quality of the Soviet term "normalization of relations" which emerges in such analysis. As the Soviets understand it, true "normalization of relations" constitutes the establishment of relations on the basis of "peaceful coexistence." As we have seen, "peaceful coexistence" is the Soviets' preferred form of "struggle"—one that allows the "peace-loving forces" to engage in "ideological struggle." However, if "reactionary forces" try to engage in what they understand as legitimate ideological struggle, the Soviets term their actions "psychological warfare" and "interference in the internal affairs of the USSR"—in short, actions that do not correspond to true "peaceful coexistence," and true "normalization of relations." What the Soviets are seeking, then, as expressed *in their own language,* is the institution of a code of international relations which grants them certain privileges of struggle which it simultaneously denies to the United States. When the "opponents of detente" ask equal access to these privileges, they are said to be calling for "concessions" on the part of the Soviet Union.

Soviet analysts perceive several American negotiating tactics as having been devised in the same spirit as "limited detente." One of these tactics is the manipulation of the concept of the "essential equivalance" of strategic forces, a criterion, according to Secretary of Defense James Schlesinger, by which the size of the American strategic arsenal must be determined. This concept is said to be the Defense Department's sine qua non for stability in the military balance and the continued relaxation of tension.[370] At first glance, Soviet analysts say this concept "provokes no objections," for it appears to accord with the principle of "equal security" and the renunciation of attempts to gain "unilateral advantage."[371] However, when Secretary Schlesinger begins to draw practical conclusions about the strategic balance, "it immediately becomes clear that in a number of 'critically important' parameters, the United States allegedly 'lags behind' the Soviet Union and that this 'gap' may 'increase intolerably' in the near future." This realization leads the secretary to recommend that the United States undertake measures to seek "essential equivalence" to redress the situation. In the Soviet view, the measures justified by this concept amount to "forging ahead with the arms race." "Essential equivalence," then, is just another cover for the "aggressive plans" of the military-industrial faction of the American ruling class.

The second dubious negotiating tactic, described in the same 1975 article, is the use of "bargaining cards" at the SALT talks, that is, the acquisition of new weapons systems that may be sacrificed as "concessions" or traded off against Soviet weapons in the limitation process. The Arbatovs maintain that the military-industrial complex uses this tactic in an attempt to justify the "biggest current U.S. strategic programs." Like "essential equivalence," the use of a "bargaining cards" strategy is another way in which the ruling circles try to "justify the continuation of the arms race."[372] Thus, for these "opponents of detente" negotiations are said to represent "a screen for concealing one's aggressive policy."[373]

Yet another diplomatic tactic that is said to influence American policy is the attempt to use detente and negotiations for "subversive" purposes. Soviet analysts claim that with this tactic, the opponents of detente strive to use detente as a pretext for implementing the "bankrupt" doctrine of "bridge building" with its corollary calls for the "liberalization" of social conditions in the Soviet Union, the "broadening of human rights," and the introduction of "pluralism" in Communist systems.[374] The Soviets view the argument that "detente cannot be stable under conditions of ideological struggle" in this same context.[375] They hold that this American argument is tantamount to calling for "ideological peace," and as Iu. Oleshchuk observes, "Is it necessary to prove that the 'ideological peace' advanced as the best alternative is pure Utopia?"[376] That Oleshchuk describes such a situation as "Utopia," literally, "nowhere," is ironic, for the word is an interesting characterization of fully realized communism, the only situation in which, presumably, a condition of "ideological peace" could be attained.

In conclusion, one can detect distinct points of view in Soviet perceptions of the diplomatic means of American foreign policy. The traditionalists ascribe greater weight to those in the American ruling class who would oppose detente. Their intentions, as usual, are depicted as unchanging: always aggressive and protective of imperialist ambitions and positions, using whatever means possible, direct or indirect, blatant or subtle. The U.S. imperialists are always pursuing their "class interests" and the consequences for American diplomacy include the "policy of force," the policy of the "status quo," and the "aggressive" aspects of the policy of "negotiation." The realists, however, perceive an erosion of the imperialist spirit of American policy. Although they acknowledge the continued influence of the reactionary imperialist circles, they see these groups as having been superceded by those who support detente. Thus, on balance, they maintain that the United States as a whole has been "forced" to recognize "realities." As Iu. Davydov puts it: "There is no doubt that the American ruling elite feels the pressure of changes in the ratio of forces in the world, a pressure that demands that the United States limit itself to some extent, seek its place in a new world, and recognize the failure of American attempts to direct the development of humanity along an American path and the failure of its claims to becoming the dominant factor of current development."[377] As the realists see it, then, the recognition of "failure" and the attendant retreat of American "aggressive" policies, must have a demoralizing and weakening effect on the policies by which the United States exercises its leadership over the forces and the philistine values that comprise the "so-called 'free world.'" The link between this dispiriting "recognition of failure" and Washington's unprecedented conferral of legitimacy on the Soviet Union is stressed by Davydov: "To admit the *inevitability* of such evolution and of a reduction in the global capabilities of the USA means to admit the inevitability of a narrowing of its capability in the historical perspective, to admit the *reality* of another alternative for development, primarily, the socialist alternative" (my emphasis).[378] In other words, the greater the American retrenchment in the defense (or as the Soviets would say, the "imposition") of its values, the more legitimacy it grants to the truthfulness, correctness, and validity of "socialism." It is, of course, precisely this kind of retrenchment, this kind of "recognition of reality," that Soviet realists have observed during recent years. Naturally, since the American ruling classes have been "forced" into this retreat, American foreign policy, in the Soviet view, continues to balance between two "imperatives": "on the one hand, it cannot fail to consider certain realities of the changing world and the *inevitability* of adapting to them, while on the other hand, it cannot fail to take into account the fact that the political and economic aspirations of the U.S. ruling class conflict with these realities. From this we get the duality, inconsistency, and zigzags of the new U.S. foreign policy doctrine."[379]

When these words were written in 1972, Soviet realists were apprehensive about this duality. While delighted with what it saw as the Soviet victories at the Moscow summit of that year, Soviet realist commentary was marked by concern as to the "fragility" of the still nascent "detente" and lingering fears that it might have misperceived the correlation of forces and therefore misjudged the strength of the "opponents of detente." Arbatov articulated the nature of these apprehensions in his comments on the Nixon Doctrine: "When the behavioral style of the other side is such that it is possible, at any moment, for some new zigzag to occur under the influence of the domestic policy situation, it is necessary to fear that even a state of agreement which has been established as a result of prolonged negotiations might be derailed."[380] As the 1970s progressed, however, despite the usual lip service to the insidious character of the "opponents of detente," realist expressions of confidence grew. "Detente" was being "consolidated." The situation was being "stabilized" and "normalized." Detente survived the "test" of the October 1973 Middle East war; the Helsinki agreement was signed in 1975, and "security" prevailed over half of Europe. The forces of "national liberation" were victorious in Vietnam, Laos, and Cambodia, as well as in Mozambique and Angola, without much interference from the imperialists. Later, these same forces were emerging as the victors in Ethiopia, South Yemen, Nicaragua, and Afghanistan—and in these cases there was no imperialist impediment whatsoever. The "consolidation of detente" was therefore "progressing," and Soviet fears of the duality and "zigzags" of American policy diminished accordingly. "Reality" was being "recognized."

Chapter 4

U.S. Relations
with Its Allies

American alliance policy is the subject of considerable Soviet scrutiny—considerable, because the Soviets have long demonstrated an interest in finding and exploiting any cracks in an alliance system that they see as directed against their country and its "ideals." Soviet analysis is itself a demonstration of such interest, and as we shall see, its normative content underscores the degree to which it is shaped by the imperatives of Soviet ideology and foreign policy.

The Ends of American Alliance Policy

The basic goal of American policy toward its allies is, in the Soviet view, to maintain a community of imperialist interests directed against the USSR and the socialist community of states in particular and against the "progressive" forces of socialism, the national liberation movement, and the international workers movements in general. Soviet analysts maintain that there are two corollaries to this goal: (1) the U.S. desire to maintain its domination over its allies and the organizations in which they are joined, and (2) its attempts to convince those allies to share a greater part of the burden of defending imperialism. This second corollary, which in some ways contradicts the first, emerged only in the early 1970s, during which the correlation of forces shifted "in favor of socialism." Whereas traditionalist analysts predictably interpret recent alliance policy as a continuation of an aggressively imperialist course, the realists see it as yet another sign of change in American foreign policy. The new goal of sharing defense responsibilities, a function of the "partnership" component of the Nixon Doctrine, is seen as an index of the relative decline of U.S. power in the world arena and a verification of the realists' diagnosis of the change in the world correlation of forces.

The Means of American Alliance Policy

Diplomatic Means

Soviet analysts maintain that the primary means by which the United States conducts its relations with its allies is the formation of politico-military and economic blocs such as NATO and the OECD.* Within the context of these organizations, relations are based on the imperatives of the struggle between the two social systems.[1] Thus, the United States must maintain the edifice of an "Atlantic Fortress" to counter the "mythical Soviet threat," and, in order to justify such a "fortress," Washington must sustain tension by stoking the arms race and continuing its reliance on the "policy of force" and a "position of strength." Under conditions of detente, then, the continued existence of such "fortresses" is seen as a "contradiction" that has a deleterious influence on the cause of "peace" and "security."[2] As Anatoly Gromyko says, "Herein lies the great weakness of the U.S. administration's foreign policy, which is still based on reliance on military strength in Europe."[3]

To maintain its allied relations on this basis, the United States is seen as having to preserve its domination over these alliances, having recourse to various "levers" to achieve this aim.[4] Soviet analysts argue that such "levers" (found mainly in the economic, scientific-technical, and military spheres) were once plentiful and could be manipulated with comparative ease, but that the change in the correlation of forces and the onset of "detente" have rendered the problem of maintaining dominance more difficult for Washington. According to the Soviet interpretation, these changes in the international situation confronted the United States with a relaxation of the very tension that was required to maintain the cohesion of the

---

*In the following text, although NATO will be cited as the example of U.S. relations with its allies, it should be remembered that the Soviets perceive American relations with other allies by and large according to the same model.

195

"fortress." Moreover, America's allies had risen in political and economic stature and, as a result, were inclined to adopt greater independence in their foreign policies.[5] Among these "independent" policies are a "yearning" for detente and a strengthening of cooperation with the Soviet Union.[6] Such "independence," then, is listed as yet another reason why the United States tries to maintain its domination over these alliances. As Gromyko observed in 1971, it is the American fear that "European political antennae will turn toward the East, . . . not the need to 'safeguard the security' of Europeans from mythical threats," which constitutes the main reason for the continuation of American dominance.[7]

The American policy of maintaining a "symmetry of power" in Europe, then, is characterized as an effort to "isolate" Western Europe from socialist Europe.[8] The United States is said to implement this policy by playing a "neutralizing role," that is, by engaging in "blocking actions" vis-à-vis Western Europe's interrelations with the socialist countries.[9] The main diplomatic "lever" of such "blocking actions," particularly important given the new world conditions, is the use of allied organizations as instruments to influence European foreign policies.[10]

Turning to the example of NATO itself, Soviet analysts see American policy as attempting (1) to strengthen the bloc militarily and (2) increasingly to carry out a "joint Atlantic diplomacy." The NATO Council is seen as the particular vehicle of the latter aim, for it is designed to play a more effective role as the highest forum in the alliance system for "developing, agreeing upon, and coordinating the policy of the participants above all in relation to the European socialist states and also in questions of European security."[11] Given this line of argument, the Soviets conclude that the basis for the alliance and the basis for American domination of the alliance are largely identical. As Beglov explains, "It is not superfluous to note that in two decades, NATO's power has never had occasion to be put in motion in order to fulfill the sacred mission for the sake of which this organization was created—to repulse illusory military aggression." Instead, it is "utilized regularly to protect reactionary processes that take place within the orbit of Atlanticism."[12]

Soviet analysts maintain that the new worldwide correlation of forces has forced the United States to adopt the concept of partnership as a means for maintaining its international positions, and that this means has become an end in itself. As the Soviet realists see it, the trick for the United States was not just to adopt the new method of "partnership" but to be able to avoid its deleterious consequences—especially the greater independence of its allies. The inspiration for partnership, of course, came from the desire "to become liberated from the rigidity of U.S. foreign policy 'obligations.'" Having to take account of both the greater stature of its allies in the capitalist world and the limitations that the new correlation of forces placed on its ability to influence international events, the United States sought to share some of the burdens of the "defense of the so-called free world." Thus, partnership is said to amount to an effort "to raise the level of American capabilities in the world arena by compensating for the relative American weakening by more extensively enlisting the forces and means of allies."[13] In addition to sharing the military burden, the United States is seen as seeking to redistribute "the moral-psychological responsibility for the fate of the capitalist system."[14] This approach, however, has raised the question of how the United States can encourage Europe to become the "second support" of the Western world while at the same time maintaining sufficient influence over the alliance to accomplish its primary purpose of preventing deviations from the orbit of American global strategy. Novosel'tsev notes that "in order to achieve this two-sided but unified goal, . . . Washington is declaring its readiness to resort to certain economic and political concessions in Western Europe and to give it greater responsibility in decision making within the framework of a 'mature Atlantic partnership.'"[15] As the Soviets see it, the use of this "framework," that is, the allied organizations over which the United States can exercise control, is the only possible diplomatic method by which these opposed goals can be accomplished.

The Soviet realists, however, do not believe that these American efforts to combine the goals of partnership and dominance have much chance for success. Their prognosis is based on the conviction that, given the new conditions in the world, the American system of alliances is fraught with "contradictions." First, there are the so-called interimperialist contradictions that stem from the intense economic rivalry among the world's capitalist states. These economic contradictions will be discussed below. Second, there is the contradiction between the American goals of dominance and partnership which Novosel'tsev points to when he notes the "many very well-founded doubts in Western Europe" about the continued American assertion of "leadership" in the face of the newly acknowledged "autonomy" of America's "partners."[16] Furthermore, the Soviets observe that the very idea of partnership presupposes a coincidence of "national interests" between the United States and its allies.[17] However as Iu. Davydov sees it, "Washington's expansionist aspirations are alien to a majority of these countries, even where their regimes have a common class background. More and more often they feel alienated from these aspirations and attempt to divorce themselves from them out of fear of being involved in some unpopular action."[18] Specifically, America's allies fear being dragged into "military adventures and international crises unleashed by Washington in different parts of the world."[19] The above-mentioned European desire for "security" and the concomitant "relaxation of tension" are also seen as deviations from any coincidence of interests between the United States and its allies, indicating that the United States must also take into account the increased "Europeanization of East-West relations."[20] Davydov argued that the October 1973 Arab-Israeli War highlighted another, no less significant divergence of interests: in this case the "realistic" foreign policy of the European countries that supported the Arabs dealt "a serious blow to this principle of future global partnership."[21]

As a result of such contradictions, the United States is said to fear an erosion of the very "foundations on which the structure of the USA's postwar Atlantic policy in Europe has been based."[22] If genuine partnership is to prevail, with its implied "autonomy" for the European states, then, given the new conditions of "detente" and the European aspiration for "security" and "cooperation" with the Soviet Union and socialist Europe, the very raison d'être for NATO allegedly disappears. Davydov looks at the erosion of the basis for the alliance from another perspective. He observes that, before the Nixon Doctrine and its calls for partnership, America's allies were ready to "recognize American hegemony" in return for "obligatory American intervention" in case revolutionary situations or other threats arose.[23] With the Nixon Doctrine, however, Washington sought a liberation from the rigidities of its old and sometimes obsolete treaty obligations. Thus, Davydov characterized the new American policy as one guided "by [Washington's] current-day goals in every concrete decision-making case, and not by the nature of treaties signed decades earlier." It was a more pragmatic policy, one for which the United States to have "greater freedom of action," "greater flexibility," and a "broader choice of alternatives." Davydov concluded that, as a result, "if the automatic obligation to intervene disappears, the ruling circles of the particular U.S. ally immediately face the question whether the alliance is necessary, and what is the significance for these regimes of recognizing the leadership of the United States in the capitalist world."

It should not surprise us that these observations on the contradictory nature of the American alliance system conform to the normative pattern of much of Soviet analysis. Since the Soviet Union has not and does not like the existence of blocs such as NATO, which add to the strength of its imperialist opponents, it pursues a policy that attempts to exacerbate their internal contradictions and give them wide publicity. The policy of "detente" of course fits Soviet purposes well, for it states that international tension, in the form of arms race or threat of war, no longer exists and thus, by implication, asks why NATO needs to be maintained. Indeed, Soviet logic makes a great deal of sense, and the policy of detente appears to have been a good try at dissolving NATO. However, the unprecedented military buildup by the USSR and its adventurism in Afghanistan, Ethiopia, and elsewhere pierced the comfortable vacuum of this reasoning and restored the context of the true international situation. And, one might add, the Soviet realists do not delude themselves by permitting the ultimate, desired results of their detente strategy to masquerade in their own minds as the current reality of U.S. policy. As Davydov implies, although the United States has recognized certain "realities" of the new international situation, its ruling circles are not so foolish, from their "class" point of view, as to ignore the rising threat to the NATO alliance and ultimately to their own very existence. Under these conditions, they cannot permit their allies to go free. As Davydov explains: "The USA cannot rely on a real 'partnership,' but only on the kind of partnership which can be maintained by new, although possibly more refined, forms of dependency of these countries on the United States."[24] Thus, as the Soviets see it, the future of allied relations will be determined by the interaction between the claims of American dominance with its attendant "levers" for the creation of "dependence relations," and the European desire for "independence."[25]

Ideological Means

Soviet analysts hold that the ideological means by which the United States tries to maintain its alliance relations and preserve its dominance over them are exercised primarily within the framework of the NATO alliance. Operating under American tutelage, the "NATO machine," in particular the NATO Public Relations Committee and a number of other "propaganda divisions," is said to "grind out propaganda in the member states."[26] In the Soviet view, the NATO information service uses both the official press and the private mass media and other public organizations of different countries "for the anti-communist and anti-Soviet indoctrination of public opinion in non-socialist countries" as well as, of course, for "ideological subversion" in the socialist states.[27] International research institutions that "work on problems of anti-communist strategy and tactics" are another means by which the U.S. imperialists bind their alliances ideologically. Particular attention is given to the Atlantic Institute in Paris which, according to Soviet analysts, was set up on the basis of NATO funds. Finally, the Soviets claim that ideological influence on allied relations is exercised by various nongovernmental, but imperialist organizations, including "organizations of the monopoly bourgeoisie," "political parties," and "businessmen's associations." As one commentator concludes, "U.S. imperialism endeavors to continue influencing other capitalist countries and pursue a common policy in the main areas of the class struggle."[28]

Economic Means

The Soviets believe that the United States has a number of economic "levers" at its disposal for the purpose of maintaining the cohesion of its alliances. Many of these levers seek to take advantage of the "internationalization of economic life" which has been spurred on by the "scientific-technical revolution" and the resultant progress in the "development of the productive forces."[29] One aspect of this internationalization has been the process of economic integration among many Western capitalist states, a process that the United States has encouraged and that the Soviets see as a primary means by which American alliance relations are fortified. According to Inozemtsev, integration "organically combines the interlacing of private capital from the various countries, and the long-established cooperation of the national monopolies and international monopolies with the policy of the capitalist states and the activity of governments participating in integration groupings."[30] The primary impetus, of course, behind this economic means is the alleged widening in the scope of "the class struggle ... within the imperialist countries themselves."[31] Confronted with these circumstances, the imperialists "are trying to pool their efforts in the economic, political, and military fields and oppose world socialism, the international working class and national liberation movements."[32] These organic international connections between the state and private capital are said to enable the bourgeois forces of many countries to react to any threat to the socio-economic order which may appear in a neighboring country. Thus, "economic integration," in the words of one commentator, "serves the imperialist strategy of adaptation to the new worldwide alignment of forces."[33] Two other forms of economic internationalization are identified as instruments for the cementing of American alliances: the "accelerated formation of multinational monopolies," and the appearance of "international state monopoly organizations."[34] Soviet analysts argue that the United States encourages both of these phenomena in order to provide "the basis for further expanding bourgeois international cooperation and framing imperialism's general strategy."[35]

Also at the disposal of the United States, in the Soviet view, are a set of economic "levers" whose purpose is to preserve the American domination of these alliances. One of these levers is the broader politico-military relationships that stem from the process of economic integration between the allies. As Inozemtsev notes, these growing economic ties "help to intensify political and military cooperation and the formation not only of economic groupings but also of military-political blocs."[36] For example, although the United States is not a member of the EEC, its promotion of European integration, furthermore, is said to involve the "use of force, breaches the cohesion of NATO under American domination. Economic integration, furthermore, is said to involve the "use of force, breaches of the independence and sovereignty of nations and rivalry between opposing groupings,"[37] as well as the "subordination of the relatively weaker participants in integration to the stronger partners."[38] Thus, Soviet analysts conclude that economic integration provides the very structure of "force relations" which the American imperialists find so propitious for the successful pursuit of a "divide and rule" policy. In other words, the very integration of capitalist states such as those in the EEC is fraught with enough "contradictions" and antagonisms that the United States can still divide and thereby control them.

Soviet analysts list three more economic "levers" that can be used to preserve American dominance. The first is the very existence of a "tremendous amount of direct capital investment."[39] As was noted in the previous chapter, direct capital investment is seen as one of imperialism's chief methods of political-economic control. Second, the Soviets note that the dollar is the major capitalist reserve currency and stress the control implicit in this fact.[40] Finally, the Soviets acknowledge more "crude" forms of pressure. E. Shershnev, for example, cites the various American "threats" posed in late 1971 "with the aim of exerting influence on its allies and creating favorable conditions for its own exports."[41]

The Soviets see few economic means with which the United States can try to fulfill its corollary goal of "partnership," for they view partnership primarily as a sharing of the imperialist military burden. The Soviets do distinguish, however, two forms of partnership in the economic sphere, one of which is the sharing of the foreign aid burden. According to Zakhmatov, the partnership approach strives for an increasing transfer of expenditures for Third World assistance to America's industrially developed allies.[42] One of the primary methods by which Washington tries to accomplish this task is by shifting the channel of foreign assistance from direct American grants and loans to indirect payment through international organizations under American control. This approach is motivated by the expectation that it will be possible to mobilize the efforts of other countries and pass a significant part of the aid burden on to America's allies. Then, as Zakhmatov declares, "by controlling distribution of assistance through international organizations more rigidly, American representatives hope to direct the capital invested by other countries in their own interests."[43] The second economic form of partnership is perceived to be a consequence, generally speaking, of the "crisis of capitalism," and more particularly, of the U.S. failure to realize the goals it sought in issuing the above-mentioned "threats" to its allies in 1971. In the Soviet view, this form of partnership boils down to the sharing of American economic difficulties. In the early 1970s, according to several commentators, this approach was manifested in the floating of the American dollar and the abandonment of the international economic order that had been devised at the Bretton Woods Conference.[44]

In spite of all these U.S. efforts to maintain alliance cohesion while pursuing the goals of domination and partnership, the Soviets discern various fundamental "contradictions" in American-allied relations. First of all, American policy toward integration is seen as contradictory. As Novosel'tsev has observed, the United States on the one hand feels "compelled" to encourage the expansion of such groups as the Common Market and to "intensify integration processes" as an element in its struggle against world socialism.[45] On the other hand, the United States increasingly feels the discomforts of competition with its new integrated capitalist rival,[46] for integration is not only "a system of deep-going measures" to tie participating countries into a "single economic complex," but also a method designed "to oppose" any countries outside the grouping.[47] As Inozemtsev notes, this competition proves to be even more aggravating to the imperialists on account of the "relative weakening of the U.S. positions in the world capitalist economy" and the concomitant strengthening of its West European rivals and Japan.[48] Another commentator notes that "sharp disagreements" exist between the United States and the Common Market: "The U.S. monopolies are out to undermine the latter primarily from within, taking advantage of privileges granted to foreign investors."[49] The "intensified flow of U.S. private investment to Western Europe" and the consequent "subjugation by American capital of a number of large companies in France, Belgium and other countries" are policies that allegedly serve this purpose.

Interallied contradictions also occur, of course, in the sphere of "competitive struggle" for world markets. Soviet analysts maintain that these contradictions have always existed among the "capitalist vultures," but that they have been greatly exacerbated by the new correlation of forces. This change has led to "the sharp territorial reduction in the sphere of capitalist domination owing to the formation and development of the world socialist system," a process that leaves the imperialists with fewer areas to "exploit" and "plunder."[50] This argument clearly implies that those who live under "collective security" of the communist kind are "secure" from the capitalists' rapacity—a rapacity that, in the Soviet view, must consequently restrict its loathesome plunderings to the beleaguered corridors of the rapidly shrinking "free world." The result is an intensifying struggle among the imperialists for the remaining crumbs of this non-"secure" world. In the Soviet view, this interimperialist struggle is, in a sense, a "progressive" development. Thus, Soviet analysts argue that the economic and political dislocations that the imperialists necessarily suffer in the course of their struggle make them begin to appreciate the "benefits" of the "stable" "socialist economy." In the words of one commentator, "The general crisis of capitalism and the intensifying competitive struggle between the monopolies for markets are heightening the interest of many capitalist countries in contacts with the socialist market, whose capacity is steadily growing and which is free of market fluctuations."[!][51] Inevitably, this magnetic attraction is the cause of more "contradictions," ensuring "the failure of the innumerable attempts to make capitalist countries pursue a common strategy."[52] Inozemtsev summarizes the Soviet view when he writes that alliance relations in the economic sphere are characterized by "the close interweaving of cooperation and struggle, of joint action and clash of interests."[53]

Scientific and Technical Means

As noted earlier, Soviet analysts identify the scientific-technical revolution as a weapon by which American ruling circles seek to counter the "internal contradictions of capitalism." By the same token, the Soviets view the American use of science and technology as a means of U.S. alliance policy—one that can be used both to cement alliances and to fight the "international workers movement" as it appears within allied societies. According to one commentator, scientific experience and increased technical knowledge are major factors in the "objective material foundation" of integration that the United States encourages among its allies.[54] Soviet analysts maintain that the scientific-technical revolution stimulates "progress in the development of productive forces," and thus leads to "important changes within the system of links between individual national economies."[55] The result is "more extensive scientific and technical exchanges between the advanced capitalist countries" and an "intensification" of the internationalization of economic life— developments that fit the American scheme of promoting alliances through economic integration.

At the same time, however science and technology are said to constitute a "lever" by which the United States maintains its dominance over its allies.[56] U.S. scientific and technical supremacy over its allies leads to a "technological gap" between them.[57] Furthermore, as Novosel'tsev argues, this gap is not simply a function of private economic phenomena but also results from a "U.S. state policy which is consciously directed to deepening this gap in its favor and financing efforts by American monopolies with federal budget capital."[58] Since American capital is "predominant" in "those sectors of Western European industry which determine the development of scientific-technical progress," the deepening of this gap "may lead not only to preservation of the backwardness, but also to preservation of a foreign (in this case American) control over a significant part of the national wealth of particular Western European countries."[59] As another commentator points out, the far-flung network of U.S. businesses located abroad allows the United States to play a large role in determining "the rate of scientific and technical progress in the rest of the capitalist world."[60] As a result, it can "[obstruct] the unfolding of the scientific and technical revolution in the most developed capitalist countries," thereby preventing any "progressive" changes that may result from the scientific-technical revolution and also allegedly creating a situation whereby its allies are increasingly dependent on it economically as well as in science and technology. Gromyko argues that one of the chief goals of the "New Technological Policy," for example, is "to put into effect mutually advantageous projects which are beyond the powers of any one country."[61] In the context of the "technological gap," this policy is one of the "new levers by which to make other countries dependent on American capital."[62]

The American attempt at "partnership" has few manifestations in the sphere of science and technology, the one important example that Soviet analysts cite being the sharing of the expense of the space program. In this regard Gromyko points out that the United States had concluded some 250 agreements with 35 countries in the fields of space research and aeronautics.[63] Such agreements are designed, according to Gromyko, not only "to make [the U.S.] space programs less expensive," but also to pursue "far-reaching strategic goals of a political nature which are based on a desire to tie other states to American space programs and avert the development of national space research programs in those countries."[64] Here, then, "partnership" and "dominance" blend into a single policy.

As can be expected, "the Soviets maintain that these insidious American scientific and technical policies sharpen "contradictions." Thus, for example, the dependence relationship of America's allies contradicts their desire for "independence." As Novosel'tsev notes, American "control" over much of its allies' national wealth is increasingly perceived "as a political problem linked with material support for the possibility of independently disposing of one's own national resources to achieve one's own foreign policy goals, especially when they are at odds with U.S. goals."[65] Finally, the application of the scientific-technical revolution to the competitive struggle among capitalist allies deepens the usual "interimperialist" economic contradictions. Since competing monopolies can ignore this revolution only by risking "catastrophic consequences," Western allies are evidently trapped by the inexorable forces of historical "progress" and must suffer all the consequent "contradictions" inherent in their system.[66]

Military Means

America is also said to possess military "levers" that serve the goals of alliance cohesion, dominance, and partnership. As noted earlier, Soviet commentators hold that the military aspect of American alliances is motivated by the same factors that have brought the alliances themselves into existence: the threats of Soviet aggression, the national liberation movement, and the international workers movement. In order to maintain these alliances, the United States is forced constantly to invoke these threats, and to use the military

branches of its alliances to perpetuate these "myths" and the atmosphere of "war psychosis." The result is the active use of military
maneuvers and the joint planning of military strategy.

The Soviets see two primary military levers that are designed to
preserve American dominance over its allies: nuclear guarantees
(the American nuclear "umbrella"), and the U.S. military presence
on allies' territory.[67] As Davydov observes, "Washington has always
considered that the continuation of West European military dependence on the United States—a dependence embodied in NATO
—is a means for insuring permanent U.S. leadership and a guarantee of the unity of the 'Atlantic World.' "[68] Clearly, Soviet analysts
believe that such military patronage is designed to counter the
"imaginary Soviet threat." What may not be immediately clear to
the Western reader, however, is the Soviet argument that these
same military "levers" counter the "national liberation movement"
or the "international workers movement"—a view that is based on
the Soviet reading of American anxieties about the strength of its
commitments. Characterizing these feelings as a "guiding star" for
American policy, Gromyko writes that Americans think that

> any noticeable relaxation of the U.S. military presence in Western
> Europe would have the most "unpleasant consequences" for the
> United States because of the weakening of NATO's 'defense' po-
> tential, since the West European participants could also reduce
> their military contribution in wake of the main partner. All this
> would have a "destabilizing effect" on the situation in Europe.
> There would be a "decline" of confidence' in U.S. commitments.[69]

Gromyko goes on to make clear that, in the Soviet view, the
American fear of a decline in European confidence is nothing more
than a fear of increased "realism" among Europeans, that is,
anxiety about their desire for "collective security" and a consequent shifting of their "political antennae" toward the East.[70] In
short, any decline of European confidence in American commitments
indicates a decline of confidence in capitalist-imperialist interests and
values and an increased willingness to consider the socialist "alternative." Similarly, a reduction of European military preparedness represents the European "desire" for a "relaxation of tension," peaceful
coexistence," "cooperation" with the Soviet Union and socialist
Europe, and therefore, "security" under the benevolent blanket of

socialism. At the same time, "peaceful coexistence," the Soviets' preferred form of struggle against capitalism and democracy, provides the most propitious conditions for the growth of the "international workers movement" in America's developed allies and of the "national liberation movement" in those less-developed allies who "strain" under the "burdens" of American "neocolonialism." Under these "peaceful" and "relaxed" conditions, these "movements" can not only flourish independently but also receive, with increasingly less imperialist interference, the "generous" and "high-minded" "support" of the Soviet Union and the socialist "community" of states.

As discussed in Chapter 3, the Soviets see "partnership," the greater sharing of military responsibilities, as another goal of U.S. alliance policy. They interpret the so-called Vietnamization program of the early 1970s as an example of such partnership which proved to be a "bankrupt" fiasco.[71] The success of partnership is said to depend upon the coincidence of interests between the United States and its allies, but the Soviet analysts do not distinguish a single country in the world whose interests coincide with America's to the requisite degree. In their view it is Israel that comes closest to fulfilling the conditions for such a relationship, and they characterize U.S.-Israeli relations as an example of "partnership in action." As Kremenyuk notes, "The political and ideological prerequisites for converting Israel into a U.S. 'partner' in the Near East, that is, into an instrument of the struggle against progressive transformations in the Arab world, have existed for a long time."[72] He adds that this Israeli "foreign policy line . . . has always coincided in general with the policy goals and methods" of imperialism vis-à-vis the Arabs.[73] Thus it is "no accident" that Israeli "aggression" in 1967 was directed against those Arab states that constituted "the vanguard of the national liberation movement of the Arab peoples," an act that "fully corresponded to U.S. interests."[74] Nevertheless, despite all their shared "interests," Arbatov, writing in 1971, could not accept the idea that Israel was the "ideal model" of a partner for the United States. He pointed out that, to begin with, Israel "can press too strongly upon the American government itself," not only on an international basis, but also from within, "by means of Zionist circles in America."[75] Second, Israel's hawkish line toward the Arab countries puts the United States "into too much conflict with those countries, limiting for the United States the possibilities of intrigues in the Near East." Finally, Arbatov voices his doubts as to whether the United States completely controls Israel in all situations. "One cannot preclude the possibility," he writes, of a situation in which "the tail wags the dog." At the same time, he cautions that "Tel Aviv's 'independence' should by no means be exaggerated." It is noteworthy that Arbatov surrounds the word "independence" with quotation marks, for this is a rare practice in the Soviet press. The explanation, of course, is that in the Soviet lexicon, true independence means independence from the clutches of capitalism and imperialism and a coincidence of interests and ideals with socialism. Since Israel's foreign policy goals, while "imperialist," do not always coincide with those of the United States, Israel's is one of the very rare cases of an "imperialist" policy "independent" of that of the United States. That Israel happens to be by and large a socialist country, yet truly democratic, is not a favorite topic for discussion in the Soviet press.

Since they hold that no country's interests ever coincide completely with those of the United States, Soviet analysts conclude that the whole doctrine of partnership is "contradictory," especially with regard to the American goal of retaining its dominance over its allies by maintaining their military dependence. Davydov has noted, for example, that even while militarily dependent, Western Europe became not only an economic but also a political rival of the United States—especially during the last stages of the Vietnam War and the October War in the Middle East.[76] This increased political "independence" is a "contradiction" that the United States has tried to resolve by proposing a "New Atlantic Charter" that contains two basic principles: (1) that Western Europe "acknowledge the interdependence of the economic, political, and military problems of inter-Atlantic relations, and, as a result, make concessions to the Americans in the projected currency-financial and trade talks between the United States and the EEC"; and (2) that Western Europe "support the U.S. global policy for the 'defense' of the capitalist world in other areas."[77] Davydov argued that these principles amounted simply to the "old U.S. concept of the unity of the 'Atlantic world,' in which, as previously, the United States would have the decisive say"; but the Europeans recognized this proposal as another design to restrain their "development along the path of greater political independence." As a result, Davydov claims that the United States attempted to "blackmail" Western Europe with one of its "levers"—the "threat of the withdrawal of U.S. troops"—in order to bargain for economic concessions.[78] It is interesting to observe that, once again, the Soviets characterize as "blackmail" the threat to withdraw the very forces that are preventing Europe from growing "independent." Evidently the doctor is blackmailing the patient by threatening to cure him.

Despite all the talk about "sharing the burden" in Europe, then, Novosel'tsev notes that no "Europeanization" of the "Vietnamization" kind has taken place.[79] Moreover, "The Nixon Doctrine," with its concept of partnership, "does not answer the question of why the American military presence should be preserved in its entirety in exactly the countries which the authors of the doctrine recognize as 'mature partners.' "[80] This question, of course, is especially apropos given the fact that conditions of "peaceful coexistence" and European "security" obviate the need for any military presence whatsoever! The Soviet conclusion, once again, is that American alliance policy and its military aspect are "profoundly contradictory."[81]

Conclusion

As one can see, there is a remarkable amount of agreement between traditionalist and realist analysts on the subject of U.S. alliance policy, so much so that it is difficult to isolate their differences thematically. Their agreement is a function of the Soviet view that an alliance such as NATO exists, first, to resist the putative Soviet threat and, second, to enable the United States to dominate its allies. The Soviets thus argue that the alliance depends upon a supposed Soviet threat and that, so long as the alliance continues to function, it reflects the influence of those in the American ruling class who still hold such "unrealistic" and reactionary views. On this score the realists have no choice but to conform to the traditionalist view. Similarly, both Soviet schools of thought agree that the alliance serves the U.S. goal of maintaining its dominance over its allies. (The reason, of course, why the realists have no choice but to agree with their traditionalist colleagues is that these views are the product of ideological tenets that are so basic to Soviet politics that there is no room for disagreement.) Since the alliance is designed "to protect reactionary processes which take place within the orbit of Atlanticism," its very existence is further testimony to the influence of "unrealistic" American elements. This view enables the traditionalists to take the lead in explaining the successes of so many of the "levers" by which the American reactionaries cement and dominate their alliances. The realists, again, have no choice but to agree.

On the subject of U.S. alliance policy under conditions of the new correlation of forces, however, the realists have led the discussion, emphasizing the significance of the policy of partnership. Regardless of the extent to which they must argue that the continued existence of the alliance is an unrealistic course, they maintain that the effort to share economic and military burdens is another sign of American weakness. The United States must now seek the cooperation of its allies to do what it could once do by itself and, in the process, new interimperialist contradictions have arisen. To begin with, the goals of dominance and partnership are incompatible and, furthermore, the success of partnership depends upon a coincidence of interests which does not exist. Thus, while the realists must agree with the traditionalists that the continued existence of such an alliance as NATO is a sign of "unrealism," they can point to evidence that suggests that the new correlation of forces has weakened the United States sufficiently to block its prospects for success in exploiting its alliances for imperialist ends.

Chapter 5

U.S. Relations with
the Third World

The Ends of American Policy toward the Third World

According to Soviet analysts, the main goals of U.S. policy in the Third World are to maintain the positions and influence of American monopoly capital and to crush any political threat to these interests. The Soviets argue that in preserving the monopolies' influence, Washington seeks to guarantee its continued access to raw materials, cheap labor, and the other benefits of economic "exploitation," as well as to maintain strategic strongholds for the struggle against socialism and the "national liberation movement." In the past these "imperialist" goals were achieved by the direct methods of colonialism; but now that the "progressive" and "peace-loving" forces have effectively "exposed" such methods, the imperialists have been forced to resort to the "indirect" and "covert" means of "neocolonialism" to accomplish their greedy ends.[1]

The Means of American Policy toward the Third World

Ideological Means

Soviet analysts identify various ideological means by which the United States seeks to create the most propitious conditions for imperialist exploitation and to fragment the "national liberation movement." These means include: the dissemination of anticommunist propaganda (as discussed in Chapter 3), "ideological sabotage" (clearly some sort of perfidious activity that, despite its opprobrious title, Soviet analysts leave undefined), and the exploitation of nationalism.[2] The manipulation of nationalism is the most important of these ideological weapons, and Soviet commentators detect a parallel between its application to Third World countries and its use as a means to split the ranks of the socialist community.

Soviet analysts claim that there are many varieties of nationalism but that each of them presupposes the existence of a class or hierarchical society. The variety that one encounters in countries "fighting for social and national liberation" is said to be unique in the history of nationalism.[3] In these societies nationalist tendencies "are influenced by the degree of class differentiation, the variety of economic forms, the long record of economic and political dependence and concomitant underdevelopment of social-ethnic communities, and the politico-ideological influence of imperialism."[4] Nationalism of this kind is said to affect "reactionary" and moderate members of the national bourgeoisie, the more "radical" and "progressive" members of the revolutionary-democratic trend, as well as tribal leaders and other members of the "local oligarchy," including "feudal lords," "estate owners," and the "bureaucratic apparatus" connected with the "exploiting element."[5] The nationalistic trends themselves may take the form of "religious nationalism," "black or colored racism," or "continental nationalism"—forms and trends that are said to be rooted either in a "resistance to revolutionary change" or in a "resistance to colonialism and neocolonialism."[6] Regardless of its form, however, Third World nationalism is "adroitly exploited by international monopoly and local oligarchy to consolidate their domination and weaken the national liberation movement."[7]

Soviet analysts admit that the "local oligarchy" participates in this exploitation of nationalism, but claim that it assumes a "contradictory" position vis-à-vis the imperialists—taking an "inconsistent attitude . . . toward the national question."[8] The anti-imperialist element of their attitude is said to derive from "the bourgeoisie's reluctance to share profits with foreign imperialism." This "contradiction" in the attitude of those elements that sometimes cooperate with the imperialists leads one Soviet commentator to conclude that "all forms" of nationalism are, in effect, "a social protest against colonialist oppression."[9] The key distinction in the Soviet analysis of nationalism, then, is that between the nationalism of "oppressor nations" and the nationalism of "oppressed nations."[10]

Soviet commentators argue that the American strategy of "reliance on nationalism" depends primarily on the sensitivity of "national feelings" and the consequent ease with which they can be manipulated. As one analyst observes, by "exploiting 'dangers' to national values and unfolding subversive campaigns on the plane of 'national interests,' imperialism can expect a massive and receptive audience and, consequently, an opportunity to misguide the public by substituting nationalist for national interests." This statement depends upon the Soviet distinction between "national" and "nationalist," the former being a "natural, social phenomenon" and the latter being more "reactionary."[11] With this distinction, which is made with elaborate theoretical contortions, the Soviets seek to enlist "national" spirit in the service of the world's "progressive" movements in order to counter the "imperialist" effort to enlist "nationalism." This is the distinction that the Soviets underline by contrasting the term "*national* liberation movement" with the "*nationalist*" forces that are exploited to serve imperialist purposes. The distinction, however, is noticeably obscure, a problem that even Soviet analysts sometimes seem to admit, as in the previously cited statement that "nationalism represents a special danger for the process of the revolutionary transformation of the world."[12]

Soviet writings on nationalism stress that the imperialists perceive the Third World as an ideological battleground in the struggle between the two social systems. The strategy of relying on nationalism is thus said to have a theoretical basis in "bourgeois ideas about the character of social development."[13] Applied to the Third World these ideas, of course, envision conditions advantageous to the flourishing of "exploiter relations." The use of nationalism, then, is seen to be a means of maintaining these conditions in the traditional imperialist manner of "divide and rule."[14]

Economic Means

In the Soviet view, "neocolonialism" is primarily an economic policy whose methods are designed to keep the Third World on the "capitalist road of development" and to maintain the "unequal relations" that are the basis of successful "exploitation."[15] Primary among the means of American Third World policy, according to the Soviets, is foreign aid. A form of capital export (implemented by the state rather than by the monopolies), American aid is said to be a kind of "political and economic bribery" through which

American imperialism tries to "secure for itself military-strategic positions" in those countries to which the aid is assigned.[16] All American aid thus has "a political lining," that is, it is determined by the priorities of imperialist foreign policy and not by the economic needs of the recipient countries.[17] Aid that appears to be targeted for the genuine economic development of these countries is susceptible to the same Soviet accusation—it is allegedly motivated by "Washington's fear of losing prestige among some of the developing countries, a prestige that has already declined as a result of the fact that the United States frequently has used its 'aid' for purposes that have no relation to economic development."[18] The Soviets naturally regard this "decline in prestige" as the concomitant of the Third World's increasing shift toward an "independent course of development." It is alleged that this shift has led the entrepreneurs of the U.S. monopolies to curtail the expansion of their activities in these countries and, as a result, U.S. government aid has become "the forced substitution for private capital."[19] American aid is thus designed to prevent further Third World shifts toward "independence"; in other words, to "neutralize the national liberation movement."[20]

Primary among the political, military, and economic strings that are always attached to American foreign aid is the insistence that the governments that receive this aid protect and foster a beneficent climate for investment and capitalism in general.[21] The Soviets maintain that this requirement limits the countries that can receive this aid to those that the United States deems "stable," that is, to those that are "acceptable to the neocolonialists."[22] Soviet analysts claim that American aid is also dependent upon the requirement that it be used to buy American goods. When the aid takes the form of loans, this requirement is said to "lead to a situation where American credits become increasingly burdensome to the parties receiving the loan, depriving them of the opportunity to use the international division of labor and purchase the goods in countries which have lower production costs."[23] Other "strings" include the demand that the recipient supply manpower to be used as "cannon fodder" in American foreign military "adventures" and the insistence that it accommodate American desires to maintain military bases on its soil.[24]

Soviet realists argue, however, that the new correlation of forces and the "crisis of capitalism," have forced the United States to adopt certain changes in its foreign aid policy. As a result of these changes, the United States has invoked the concept of "partnership" to require that Third World countries rely more upon themselves. The change in payment for agricultural products is cited as an example of this development. Soviet analysts maintain that whereas most of these products supplied to Third World countries under the auspices of aid programs were once paid for in local, unconvertible currencies, the United States has recently been demanding that "payment for these deliveries be made in hard currency."[25] Another example of this kind of partnership is U.S. pressure on Third World countries to "make greater sacrifices" to strengthen the capitalist system—sacrifices handily imposed by the United States as it shifts aid from subsidies to loans and introduces less favorable conditions for obtaining these loans. Soviet analysts cite copious examples of the ever higher interest rates charged by American lending institutions.[26] They argue that the resulting burden has created a situation in which "more than half of the new loans obtained from the USA are used by these states to pay off their basic debt and interest charges, thus increasing their direct material dependence on the USA."[27] Moreover, it is said that the good graces of the USSR provide the only hope of respite for these beleaguered countries. As Zakhmatov explains, "Under the influence of the practice of the Soviet union, which gives 'Third World' countries inexpensive long-term loans, U.S. officials have often announced their intention to reduce the interest rate charged on loans."[28] Despite these declared intentions, interest rates, as well as the proportion of loans to subsidies, are seen as having increased—thus leading to the "even greater enslavement" of these states, a situation that "increasingly deprives them of economic independence."[29] Finally, the new American recognition that the Third World should rely less on American development strategies and more on its own conceptions of what would be successful for development is cited as another example of the partnership approach to U.S. aid policy. This policy is described as an admission of Washington's "failure" to "dictate its will" to the Third World. As Zakhmatov notes, however, this change does not mean that U.S. ruling circles have abdicated their efforts to influence the course of Third World development, but only that they are assigning private capital a greater

216

responsibility in these matters: "By involving the resources of private American capital, stimulating the initiative of the private enterprise of the developing countries, and organizing cooperation between them, the U.S. government figures to influence the Third World countries and force them to choose a capitalist path of development."[30]

In short, the realists argue that as the crisis of capitalism deepens, as the "realistic U.S. circles increasingly admit the failure of the American path of development, and as the developing countries become increasingly "independent," American policy becomes increasingly unsure of itself—inconsistent and haphazard. The United States first tries to export state capital to those areas that private capital considers too risky, but when state action fails, the government again resorts to private efforts. According to Soviet thinking, both methods are bound for failure because the changing correlation of forces is creating a "no exit" situation for American capitalism.

Soviet analysts claim that another change in U.S. foreign aid policy is the increased use of international and regional organizations over which the United States "keeps a dominating position."[31] They argue that this attempt to "camouflage" U.S. policy is a response to the "exposure before the entire world of the neocolonialist, mercenary nature of American aid." By using such organizations, the Americans allegedly hope that the developing states will adopt a more neutral attitude toward U.S. aid.[32]

The main international organizations used by the United States for such "mercenary" purposes are the World Bank and its affiliates, the regional development banks, and the International Monetary Fund (IMF). In his major study on "neocolonialism," V. Vakhrushev has summarized the traditionalist view of the various activities of these international organizations in a complete and coherent fashion. The following analysis of Soviet views of the development banks and the IMF draws heavily on his study.

Vakhrushev describes the World Bank as "a large and flourishing capitalist enterprise" that operates under the "domination" of the United States and seeks the "financial fettering of the countries which turn to it for loans"—a "fettering" that binds these countries to the capitalist system and leaves them prey to the plunderings of the monopolies.[33] The key feature of the bank's policy is the "onerous conditions" of both a political and economic nature which it attaches to its loans—conditions that become the very "fetters" of its debtors' "enslavement." While the economic conditions primarily take the form of high interest rates, the political conditions are somewhat more varied. The bank's charter, the "Articles of Agreement," stipulates that "political activity" on the part of the bank is "prohibited," but Vakhrushev claims that "this principle is . . . not observed." Instead, the "monopolies" allegedly go out of their way to use the bank to: "facilitate the expansion of private monopoly capital in all continents; to install capitalist systems in the developing countries and consolidate the strongholds of imperialism there."[34] The political conditions imposed on developing countries, then, are said to involve different kinds of "intervention into the internal affairs" of these countries.[35] One form of this intervention is the investigation of a given country's economic and political situation to determine whether it qualifies for a loan. Vakhrushev characterizes such an investigation as a "humiliating procedure." The bank's requirement that a potential borrower restore stability to its economy and exhibit evidence that it is taking appropriate steps for such stabilization is another form of such interference— one that the Soviets term a "crude pressure."[36]

The bank's intervention into others' internal affairs also takes a more "subtle" form. Whereas the bank is portrayed as officially supporting the industrialization of the developing countries, Vakhrushev argues that, in fact, it only allows them to achieve a scale of development which "does not represent any threat to the position of monopoly capital in the country concerned."[37] This bank's policy amounts to an effort "to impede the consolidation of the state sector in the economy of those countries which is less vulnerable to pressure on the part of foreign private capital." Furthermore, this policy of purposeful "restraint" of Third World economic development is said to fulfill one of the primary purposes of "neo-colonialism"—"the retention of the developing countries for as long as possible as sources of raw materials for the imperialist powers."

Vakhrushev contends that the World Bank performs a number of different functions in its capacity as a "tool of neocolonialism," the most important being the granting of loans that have "strings attached." He alleges that these "strings" invariably require that the recipient country do business with the Western monopolies that supply it with goods and services. At times the bank assumes the role of "mediator" in international financial disputes, the usual result being an agreement according to which a Third World country must compensate foreign monopolies whose operations it has nationalized. Once again, Vakhrushev argues, the bank is "serving the monopolies' interests." Noting that the bank frequently dispatches "missions" to work on projects of "technical aid" and "economic planning" in developing countries, Vakhrushev observes that these missions often have "imposed their 'advice' on these countries."[38] Such missions are thus another of the methods by which the bank functions as a tool of neocolonialism.

Allegedly in response to the "onerous" terms of World Bank loans, which supposedly prevented many developing countries from participating in the bank's business, the United States is said to have initiated the establishment of two affiliates of the bank: The International Finance Corporation (IFC) and the International Development Association (IDA). Officially, these organizations are designed to grant loans with "far less onerous terms" than those of the World Bank. In fact, however, despite their beneficent appearance, these organizations attempt to lure developing countries into joining the bank and thus becoming "shackled" to its operations.[39] There is an IDA ruling that its credits should have "no strings attached," but Vakhrushev observes that "this is seldom observed, as stands out particularly clearly in the case of the United States, which uses IDA to secure markets for its commodities."[40] Furthermore, Vakhrushev notes that "when granting credits, IDA demands that the borrower spend them only on projects agreed on in advance, in other words the borrower country is not free to use the money received in the form of IDA credits as it thinks fit."[41] To disguise its activities further, the World Bank allegedly uses other international organizations as a cover, "attempting to dissolve" its activities in the programs of these more "popular" agencies. For example, it is said to "use the image and authority of UNESCO" and other U.N. bodies "in order to consolidate its influence in the developing countries."[42]

Vakhrushev's analysis of this subject stresses that "political considerations" determine the World Bank's attitudes toward developing countries.[43] As a result, the bank's preferred choices for receiving credit are those countries that are most "congenial" to capitalism. As Vakhrushev describes it, however, such "preferential" treatment amounts to "discrimination" against other, more "independent" countries and is therefore to be condemned. He speaks, for example, of how the "utterly unacceptable terms attached to these loans, including political terms, have made them inaccessible for a number of developing countries," as though "accessibility" to loans from such an exploitative capitalist enterprise were somehow desirable.[44] The upshot of Vakhrushev's argument is that the World Bank is damned because it gives out loans and damned again because it does not give out loans. One would think, under the circumstances, that the poor "independent" countries that suffer from such odious discriminations would seek shelter under the Soviet wing, which boasts such advantages as "peace," "security," "generous financing" (with such solid currencies as the ruble), and the "high quality" products of the "vibrant" Soviet industrial complex.

Vakhrushev maintains that the United States also attempts to dominate and exploit the Third World by seizing commanding positions in regional development banks. Though most of these banks are said to have been established by developing countries in order to "limit their dependence on the World Bank," "U.S. financial circles went out of their way to seize a dominating position" in most of these banks.[45] In the case of the Inter-American Development Bank (IDB), Vakhrushev contends that the United States put up the lion's share of the financing, and as a result, "the Latin American countries have not achieved those goals which they set themselves when establishing the IDB: its creation has not diminished their dependence on the World Bank, the IMF, or the U.S. monopolies."[46] Instead, the IDB is seen as providing the United States with yet "another lever for intensifying its financial fettering and exploitation of Latin America." The case of the African Development Bank (AFDB), however, provoked a different situation. Its thirty-plus members are said to have founded the organization as a "protest against the domination of the World Bank by the leading capitalist countries," a move that is characterized as a "forceful demonstration of African solidarity, an attempt to stand up to neocolonialism." Although the U.S. monopolies did not seek to gain domination over this organization, the World Bank "started stepping up its activities" in Africa, leading Vakhrushev to suspect that "one of the reasons for the World Bank's intensification of its activity in Africa is to create more difficulties for AFDB which naturally is in no position to compete with the World Bank and is compelled to engage in cooperation with the latter."[47] Thus, no matter what the contingency, the U.S. neocolonialists "are taking all possible steps to turn regional development banks into instruments of their own policy."[48]

Vakhrushev views the International Monetary Fund as yet another tool of American neocolonialism. He stresses the IMF requirement that each member country agree to set the par value of its currency in terms of gold and American dollars and argues that the article in the Fund Agreement which makes this requirement is "the pivot for all U.S. ruling circles' plans of consolidating forever the domination of the dollar and making all other currencies dependent on it.[49] Working from this foundation, the IMF is said to pursue several tasks, the most important being "to 'save' capitalism, implant and consolidate private enterprise, and bolster the financial domination of monopoly capital in currency and foreign trade dealings."[50] This aim is pursued primarily through IMF support of the monetary and financial system of "international imperialism," support that ensures the "stability" of the currencies of the United States and its partners in imperialism. Vakhrushev points out that if the currency of a major imperialist country is suffering a crisis, the IMF steps in to "rescue" the currency and therefore the health of the capitalist structure of its parent country. This practice makes the IMF particularly odious to Communists, because it helps to counter the very circumstance that, according to Lenin's famous maxim, erodes the foundations of capitalist order. In Vakhrushev's view, the IMF also seeks to eliminate foreign exchange restrictions that hamper the growth of world trade. Once again, however, the IMF's concern is "first and foremost the interest of the leading imperialist powers." Allegedly, the IMF tries to "facilitate their seizure of markets and secure the lowest possible prices for raw materials from other countries and high monopoly prices on the commodities sold by themselves."[51] This goal is pursued in part by creating a "favorable 'preinvestment' climate for the monopolies and banks" in the developing countries.[52]

The IMF allegedly uses a number of methods to create auspicious conditions for imperialist exploitation. One such method is its demand that a country devalue its currency in relation to the dollar.[53] Again, Vakhrushev alleges that such demands benefit the "monopolies," for devaluation raises the cost of living through inflation and lower real wages and living standards, thereby creating conditions whereby the monopolies can "make the most of the situation." The monopolies pay the devaluing country's workers lower wages (as expressed in dollars) and export their own commodities to that country at higher prices. At the same time, the devaluing country becomes "more dependent on the dollar," "more dependent on foreign aid," and thus more susceptible to the "exploitative" techniques of the international lending institutions.[54]

Another method by which the IMF creates conditions that favor imperialist exploitation is by demanding the "introduction of wage freezes."[55] This demand is said to be directed "first and foremost towards securing maximum possible profits through the exploitation of the working people and advantages from inflation for the foreign monopolies."[56] As Vakhrushev observes, the IMF missions "usually disguise this demand with references to one of the 'theories' of bourgeois political economy to the effect that high prices are meant to be the result of increased wages. The untenability of this 'theory' has long since been demonstrated." Vakhrushev argues that, in fact, "it is precisely devaluation, for which the IMF keeps pressing, that constitutes one of the main causes of rising prices, particularly in those countries whose economies are extremely dependent on imports."

This argument is a notable illustration of the typical Soviet technique of twisting economic theories to suit communist purposes, making the "imperialists" look bad in the process. In this case, Vakhrushev declares that devaluation, not wage hikes, is the "cause" of inflation. While he is correct about wage hikes, the author is wrong about the relationship between devaluation and inflation, for, like wage hikes, devaluation is a by-product of inflation—more specifically of the differing rates of inflation between two currencies. In fact, however, Vakhrushev himself provides evidence that his "error" may well be deliberate. In another context he correctly observes that it is illusory to use devaluation to increase exports and foreign currency proceeds (and by implication, to decrease imports) for the ultimate purpose of remedying a balance of payments deficit: "Experience was to show on this occasion as be-

222

fore that this measure provides no reliable solution for a balance of payments crisis."[57] In the light of this statement, it would appear that Vakhrushev's argument that the imperialists are benefiting from Third World currency devaluations is disingenuous. This possibility should not surprise us, since such Soviet "scholarship" must fulfill the imperatives of Soviet propaganda, creating a mix of truth and lies which allows the reader to conclude: "This can't be all wrong."

Vakhrushev points out several other methods by which the IMF facilitates imperialist exploitation. Among these are its demands that developing countries eliminate "artificial industry," that is, industries, usually run by a country's government, which are overly dependent on imported raw materials and thus unprofitable. With these "demands" the IMF allegedly seeks to "implant and consolidate capitalism and private enterprise" in these countries. Vakhrushev characterizes these calls for the closing of unprofitable Third World industries as an "attempt to hold back the advance of their own [the Third World's] young industries."[58] It is significant that Vakhrushev's detailed study provides no example of a single instance in which the IMF recommended that the development of a truly "infant industry" be stunted. In the absence of any such example, it is interesting to note here that unprofitability is apparently an index of historical "advancement." Such reasoning, although rarely expressed so frankly, is a natural corollary of the Soviet view that historical "progress" flourishes during the "crisis of capitalism," one of the main features of which is the increasing unprofitability of business enterprise.

Related to its calls for the elimination of artificial industry is the IMF "slogan" demanding that developing countries " 'free their economy from government control.' "[59] Vakhrushev sees such demands as an example of "crude interference in the internal affairs of the developing countries," and claims that they amount to a "call for elimination of the state sector so as to facilitate expansion of the foreign private capital in these countries." Similar IMF "demands," said to be more "subtle" and "attractive at first glance," include "the stipulation that the state budget be 'adjusted' and 'bureaucracy eradicated.' " The "insidious" quality of these demands is their requirement that the state budget be "adjusted" through "excessive currency emission" and the "eradication of the bureaucracy." The latter is to be achieved by "mass dismissals of blue- and white-collar workers from state-owned enterprises," a process that results in "mass unemployment." That the Soviets should be concerned about "excessive currency emissions" in light of the high premium they place on inflation as a "revolutionary" vehicle is revolutionary indeed.

Finally, Vakhrushev alleges that the IMF asks all Third World countries to "restrict social legislation"—legislation that the IMF sees as a luxury that these countries cannot afford. He argues that such restriction means "cuts in state allocations to education, health services and social maintenance, etc., or in other words, a violation of the working people's basic rights in the interests of foreign and local private capital."[60]

In addition to foreign aid and the use of international organizations, Soviet analysts list several other economic methods by which the United States advances its neocolonialist policy toward the Third World. Since the opportunities to use the old, direct methods of colonial imperialism are "progressively declining," the United States is forced to utilize "more flexible and masked forms" of neocolonialist "expansion," whereby it is willing to "compromise and make concessions, and actively seek agreement with national capital."[61] Such "flexibility" includes, for one, the shifting of attitudes toward the state sector of Third World countries which, although formerly shunned by the imperialists, is now seen as a potential "catalyst" that can "speed the growth of private-capitalist relations."[62] Another "flexible" method is the formation of partnerships with local industrialists through the creation of joint stock companies, various forms of technical cooperation, and the selling of shares to smaller local enterpreneurs. Using these methods, the U.S. monopolies allegedly "subordinate large volumes of national capital to their influence, strengthen their position in the developing countries' economies, and establish covert control over [them]."[63]

The new methods of neocolonialist penetration include various other forms of capital export, among which is the creation of international private funds, consortiums, and corporations "designed to secure favorable 'pre-investment' conditions for the monopolies" in the Third World states. These funds and consortiums are used for the dispersal of small loans and the export of portfolio capital.[64] The granting of loans and credits, as mentioned earlier, is seen as another of neocolonialism's methods. Increasingly, however, Soviet analysts argue that these loans are manipulated so as to shift the risks onto either the U.S. government or, more often, the government of the recipient country.[65] They allege that similar tactics are also used to shift the risk of direct investments.[66] Yet another method of capitalist "penetration" is the "approximation of financial bodies to the objects of oppression and exploitation,"[67] a procedure by which the monopolies and banks continually establish branches and departments in the developing countries, thus enmeshing themselves even further in their economic life. The imperialists are also accused of engaging in the "export of know-how," which L. Klochkovsky calls "a deadly weapon in the battle to strengthen the foreign investors' influence in the developing countries' economies."[68] This "know-how trade" involves the export of scientific and technical information, patents, licenses, and trademarks. These licenses and patents are often said to be subject to agreement among the imperialist powers—agreements that Soviet analysts describe as "a new form of private international cartels." These agreements thus become a new weapon with which the imperialist powers can divide Third World markets among themselves.[69]

Soviet analysts argue that, once they have penetrated Third World economies, the imperialists have numerous methods of exploitation at their disposal. Writing in 1973, Anatoly Gromyko argued that this exploitation had reached such proportions that for every spoonful of capital injected into the Third World by the imperialists, seven spoonfuls are extracted.[70] Evidently, one should expect an analogous imbalance in the balances of payments between these countries and the imperialists! One of these methods of exploitation, the manipulation of foreign exchange and finance, has already been outlined insofar as it is used by the World Bank and the IMF. Soviet analysts argue that similar practices are characteristic of the exploitative techniques of private American banks and financial institutions. Like the international financial organizations, they allegedly seek to increase the indebtedness of developing nations and thereby secure their subordination.[71] Yet another of neocolonialism's methods is to regulate which industries and industrial skills develop in Third World countries.[72] The imperialists can transfer various labor-intensive and "dirty" industries to the Third World so that others can do their "dirty work."[73] Furthermore, they can exploit the workers in these industries by paying them low wages.

Trade, according to the Soviets, is another instrument of neocolonialist exploitation. Thus, the imperialists are said to utilize nonequivalent exchange," "artificially imposing the lowest possible prices on the produce and raw materials of the developing countries, while charging the highest possible prices for the industrial products that they sell to these countries.[74] A related tactic is the use of the so-called price spread, according to which the terms of trade gradually worsen for the developing countries in favor of the monopolies.[75] The imperialists are also accused of exploiting freightage, taking advantage of the fact that few developing countries have their own merchant fleets, and charging extortionary fees for the transportation of their imports and exports.[76] Yet another means of exploitation through trade is the practice of dumping and "disguised dumping."[77] Perpetrated mainly with agricultural products—the mass sale of surpluses under the pretext of aid—American dumping is said to: disorganize the internal markets of the developing states; lead to "sharp fluctuations in agricultural production causing the ruin of millions of peasant holdings"; cause "stagnation in local agricultural production"; and cause losses in these states' budgets and intensified inflation.[78] Having accomplished these sundry dislocations, the monopolies (which have been aided by the U.S. government) can "gain a firm foothold" in the private sector of Third World economies.

While making the developing countries dependent on American trade and financing in these different ways, the United States is said to practice protectionism to make itself less dependent on imports from these same countries.[79] Vakhrushev argues that such barriers are a serious obstacle to the development of Third World economies.[80] The alleged U.S. purpose, of course, is to maintain the continuing pattern of "unequal relations" between "oppressors" and "oppressed." Soviet analysts note, however, that the "honest policies of the USSR" and the example that they set, as well as the pressure from such internationl organizations as UNCTAD, have "compelled" the United States to make certain trade concessions to the developing countries.[81] Having said this, however, Soviet commentators go on to claim that even these concessions, which include preferential tariffs, reflect nefarious U.S. motives. As one commentator says, in granting such preferential tariffs the imperialists "seek to gain political prestige and pose as champions of economic progress of the developing countries." Furthermore, they hope to gain even greater economic advantages at Third World expense by stimulating these countries' exports so that they may "clear their huge debts to the imperialist creditors," and by revitalizing the local branches of the monopolies in order to take advantage of the improved business climate.[82] Thus, no matter what the imperialists do—whether they stimulate or stifle Third World industry— they are "exploiting" these countries.

Soviet analysts also argue that economic methods play a significant role in the neocolonialist struggle to suppress the "national liberation movement," and that they may take the form of either prophylactic or combative action. The preventive methods at neocolonialism's disposal generally consist of measures to create a climate hostile to the spread of the national liberation movement. The imperialists allegedly think that an increase in the monopolies' activities in the Third World constitutes just such a measure. In the words of one Soviet commentator, "The ruling bourgeois circles believe that every private monopoly enterprise there promotes a number of associated small local capitalist enterprises, and that this helps consolidate the internal reactionary forces," which thus become the neocolonialists' vanguard against the "progressive forces."[83] Another preventive method is for the imperialists to draw the developing countries into economic blocs and common markets. In this way, not only do they increase these countries' dependence on the world capitalist economy, but they create new institutional bulwarks against revolutionary changes.[84] Finally, as we noted earlier, Soviet analysts interpret U.S. foreign aid to the Third World as another attempt to "neutralize" the national liberation movement.[85]

The Soviets identify only one important economic weapon for combative action against national liberation movements—a weapon that they characterized in 1975 as "new." Before the change in the correlation of forces, the imperialists were free to exercise their will over developing countries through the direct and "crude" methods of "force," but the new conditions have "forced" them to adopt more "covert" and "subtle" means, such as those in the economic sphere. Their "new" method is the "illegal import of foreign currency" into a country where the "movement" is effecting "social changes." Soviet analysts claim that this method was used by the U.S. imperialists against Chile when it was undergoing such "progressive" changes. Dollars are said to have been sold on the black market by CIA agents at a speculative exchange rate 800 percent higher than the official rate.[86] Evidently the imperialists have finally learned one of the oldest tricks in the communist book for the successful disruption of a society.

Scientific and Technical Means

The United States, as the Soviets see it, has a number of scientific and technical means by which it can make developing countries dependent on the United States and capitalism. As was noted earlier, the "New Technological Policy" of the United States was designed, according to the Soviets, to use America's position of scientific and technical superiority to "tie" other countries to its development in this sphere, thus establishing a new form of domination-subordination relations.[87] Arbatov argues that when this policy is applied to the Third World—countries that cannot create a sufficiently powerful scientific and technical potential of their own—these countries confront a choice: either to fall seriously behind in this field and face the undermining of their competitive positions and "economic enslavement to a more developed country"; or to tie themselves to a country that possesses a much more powerful scientific and technical sector.[88] If a country chooses the latter path, Arbatov claims that it does so "at the cost of forfeiting a part of [its] economic and political independence." In the Soviet view, such dependence is the precise aim of the U.S. imperialists.

One of the chief means for implementing this policy is the "deliberate policy" of restraining the scientific and technical development of Third World states.[89] Among the ways in which this policy is carried out are: "barring or limiting the use of progressive technology," "exporting obsolete and worn-out equipment," "selling ... production secrets which have lost their value in the West," "restricting the export of licenses," and "discriminating against local personnel."[90] All these methods, of course, are perpetrated by the worldwide network of American businesses which "can largely determine the rate of scientific and technological progress in the rest of the capitalist world."[91] The Soviets also argue that the United

States manipulates the "green revolution"—the development of new high-yield crops and other projects to find new sources of protein—in order to increase Third World dependency. Since such agricultural and nutritional commodities are in short supply in the Third World, the United States lures these countries into "cooperation" in these projects, thus making them "dependent."[92] The development in Third World countries of agricultural-industrial complexes operating on nuclear power is a similar method cited by the Soviets.[93] Arbatov argues that the characteristic feature of most projects of this kind is the creation of "major technical systems and complexes whose normal functioning would depend for many years on the corresponding countries' cooperation with the United States."[94] Arbatov concludes, therefore, that the United States uses science and technology both "as a cheaper and more effective way of establishing these countries' dependence" and as an effective means in the "struggle for influence in the Third World."[95] He adds, however, that with the change in the world correlation of forces and the "upsurge of the national liberation movements" the opportunities for the expansion of U.S. scientific and technical means have been "considerably reduced"; the United States has "lost its monopoly" in this field because of the rise in the influence of the socialist "community."

Finally, American scientific and technical policy seeks to counter the "national liberation movements" through "technological blackmail," a tactic analagous to "economic blackmail," with which U.S. monopolies stop the export of new machinery to a country undergoing "progressive" social changes so as to disrupt its society and halt its progress. Soviet analysts maintain that this tactic is effective only when the recipient country is already dependent on the scientific and technical superiority of the United States. The most frequently cited example is the situation in Allende's Chile where, according to the Soviets, the U.S. monopolies tried to "blackmail" and confound the "progressive" regime.[96]

Military Means

Since American military means have been thoroughly discussed in a previous chapter, we need only to review a few basic points as they apply to the Third World. Soviet analysts have argued that the United States employs military means in the Third World in order to: maintain dominant politico-military positions over those countries, suppress the "national liberation movement," support puppet and other "antipopular" regimes, and secure bases for use in the struggle against the Soviet Union and the socialist community of states. They maintain that this policy of force was once used liberally and without obstacle, but that the change in the "correlation of forces" has forced major changes in the U.S. approach. Thus, Soviet realists point out that, with the rise in Soviet power and the victory of the "national liberation" struggle in Vietnam, the United States has had to resort to a policy of "partnership" with those Third World regimes still inclined to cooperate with it. According to this policy, the Third World country must supply the "cannon fodder" for any American military "adventure" in its region and utilize increased military assistance from the United States to take up a greater share of the burden of its own defense. Finally, Soviet realists argue that the shift in the worldwide correlation has forced Washington to alter its strategy of base-building in the Third World. In the words of one such analyst, the increase in Third World hostility to America's "policy of force" makes it "increasingly difficult for the United States, for perfectly understandable reasons, to maintain large contingents of its troops on the territory of other countries."[97] As a result, the United States must rely on naval bases and operations that are less conspicuous. Thus, according to the realist analysis, the changed correlation of forces has considerably diminished the opportunities for the successful use of the U.S. policy of force in the Third World.

Diplomatic Means

In addition to those diplomatic means already discussed, the United States is said to employ various forms of "interventionism" in the Third World. Interventionism is defined as the "interference in the internal affairs" of other nations for the purpose of supporting "reactionary" and "antipopular" regimes, safeguarding imperialist positions, and suppressing any "progressive" movements. The various forms of intervention include: "political blackmail," "espionage," "bribery," "deceit," the installation of puppets, the supervision of "staged elections" and the introduction of such apparently innocent institutions as research centers for the purpose of intelligence gathering.[98] In sum, interventionism is called a "policy of infamy and failures."

Conclusion

Once again, the composite Soviet picture of U.S. policy toward the Third World reveals a familiar pattern. Both traditionalist and realist analysts agree that U.S. policies reflect the basically imperialist nature of the American polity. Traditionalists such as Vakhrushev present the standard litany of the different methods by which this imperialism is carried out, and imply that since the policy is unchanged in its essentials, the United States remains a dangerous force against peace, progress, and the independence of peoples. Realists such as Zakhmatov accept this standard interpretation but they emphasize the new correlation of forces and argue that it has imposed changes on U.S. policy. Just as the policy of force had to give way to the policies of status quo, realism, and partnership, so the "direct" methods of colonialism had to yield to the more subtle, covert, and "indirect" methods of neocolonialism. The realists argue that the United States had once boldly imposed its messianic schemes for Third World development, but, after the growing "realistic" faction of the American ruling class recognized the failure of these schemes, American economic development policy became increasingly confused and desultory. Although the realists pointedly refrain from praising any of these more subtle, covert, and often directionless methods of neocolonialism, they nonetheless interpret them as a sign of American adaptation—an adaptation that could have been necessitated only by the new correlation of forces in the world.

Chapter 6

U.S. Relations with the Socialist Countries: Some Remaining Issues

As we have seen earlier, Soviet analysts maintain that in its policy toward socialist countries the United States seeks primarily to preserve capitalism's worldwide positions and to expand them wherever possible. Any such expansion, however, encroaches on the positions of socialism and the "fraternal" "progressive" movements, producing the conflict that is the basis of the struggle between the two social systems. Before the change in the correlation of forces, there was, in the Soviet view, a general consensus among American ruling circles that these "unrealistic" policies best served the interests of their class, and they pursued them with brash abandon. As the shift in the correlation of forces occurred, however, some members of U.S. ruling circles recognized the "unrealistic" nature of American imperialism and, with this development, the former imperialist consensus broke down.

At the same time, the imperialists found that it was increasingly necessary to cooperate with the socialist countries under conditions that Soviet analysts characterize with the terms "relaxation of tension" and "peaceful coexistence." These analysts argue that, since there is "no alternative to peaceful coexistence," the imperialists have no choice but to pursue a policy of "cooperation." In the Soviet view, the options suggested by the "opponents of detente," including no "cooperation" with the socialist bloc, no trade, no "sharing" of scientific information, and even the prosecution of cold war and ideological struggle, have all been rendered more "unrealistic" than ever by the changed circumstances. The Soviet insistence that there is "no alternative" to cooperation suggests that there is an increased likelihood of an outbreak of nuclear war and that, as a result, these "hardline" alternatives involve much greater risk than was once the case. Their argument clearly implies that the socialist countries will no longer tolerate such "nonpeaceful" ways of conducting international relations as the "contradiction" between capitalism and socialism. The vast increase in Soviet military means has allegedly "forced" relations between the two systems to adapt to the norms of "peaceful coexistence," and the Soviet position implies that similar military means may be required to "force" the acceptance of a new set of "peaceful" conditions should the "unrealistic" opponents of detente become predominant again. In short, the Soviet argument holds that since communism is destined to triumph by the law-abiding processes of history, it might as well do so "peacefully," and the imperialists should simply reconcile themselves to being "realistic."

According to the realist view, then, the new correlation of forces has made "cooperation" between the two systems an "objective reality." In 1973 G. Arbatov observed that "the expansion of international cooperation in economics, science, and technology ultimately is a task dictated by the objective needs of social production in all countries, regardless of the social system to which they belong. . . . No power can afford to ignore this today—and that includes the United States."[1] The United States is said to have an "objective interest" in such cooperation because it "is finding it increasingly difficult, because of the present cost, scale, and comprehensiveness of scientific and technical work, to perform research along the entire front of the advance of science and technology without cooperating with other countries."[2] Moreover, failure to "cooperate" with Moscow may well cause the United States to lose the scientific and technical struggle to the Soviet Union, which is busy "cooperating" with every country that is willing to live under the benevolent blankets of "fraternal socialist relations," "collective security," and "peaceful coexistence." As we have seen, however, what constitutes an "objective reality" for the Soviet realists is something that, not just coincidentally, corresponds to the imperatives of their perceived foreign policy interests. Soviet realists want this kind of "cooperation" very much. They want trade, scientific and technical exchanges, and all the products of American industry and agriculture which the socialist "community" of states is incapable of producing. As Alexander Solzhenitsyn has pointed out, the Soviets love it when an

American trade mission of manufacturers of the latest criminal surveillance technology comes to Moscow to display its wares.[3] Nothing could better serve the KGB's pastime of finding more "ideological degenerates" to throw into the "psychiatric" "clinics" for lobotomies or into the Gulag Archipelago. When the actions of an American company coincide with Soviet interests, it is no longer labeled with such pejorative terms as "monopoly" or "imperialist." Thus Occidental Petroleum, whose boss Armand Hammer is a longtime proponent of trade with the Communists, is called a "firm."[4] And Control Data Corporation, which was trying to sell the Soviets the "Cyber 76" computer (which is used extensively by the U.S. Defense Department) until President Carter blocked the sale, is called a "problem-solving organization"![5]*

At this point, however, Soviet thinking reveals a potential contradiction. If "force" is indeed the hallmark of all capitalist relations, and if the characteristic feature of American economic, scientific, and technical policies is the intent to create new "domination-subordination relations" (thus making other countries "dependent" on capitalism), then there is reason to assume that these same considerations determine the U.S. approach to East-West trade. In short, the Soviets' own reasoning suggests that the United States "exploits" the Soviet Union whenever the two engage in trade.

In fact, this matter has provoked a major debate between traditionalist and realist groups—a debate that, as we shall see in Chapter 7, reveals the complexity of the political forces in the Soviet Union. This debate involves another element essential to the measurement of the correlation of forces—one that is beyond the scope of this study —namely, the Soviets' assessment of their country's comparative strength, especially in terms of its economic and scientific-technical potential. If the Soviet Union can pursue autarky successfully, then perhaps there is no compelling need to seek international trade and scientific-technical cooperation. Contrarily, inability to attain self-sufficiency might necessitate trade and cooperation with the capitalist powers, but these contacts could involve unacceptable risks that, for the sake of national security, are best avoided.

The traditionalists express precisely such reservations, citing, first of all, the ideological dangers of East-West contacts. As shown in

---

*Control Data eventually succeeded in making the sale in 1979.

Chapter 3, Soviet traditionalists focus a great deal of attention on bourgeois attempts to "build bridges" and to engage in "peaceful penetration" in order to disseminate subversive ideas. The traditionalists argue that such initiatives are invariably accompanied by calls for the "free flow of ideas and information" and other efforts to "interfere in the internal affairs of the USSR." Wary of the dangers of excessive East-West contacts, an editorialist in *Kommunist* declared that "every Communist and every Soviet patriot realizes that it is his duty to struggle decisively against alien views."[6]

Other traditionalist commentators have expressed fears that the importation of Western technology is fraught with the threat of dependence on imperialism which has already become a reality for many Third World countries. Such dependences carries grave security implications for the USSR, particularly if it involves military technology. Thus, one commentator warns, "The striving in individual socialist countries to solve the problems of the scientific-technical revolution with the aid of imperialist groups of monopolies or from a position of separate 'independence' is, in practice, pregnant with the danger of dependence upon the imperialists."[7]

Finally, other traditionalists see the dangers of imperialist exploitation in that aspect of East-West trade, which they call the "brain trade." As Iu. Zhukov notes, "It is more lucrative [for Western capitalists] to buy an experienced specialist than to train him—the deal is faster, cheaper, and involves fewer risks."[8] Accustomed to this head-hunting technique, the capitalists allegedly try to obtain specialists, including scientists, engineers, and managers, from the socialist countries. In the traditionalist view, such "brain trade" is one of the purposes for which the capitalists have concocted the "troublesome, hypocritical campaign" for "free emigration" and the "complete freedom of international movement of people."[9]

The realists disagree with this analysis on all counts. Their more optimistic view of the correlation of forces—both with regard to the increasing weakness of the United States and the continuing strength of the USSR—leads them to conclude that East-West trade and cooperation will only serve to strengthen their country, which is already strong enough to protect itself from the threats of exploitation, dependence, and subversion. As Arbatov has emphasized, "The socialist community and the countries that are members of it certainly do not enter into multilateral relations with the capitalist powers from a position of 'weakness.' "[10] In the realist view, the West does not have enough "levers" to force the socialist countries to accept a deal that is "exploitative." As a result, they maintain that any trade agreement between East and West is necessarily based on "equality" and "mutual advantage," thus representing a successful utilization of the "international division of labor."[11]

Significantly, these realist commentators do not accuse the United States of grand larceny when it makes trade agreements with socialist countries. But identical agreements with any nonsocialist country are termed "exploitative" and "neocolonialist" attempts to keep the country on the capitalist road of development. Clearly, there is no possibility of "mutual advantage" in such agreements. It should be noted that "mutual advantage," like so many other Soviet terms, has one meaning for the West and one for the Soviets. In the Soviet lexicon it has a "positive" value, which is to say that it implies movement toward the realization of communist values, or "progress." In the Soviet view, then, the "advantage" that the West derives from East-West trade agreements is inherent in the "progress" that they represent—progress toward the establishment of worldwide communism and, consequently, of world "peace."

Still, the Soviets must deal with the possibility that East-West trade aids capitalism marginally by enriching some of its "monopolies." Soviet realists avoid this potential policy contradiction by arguing that whatever benefits capitalism may derive from such trade are insufficient to enable it to surmount its problems. Indeed, they maintain that the expansion of East-West trade exacerbates these problems. Such trade spurs "progress," thereby tipping the correlation of forces further in favor of socialism. In addition, this trade gives some elements in American ruling circles a vested interest in seeing that the United States not only avoids antagonizing but in fact accommodates (i.e., "cooperates" with) the Soviet Union for the sake of profits. By dividing the American ruling class into two camps—the military-industrial "monopolies" and the "realistic," "sober," and "cooperative" "firms"—East-West trade aggravates capitalism's internal contradictions.

These are the reasons that the realists advance in support of their contention that any "bridge-building" strategies the United States may employ are "doomed to failure." As Arbatov has noted, those who try to use economic, scientific, and technical policies to erode or soften up socialism ideologically act "in vain."[12] He observes that even some Americans, who would like to use trade and other exchanges to effect a liberalization of socialism, have acknowledged the futility of such hopes and have remembered that when the isolated Soviet Union enlisted foreign specialists to help its industrialization policy during the 1930s, this policy "influenced neither the character of its socialist system nor the ideological atmosphere in the country." Arbatov concludes that it is "much more fruitless . . . to build calculations on such a foundation today, now that there exists a dynamic world system of socialism which not only produces one-third of the world's industrial output but is also exporting the products of its scientific and technical thought to other countries on an increasingly extensive basis. Arbatov is therefore fully confident that trade and "cooperation" can take place under the proper controls.

Such controls, of course, include internal restriction on the activities of Soviet citizens and restrictions, in the form of bilateral agreements, on those foreigners who deal with the Soviets. The realists' confidence in the efficacy of these external restrictions and agreements is exemplified by V. Sobakin's declaration that "the wider the sphere covered by such agreements, the narrower are the possibilities of an imperialist, great-power policy."[13] It appears, then, that so long as the United States follows its usual imperialist policy, any agreement it makes with the socialist countries constitutes a brake on the "reactionary" forces while allowing the "progressive" forces to "progress." Such agreements are thus a corollary of "peaceful coexistence" and the only obstacle that may confront the "peace-loving" forces is that of actually persuading the imperialists to make an agreement for the sake of "detente." From the realist point of view, however, this problem is becoming less and less serious; not only are all the "objective realities" of the world situation "forcing" the imperialists to "agree," but the United States "was able to be *convinced* that far from all of the problems that it encounters can be resolved by fighting against socialist countries and communism" (my emphasis).[14] They argue that the crisis of capitalism, interimperialist contradictions, and the "great diversity in the developing countries" have emerged and "upset the black and white concepts about the world which stem from frantic anticommunism."[15] Thus, according to the realists, the United States is becoming "reasonable" enough to be persuaded that the struggle against communism is not only futile but also rather silly. History, after all, follows a single, law-abiding path, and it is therefore fatuous for the capitalists to struggle on basis of the "black-white concepts of frantic anticommunism" when they can "progress" much more successfully on the basis of the "black-red" concepts of anticapitalism.

Chapter 7

Traditionalists
and Realists

As we have seen, there is a divergence between the traditionalist and realist perspectives in Soviet analysis of American foreign policy. This situation (and the author's ascription of "traditionalist" and "realist" labels to the analysts who hold these views) can lead one to conclude that there exists an ongoing debate between two distinct and easily indentifiable policy groups within the Soviet Union. To avoid any impression that Soviet political differences are so sharp, we must clarify several issues. First, we must attempt to determine which elements of the Soviet political process constitute each group. Second, we must assess the relations between the two groups in an attempt to see if there are any ways in which one dominates the other. Having examined the various interpretations of the debates between Soviet factions, we may come to a better understanding of the policy positions that animate Soviet political discourse, and ultimately, Soviet foreign policy.

The Western literature on this subject reveals a variety of interpretations, each of them plausible, of what I have called the traditionalist-realist disagreement. Different scholars and policy makers have termed it a conflict between "Left" and "Right," between "hawks" and "doves," or between "orthodox" and "revisionists." Morton Schwartz, for one, characterizes it as a conflict between two distinct tendencies: "one aggressive, militaristic, suspicious of the United States, hostile to detente; the other, sober, moderate, concerned less about the danger of war with the United States than the benefits of mutual collaboration in specific areas."[1] Whereas the former are said to be conservative and ideologically orthodox, the latter, "moderate" forces "do not see this country as threatening basic Soviet security interests, . . . they do not regard us as weak, passive or isolationist."[2]

Vernon Aspaturian in effect characterizes the same basic conflict as one between guns and butter.[3] On the one hand, he identifies three distinct "demand sectors" that make up the Soviet "military-industrial complex": (1) the "ideological demand sector (the ideologues and conservatives of the Party apparatus)"; (2) "the security demand sector (the police, armed forces, and defense industries)"; (3) "the producer demand sector (heavy industry, construction, and transportation)." On the other hand, there are three other sectors that focus on a different set of concerns: (1) "the consumer demand sector (light industry, consumer goods industry, trade, and housing"; (2) "the agricultural demand sector"; and (3) "the public services and welfare sector." Aspaturian maintains that these two coalitions tend to compete with one another for budgetary allocations.

Working from Aspaturian's general framework, Robert Donaldson analyzes the conflict as it centers around the issue of detente.[4] While the proponents of detente stress the beneficial possibilities of cooperation with the West, the opponents of the policy are concerned: (1) that Moscow may abandon its commitments to its socialist allies and the national liberation movement; (2) that detente may become a vehicle for bourgeois subversion and interference in Soviet internal affairs; (3) that because the "imperialists" are untrustworthy, it is dangerous to do business with them; and (4) that tactical compromises with imperialism may be interpreted as a sign of Soviet weakness.

Other terms, used to characterize Soviet traditionalists, include Klaus Mehnert's "anti-detenters," who see the danger of Western ideological infection in detente,[5] and Roman Kolkowicz's "Red Hawks," who believe in the possibilty of victory in nuclear war. In addition, characterizing the Soviet military as an interest group, Kolkowicz emphasizes the insularity and narrow professionalism of the Soviet military, and hypothesizes that the importance of the military declines during periods of detente. In his opinion, this circumstance impels the military to support heavy industry and high levels of international tension "in order to provide the rationale for large military budgets and allocations."[6] In his study of the period before 1970, William Zimmerman wrote that this traditionalist group was composed of military men "with a stake in continued heavy military spending," "old ideologues," and "persons whose career patterns suggested a favorable disposition to domestic reactionary policies." For these groups, according to Zimmerman, "the war in Vietnam was not an isolated event, but evidence that the United States confronted Soviet interests in revolution in every corner of the globe."[7]

Vladimir Petrov believes that the conflict is between the "Neo-Stalinists," who argue for employment of every means to weaken the United States and its allies, and a more friendly group who press for cooperation with the West in order to reduce military spending and thereby obtain the means for modernizing the Soviet economy.[8] These latter forces are said to believe that a decrease in anti-American propaganda will relax cold-war attitudes in the United States and thus enhance the Soviet Union's security. In a similar vein, Marshall Shulman posits a conflict between the "champions of economic modernization," who support the policy of peaceful coexistence, and "military interests and the orthodox Party apparatus whose vested interest in an 'imperialist enemy' is combined with a fear of the effect of modernization upon the system."[9] The military services are said to resemble their American counterparts citing national security and mistrust of the United States and the SALT process to justify their claims on the national budget. The principal sources of opposition to peaceful coexistence, according to Shulman, are the "orthodox wing of the Party," with its large ideological apparatus, and the political police. For these groups, detente holds the danger of "a weakening of the ideological elan which is their stock-in-trade, an opening of the country to influences which they can only regard as 'subversive,' increased trouble with intellectuals and nationality groups, and an erosion of the image of the 'imperialist threat' which legitimizes their power and on which their careers depend."[10] Furthermore, these groups believe that an abandonment of autarky may lead to a fatal dependence on the imperialists, that detente will weaken Soviet political control both at home and in Eastern Europe, and that foreign trade will not be very productive.[11]

Consistent with most of these analyses is that of Alexander Dallin, who has elaborated on the differences between the Soviet "Left" and "Right." Declaring that "the traditional dichotomy into 'Left' and 'Right' is an inadequate diagnostic tool," Dallin maintains nevertheless that "it is descriptive of profoundly divergent attitudes which, in their extreme manifestations, reflect conflicting values and orientations."[12] He warns that, however close the "congruence of cleavages over foreign policy approaches with those over other issues," not all politicians assume ideologically consistent postures on all issues. Having voiced these caveats, Dallin proceeds to summarize the differences between those usually categorized in the Soviet Left and Right:

Left	*Right*
Goal Orientedness (utopianism)	Pragmatism
Optimism	Pessimism
"Red" (partisanship)	"Expert" (rationality)
Transformation	Stability
Monolithism	Pluralism
Politics	Economics
Mobilization	Normalcy
Heavy Industry	Consumer Goods
Uneven ("breakthrough") Development	Even Development
Central Command Economy	Market Economy
Cultural Revolution	Tradition Persistence
Tension-management	Consensus-building
Dialectic ("the worse the better")	Linear ("the better, the better")
Centralization	Decentralization
Violence	Gradualism
Three-class Alliance Strategy	Four-class Alliance
Inevitability of International Conflict	Avoidability of Conflict
Voluntarism	Determinism[13]

With this general framework, Dallin highlights the major policy cleavages: (1) "the predisposition to make different assessments of the correlation of forces"; (2) "the tendency to link certain readings of reality to other, seemingly unrelated, policy positions"; (3) the course of Soviet strategy toward the noncommunist world, with positions ranging from offensive revolution to detente, bluff, and compromise; (4) the question of whether one can do business at all with capitalism; (5) the debate over the nature of international tensions; and 6) the question of what constitutes the wisest alliance policy.[14]

Although each of these interpretations of the Soviet foreign policy debate is slightly different in emphasis, they represent a fairly strong consensus. A composite picture of these "orthodox" American interpretations would indicate that there are two primary policy groups in the Soviet Union. The first is the ideologically orthodox, aggressive, hawkish Left, a group that includes Party ideologues, members of the security apparatus, and the Soviet military-industrial complex. This group is skeptical of deterrence and detente, distrustful of the West, wary of ideological subversion and economic dependence on the West, inclined toward autarky, supportive of heavy industry, high military budgets, and continued domestic oppression, and prone to believe that military confrontation or war with capitalism is inevitable. It has a vested interest in the continued existence of an imperialist enemy, and is optimistic about opportunities that can be exploited politically and militarily in the international arena—a manifestation of its general confidence in the inevitable victory of socialism. The second group is the more pragmatic, rational, moderate, and dovish Right—a group reconciled to the necessity of deterrence and detente in order to avoid nuclear war. As such it is inclined to seek avenues for cooperation with the West, confident that East-West trade is beneficial to the economic modernization and security of the USSR, supportive of the light industry and consumer goods sectors, confident that war with the West is avoidable, and realistic about the continued strength of the United States as a pluralistic, democratic-capitalist state and defender of its international interests. As a result, this group is more pessimistic about the prospects for revolutionary success in the international arena in the foreseeable future.

There is, no doubt, a great deal to commend this composite orthodox American interpretation; indeed, a substantial portion of the documentation in this study attests to its validity. That the positions taken by each of the two broader Soviet schools of thought are intellectually quite consistent makes them all the more plausible. Furthermore, such a "Left-Right" divergence corresponds with certain historic splits in the Bolshevik ranks, a salient one being the conflict between Lenin and Bukharin over the terms of the peace treaty with Germany in 1918. Bukharin, as one of the "Left" Communists, opposed peace on the grounds that the Bolsheviks owed their first allegiance to spreading the world revolution. Lenin, however, being more realistic about the meager prospects of success, ultimately prevailed upon his colleagues to accept the treaty terms so that the Bolsheviks could consolidate their fragile rule over Russia.

Finally, a number of scholars maintain that there is a considerable congruence between the dominant themes in the Soviet press and the actual foreign policy of the Soviet Union. There has been a general consensus among Western scholars and commentators that the Soviet "Right" (to use a term that summarizes the orthodox American approach) has been the dominant group in the Kremlin and that the general pattern of Soviet foreign policy reflects their power. Indeed, Moscow has continued to pursue a policy of detente, peaceful coexistence, and East-West trade, sparing no effort to emphasize the mutual benefits of such cooperation. It has ostensibly accepted the principles of mutual deterrence by engaging in SALT negotiations, and by heralding the most important of the "Basic Principles of Relations" between the United States and USSR— peaceful coexistence—the Kremlin appears to have rejected the idea that war is inevitable between the two social systems. Finally, and perhaps most dramatically, the Kremlin apparently demonstrated its moderation during the two most "provocative" American acts of the 1970s: first, by refraining from retaliation after the mining of Haiphong harbor in the spring of 1972 and proceeding with the Moscow summit several weeks later, and second, by renouncing direct involvement in the 1973 Mideast war when the United States conducted its massive airlift to Israel.

Despite this compelling support for the orthodox American interpretation of the Soviet "Left-Right" split, there is a striking lack of evidence to support a number of its key elements. For example: (1) Where is the evidence that the Soviet military constitutes a major segment of the anti-detente "Left"? (2) Where is the evidence that the dominant "Right" is distinguished from the more hawkish "Left" by its opposition to high military budgets? Or, if such evidence can be produced, where is the evidence that demonstrates the dominance of the moderate "Right" when it comes to decisions on defense budgets? (3) Where is the evidence that the hawkish "Left" can be distinguished from the moderate "Right" by the greater interest it has invested in the maintenance of an imperialist enemy?

(4) And where is the evidence that the Soviet "Left" of today is more optimistic than the realistic and therefore putatively pessimistic "Right"?

The Military and Detente

Those who seek support for the thesis that the Soviet military constitutes a major element of the anti-detente "Left" can find a wide variety of statements by high-ranking military officers which demonstrate a profound suspicion of the United States and call for continued vigilance by the Soviet armed forces. The military press is replete with articles entitled "New Doctrine, Old Plans" or "Old Wine, New Bottles" which warn the Soviet public against harboring any illusions about the new policies and intentions of the United States. As Marshal Andrei Grechko stated early in 1974, "The world has changed but the aggressive misanthropic nature of imperialism has remained unchanged."[15] In contrast with the realist analysis (that although the fundamental nature of imperialism has not changed, it has been forced to adapt to the new correlation of forces [see Arbatov's analysis on pp. 101, 102], the military position thus appears to demonstrate a suspicion of the United States so deep-seated that it must represent a policy stance opposed to detente. Equally plausible is the contention that the Soviet military is a narrowly professional interest group whose role in Soviet life is diminished by detente. Finally, if one adds to such evidence and conjecture the numerous instances in which Soviet military spokesmen have criticized deterrence, supported the possibility of victory in nuclear war, posited the inevitability of war as the underlying premise of such positions, and warned against dependence on the West for military technology, then it seems that one *must* conclude that the military constitutes a homogeneous bloc against detente, SALT, and East-West trade.

But cannot this evidence be used to support a different interpretation? Isn't it just as likely that all these policy statements by military spokesmen are largely a function of their bureaucratic duties, specifically that of maintaining a high level of vigilance among all who are responsible for the country's security? It can be argued, after all, that when Marshal Grechko emphasizes the unchanged nature of imperialism, he is interested primarily in disabusing his subordinates of any illusions that they might entertain about the

United States, especially in the relaxed climate of detente. When other commentators criticize deterrence and defend the possibility of victory in nuclear war, they may well be performing the same task. After all, to what, other than morale and vigilance, does Lt. Col. Ye. Rybkin refer when he declares that "the *a priori* rejection of the possibility of victory [including, specifically, victory in nuclear war] is bad because it leads to moral disarmament, to disbelief in victory, to fatalism and possivity"?[16] A similar process seems to be at work when Boris Ponomarev seriously discusses the possibility of the rise of "neofascist elements" in the capitalist world and warns of increasingly frenzied attacks on socialism (see above, page 95). Such talk is a bureaucratic imperative of his position as the head of the Central Committee's International Section, with responsibilities for supervising the agents of world revolution.

The theory that the Soviet military constitutes an interest group whose narrow professionalism demands opposition to detente also provokes certain questions. To a degree this theory assumes that the military wants things that the Party does not want and is usually in a position to exert enough pressure on the Party to get most of them. In a skeptical response to this assumption William Odom has raised several important points. First, he questions the validity of the "interest group" theory of Soviet politics, noting that excessive concentration on the study of the influence of Soviet interest groups tends to emphasize political factors of "peripheral significance" at the expense of those of "critical importance." He maintains that it is of critical importance that the central Party leadership makes all important policy decisions—a fact that reduces to "peripheral signficance" the kind of influence that "interest groups may exert.[17]

Elsewhere, with specific reference to military-Party relations, Odom disputes the assumption that President Brezhnev's relation to the Soviet military is analagous to an American president's relation to the Defense Department.* He first notes that the historical

---

*This assumption, according to Odom, is inherent in two similar laments on the difficulty of achieving arms control: one by Secretary Henry Kissinger, "Both sides have to convince their military establishments of the benefits of restraint, and that does not come easily to either side"; and the other by James Reston, "Neither Mr. Nixon nor Mr. Brezhnev is now strong enough politically to compel their military establishments to cut defense budgets or take chances for peace."

record reveals that "although military considerations have dominated Soviet foreign policy-making, Soviet marshals and generals have not."[18] This situation is explained in part by the fact that Soviet Party leaders, including Brezhnev, have inherited and continued a quasi-military mode of leadership and policy making. Noting that the predominance of military considerations is clearly demonstrated in Soviet economic policy, Odom reminds us that "the Soviet centrally planned, command economy is a war-mobilization economy. Soviet historians miss no chance to emphasize its superiority over Western models precisely for this reason."[19] This economy, of course, is directed by the Party and not by the military, and as a consequence, it is the Party that makes the key decisions as to how to maintain the recently sagging rates of growth and technological development at levels sufficient to sustain the military priority. The Party has had two alternatives in any attempt to solve this problem: (1) economic reform of the kind proposed by E. Liberman and others, which would remove those features of the command economy, such as the central pricing system and the prohibition of profits, which hinder the efficiency of the resource allocation necessary to promote growth and technological development; and (2) the importation of foreign technology to increase labor productivity, growth, and the Soviet military potential. For a variety of reasons the Party has consistently chosen the latter option ever since the New Economic Policy of the 1920s. The importation of foreign technology allows the Soviets to maintain their command economy without having to effect any market-oriented reforms—reforms that would be truly revolutionary, for any dismantling of the central pricing system would unleash the market forces of supply and demand. These forces would in turn decentralize all economic decision making, thereby diluting, perhaps even decimating, the political power of the Party and diminishing its ability to retain a high military priority. The unreformed command economy, however, remains at the service of war mobilization. Odom concludes that the Soviet Party and military see considerable advantages in the policy of peaceful coexistence because it permits both the survival of the command economy and the importation of foreign technology.[20]

In an observation that further confounds the idea that the military is an independent force opposed to detente, Odom suggests that the economic managers are a group more likely to oppose detente than the military. Rather than single out just those managers of heavy industry, he refers to the broader group of managers who would feel, and have felt, considerable discomfort as a result of the influx of new, foreign technology. Among the results of such a policy that the tradition-bound Soviet managers fear are: organizational change, the loss or displacement of thousands of jobs, the movement of offices away from large cities to remote areas that are closer to production activity, and the general uncertainty that stems from the introduction of any new technology.[21]

The Dominance of the "Right" and Defense Budgets

The notion that the dominant "Right" opposes the hawkish "Left" on the size of Soviet military budgets should also be treated more skeptically. We do have numerous documented cases in which top Soviet officials have advocated investment in light as opposed to heavy industry, and it is reasonable to assume that such advocacy constitutes a call for decreased military spending. Sometimes the advocacy for lower military spending is quite explicit, as Vernon Aspaturian has found in these quotations from K. P. Ivanov and P. V. Sokolov:

> Experience has proven that only under conditions of a relaxation of tension is it possible to concentrate a maximum of resources for accompanying the plans for building of communism.[22]

> There are objective limits to military spending, and if they are exceeded, this will have a negative effect not only on expanded production, but also on the strengthening of defense. . . . It is essential to observe definite ratios between the output of armaments and producer and consumer goods. . . . An expansion of military consumption beyond permissible boundaries does not lead to a strengthening of the military power of a state, but to its weakening and an inevitable breakdown of the economy as a whole and military-economic potential in particular.[23]

As for the opposing view, Aspaturian quotes General Major A. Lagovskii, who implies that no ceiling should be put on military spending: "Everyone will agree that an army that does not train itself to master all arms, all means and methods of warfare that the enemy possesses, or may possess, is behaving in an unwise or even criminal manner."[24]

The conclusive identification of the elements of the Soviet leadership which subscribe to each view, however, is not so simple a task. Aspaturian hypothesizes, for example, that the late premier Kosygin was an advocate of lower military spending, citing his 24th CPSU Congress report on the Eighth Five-Year Plan as evidence. In that speech, Kosygin revealed that the military establishment had absorbed nearly 25 percent of the funds available for economic development over the preceding five years." Aspaturian reasons that the premier made these remarks "in an attempt to show that development of the consumer sector had been frustrated by the voracious budgetary appetites of the military spokesmen present at the Congress."[25] But where is the evidence in Kosygin's protracted speech that he thinks military spending is excessive? Is the mere fact that Kosygin cites the defense spending figure of 80 billion rubles sufficient evidence to support such a conclusion? On the contrary, a few heavy-industrial excavations into Kosygin's soporific *copia verborum* reveal remarks that suggest either opposition or neutrality on the issue of lower military spending. He begins by offering an explanation for increased military spending:

> We must not fail to take into account the fact that the country's economic development in the period of the Eighth Five-Year Plan took place in conditions of an exacerbated international situation. This caused the necessity of carrying out additional measures in the field of defense, and this required a certain diversion of resources and manpower.[26]

In addition, Kosygin advances a rationalization for investment in heavy industry:

> Heavy industry has been and remains the foundation of the country's economic strength and of a further increase in the well-being of the people. It ensures technical progress, the development of the entire national economy, including agriculture and the branches connected with the production of consumer goods, and also the strengthening of the Soviet state's defense capability.[27]

Aspaturian may well be correct in saying that Kosygin was a

"subtle and persistent, if not always successful advocate of shifting greater attention to the consumer sector," whereas Brezhnev has been an advocate of heavy industry and defense;[28] but their positions have not been held consistently for even short periods of time. Bruce Parrott, for example, has produced evidence of a change in Kosygin's position on the closely related question of Soviet economic and technological progress in comparison with that of the capitalist West. In 1969 Kosygin downgraded Soviet performance by emphasizing the strengths of Western economies. Two years later, in his already cited report to the 24th Congress, he praised the strength of the Soviet economy and drew a favorable contrast between its ability to develop and absorb the fruits of science and technology and that of the capitalist economies.[29] The trend of Kosygin's thinking, according to this evidence, suggests that he was becoming increasingly rather than decreasingly content with the state of economic affairs, and, as a result, less inclined toward drastic changes in the defense/consumer ratio of budgetary allocations.

In light of this information, it appears that it *is* reasonable to assume that there are factional conflicts over the size of the Soviet military budget. Due to the extreme difficulty of identifying individual leaders with one or another position, however, it is even more difficult to identify distinct "Right" and "Left" factions. Once again, it is possible that General Major Lagovskii, who declares that it is unwise or even criminal for the army to fail to train itself in all methods, is merely speaking to the bureaucratic imperatives of the military services. His remarks do not seem sufficient evidence to brand him and his military mentors as representatives of the hawkish "Left." And if Kosygin indeed tended to talk more than Brezhnev about light industry, consumer durables, and the increased efficiency of economic management, one can argue that his stance was a by-product of his bureaucratic function as director of the entire national economy.

If one accepts the hypothesis that its opposition to high military spending distinguishes the "Right" from the "Left," then one must reexamine another question: Which of the two factions is in fact dominant within the Kremlin? The orthodox American interpretation generally has assumed that the Soviet "Right" has been dominant throughout the 1970s as demonstrated by the Kremlin's consistent solicitude for detente, peaceful coexistence, SALT, and

East-West trade. If one juxtaposes the concurrent policy on military spending to these policies, however, one notices that since the days of Khrushchev Soviet military spending has not decreased in any given year and neither has the growth rate of these expenditures. Thus, what one might assume to be a policy consistent with detente and the consumerist concerns of the Soviet "Right," namely, a slowdown of the growth of military allocations, has not occurred.[30]* This fact in turn forces one to question: (1) the evidence that the "Right" *qua* Right has been the dominant faction in the Kremlin, when it appears that the Soviet "Left" has been the group responsible for military spending policy; and (2) the evidence that supports the American contention that the existing Kremlin leadership has in fact been oriented to the "Right."

The "Left" and the Necessity of an Imperialist Enemy

As noted earlier, Marshall Shulman has singled out a "vested interest in an imperialist enemy" as a distinguishing trait of the Soviet "Left"—a trait that contrasts with the "Right's" pro-detente outlook. Again, one can find differences between Soviet groups which, from outward appearances, suggest that Shulman's point is valid. As we have seen, Soviet traditionalists have placed a much greater emphasis on portraying the United States as threatening than have the realists. In particular, the traditionalists have highlighted the "ideological maneuvers of the bourgeoisie," the techniques of economic exploitation, and the dynamics of American militarism. Here again, however, one can ask to what extent such a portrayal might be a bureaucratic function of Party ideological workers charged with preserving doctrinal conformity or of military writers responsible for maintaining sufficient vigilance? There is a difference, after all, between being bureaucratically required to portray enemies and having a "vested interest" in doing so.

One might also question the reasoning behind the notion that

---

*One may observe that other actions that are inconsistent with a genuine relaxation of tensions also appear to have been the consistent policy of the Kremlin leaders. Such policies include intensified Soviet politico-military activities in Afghanistan, South Yemen, Vietnam, Nicaragua, El Salvador, Angola, Ethiopia, and elsewhere in Africa and Latin America, including the extensive use of proxy forces such as Cubans and East Germans.

251

the "Left" has a greater "vested interest" in portraying an imperialist enemy than the "Right." The purpose of such a portrayal, of course, is to legitimize a dictatorial regime that is so insecure that it needs a pervasive secret police, 750,000 border guards, Berlin Walls and total control of the media to maintain its hold on power. Such a regime needs enemies or at least the appearance of enemies, for without them, a dictator is not only unable to portray his government as a legitimate guardian of the people against mortal dangers, but less able to rally the people to his cause. Why, therefore, should one component of a regime have a greater *vested interest* in enemies than any other? Do not the "Left" and the "Right" have an equal interest in legitimizing the Soviet regime as a whole? To suggest, as Shulman does, that the Left's interest in convincing the public of the existence of an imperialist threat is the nourishment "upon which their careers depend" is to risk inflating the influence of the ideological bureaucrats or, for that matter, of the military. Such an argument would seem to emphasize a factor of "peripheral significance" at the expense of factors of "critical importance," for example, the fact that the elements of the top leadership, not their bureaucratic underlings, are fundamentally responsible for the orientation of policy. After all, Mikhail Suslov, long the Politburo's chief ideologist, did not depend upon images of imperialist threats to secure his career. And as for the army of ideological propagandists, they will continue to have jobs disseminating the Party line, no matter what it is.

The "Left" as Optimists?

Alexander Dallin noted that one aspect of the distinction between the Soviet "Left" and "Right" is each side's predisposition to make its own assessment of the correlation of forces. Specifically, Dallin observed that "the 'Left' has invariably perceived opportunities to be exploited where the 'Right' has seen none (and has charged the former with adventurism)."[31] He draws from the historical record to support his point, stating that "this was the case with Zinoviev's associates in the Communist International until at least 1923; with the militant line symbolized by Andrei Zhdanov and Josip Tito in 1947-48; and with the Maoists seeking to convince the Khrushchevites after 1957."[32] Such evidence does not, however, tell us whether the pattern holds to the same extent today. We must investigate further to ascertain whether those generally considered to be members of the Soviet "Left" continue to see opportunities where the "Right" sees none.

Morton Schwartz's answer, essentially, is that the pattern still holds. His study leads him to conclude that the "Rightist," "moderate" group in the Kremlin recognizes as never before the manifold strengths of the United States: "The military resources of the United States are known and respected as are our economic capabilities, especially in the area of 'scientific-technical revolution.' "[33] Furthermore, he notes that the Soviet "moderates" see "little evidence of a loss of will on the part of high-level American officials or, for that matter, that domestic concerns are paralyzing their ability to act." In addition, they feel that "our international interests and commitments remain considerable" and that we continue to possess the "willingness to use force where necessary to protect them."[34] Schwartz's analysis strongly implies, therefore, that because it is so fully aware of U.S. strength, the dominant Soviet "Right" is not optimistic about the international opportunities that will be available to the USSR. At the same time, Schwartz implies that the orthodox Soviet "Left," which persists in depicting an America debilitated by the crisis of capitalism, also continues to fit the historical pattern: if they indeed believe that the crisis of capitalism is deepening, they must be relatively optimistic about the opportunities that their country can exploit.

In contrast, this book argues that the roles of Soviet optimists and pessimists have been fundamentally reversed since the early 1970s. As has been amply documented in earlier chapters, a substantial portion of the disagreements between Soviet analysts involve their assessments of the correlation of forces. In case after case, the same pattern is revealed: one side offers a sophisticated, realistic assessment of both the strengths and weaknesses of the United States, while the other reiterates the traditional picture of a dangerous and exploitative imperialist force, always buttressing its statements with a dose of ritual optimism—the habitual formulations about the continuing crisis and imminent collapse of capitalism. Whereas the traditionalists stress the persistence of the imperialist threat, the realists see increasing signs of American weakness, particularly in the American response to the recognition that there has been a significant change in the worldwide correlation of forces. The realists maintain that almost every means of American foreign policy has been adapted to these new circumstances, and conclude that the result is retrenchment of American influence throughout the world. Given this perspective, there can be little doubt that it is the realists and not the traditionalists who believe that the international situation provides opportunities that the Soviet Union can exploit for its own benefit. Accordingly, the realists should be more optimistic about the prospects for revolutionary gains than their traditionalist comrades.

Realists and Traditionalists: A Harmony of Interests

This perspective on the differences between the two Soviet groups sheds new light on the nature of each of them. In fact, this perspective suggests that the terms commonly used to describe these groups may be misleading. For example, it reveals that the "moderate" or "dovish" "Right" may not be as moderate, nor the traditionalist "Left" as "hawkish" as the orthodox American interpretation maintains. For example, the traditionalists' apparently hawkish tendency to depict a threatening imperialist enemy may not only reflect a bureaucratic imperative, but may also be a natural function of a pessimistic assessment of the correlation of forces. The traditionalist impulse, then, might well be construed as comparatively less offensive and more defensive.

The same perspective also calls into question the alleged moderation of those of the realist "Right." For example, rather than opposing continued high levels of military spending, they may in fact favor them for two reasons. First, the realists fully realize and have amply documented the primary causes that helped to deter the correlation of forces: the rise of Soviet military power, the attainment of strategic parity, and the efficacy of Soviet military assistance in support of the "national liberation movement," especially in Indochina. Second, they know that the effective use of such military power can be one of the indispensable elements in exploiting new opportunities in the international arena. The fact that the Soviet "Right" has not reduced the growth of military spending over the last two decades further supports the validity of this analysis.

Recent Soviet foreign policy actions tend to corroborate this thesis. The recent Soviet politico-military offensive in parts of the Third World is very likely a logical outgrowth of an optimistic assessment of the correlation of forces. It is not unreasonable to presume, for example, that the Soviet sponsorship of Cuban troops in Angola could have been a probing action to test this new assessment. And shortly thereafter, the various Soviet, Cuban, and East German activities in Ethiopia, South Yemen, Zaire, Afghanistan, Nicaragua, El Salvador, and even Iran could have been part of a similar pattern. These instances of subversion, use of military force, and sponsorship of coups d'etat, not to mention the unprecedented military buildup of the 1960s and 1970s, cannot properly be characterized as "moderate" behavior.[35]

One can see why Schwartz decided to describe the realists as "moderate" and as having been responsible for the "moderate foreign policy line of the past half decade or so"—especially when he concludes that: "They view U.S. foreign policy today as less belligerent, less anti-Soviet, less prone to taking unnecessary risks, and generally less threatening than at any time in the past."[36] After all, if the United States is less threatening, then the USSR is more secure and presumably these conditions mitigate the suspicions and hostilities that translate into arms races and belligerence. But the connection between this line of reasoning and the conclusion that the realist group is "moderate" is tenuous. It depends upon the optimistic assumption that the Soviets will respond to a decrease in American anti-Sovietism with a less antagonistic stance of their own. Unfortunately, there is no evidence to support this assumption. And furthermore, this common line of reasoning tends to ignore some of the deeper political causes of the East-West conflict.

It *is* reasonable to assume that hostilities between two adversaries with relatively similar political structures will abate when they attain strategic parity and the formerly superior power thus appears less threatening. But is such an assumption a necessary or even likely result of parity between powers whose ideologies are not only radically disparate but hostile? Given that ideological factors lie at the root of the East-West conflict and that Soviet policy is dictated largely by imperatives of self-legitimation, only two contingencies could possibly produce an *objectively* based reduction of hostility: (1) the ideological conversion of one side or the other; or (2) the ideological convergence of both sides. Perhaps, indeed, Schwartz assumes that one of these contingencies was an integral element of the "detente" relationship of the 1970s. If one concludes that the Soviet realists have evolved toward a pragmatism characteristic of the leaders of most great powers, then perhaps there has been an ideological conversion sufficient to have obviated the fundamental ideological basis of the East-West conflict. If this is not one of Schwartz's working assumptions, he is ignoring the deeper, ideological roots of the conflict.

It is tempting to conclude that a certain ideological conversion underlies the various changes that we have noted in the traditionalist analysis of U.S. foreign policy; but there remains an important question of both substance and semantics: Are these changes so substantial that the policies derived from them cannot be reconciled with ever-increasing military spending and foreign adventurism and thus merit being described as "moderate"? Indeed, the crux of this issue is the degree to which the policies, as well as the ideologies, of the Soviet traditionalists and realists can be reconciled with one another. The greater the extent to which they can be reconciled, the more appropriate it is to emphasize their similarities rather than their differences in any discussion of the political factors of "critical importance."

On the surface it seems difficult, for example, to reconcile the pro-SALT policy with the continued high level of Soviet military spending and the active and unprecedented projection of Soviet military power abroad. SALT would appear to be a policy of the "moderate" "Right" whereas the others are policies of the hawkish "Left," but such an interpretation may be misleading. There is, after all, *no evidence* to exclude the possibility that all of these policies are part of one comprehensive strategy pursued by a single, dominant, and unopposed coalition in the Kremlin. A pro-SALT policy need not be a "dovish" policy at all, especially if it is designed to muzzle American strategic programs while giving the Soviets an opportunity to continue the development and deployment of new weapons systems. Surely this possibility cannot be dismissed in light of the facts that: (1) SALT has not in fact succeeded in the achievement of any arms reductions; (2) during the period between SALT I in 1972 and SALT II in 1979 the Soviets tested and/or deployed at least six *new* intercontinental nuclear delivery systems (SS-16/20, -17, -18, -19, -N-8, and Backfire) while the United States did

256

not deploy any; (3) SALT II was negotiated with two major loopholes that allowed the replacement of Soviet ICBMs with vastly improved and enlarged missiles; and (4) SALT II limited launchers but not delivery vehicles (e.g., missiles), thousands of which could be stored nearby and reloaded into Soviet launchers, which are uniquely capable of "cold-launch."[37] A U.S. policy that combined detente with increasing defense expenditures would probably seem utterly self-contradictory to many Americans, but the combination of these policies may not represent such a contradiction for the Soviet leaders, who, in any case, do not feel obliged to explain apparent inconsistencies to anybody.

The orthodox American interpretation, which emphasizes the differences rather than similarities between Soviet factions, accordingly tends to argue that such incongruities in Soviet policies are the result of the concessions that one faction is forced to make to another. Shulman, for example, has noted the "fundamental contradiction" between the Soviet assertions that "peaceful coexistence between different social systems is possible" and that such peaceful coexistence is consistent with, and even intensifies the "ideological struggle." Instead of weighing the possibility that these two positions may not be at all incongruous—especially if one acknowledges the Soviet view that "peaceful coexistence" is a form of struggle—Shulman underscores their inconsistency and explains that the component of "ideological struggle" is "an organizational concession to domestic cold warriors."[38] Shulman's assumption, of course, is that the moderate, dovish "Right" is the dominant group and thus in a position to make occasional concessions to the hawkish "Left." But if one looks at the whole range of Soviet policies—including the undiminished military budgets, the foreign adventurism, the barriers against emigration, the continued high levels of domestic repression, and the maintenance, without fundamental reform, of the command economy—it appears that policies on most every important issue are "concessions" to the traditionalist, hawkish "Left." Could it be that the "Left" is the dominant group that makes cosmetic "concessions" to the "Right"? Certainly those who are disinclined to describe recent Soviet policies as "moderate" might well accept this suggestion, but they would not be correct. Real differences do exist between factions in the Kremlin, and during the Brezhnev period the views of the dominant group have been somewhat closer to those of the realists than to those of the traditionalists —insofar as the two views diverge at all. But this situation should not obscure the fundamental reality of the Soviet political system, namely, that the end products of the Kremlin's policy-making process are more representative of consensus than division, of shared values rather than a struggle over differences.

Some of the differences between traditionalists and realists may seem so profound as to vitiate the above hypothesis. The debate over the inevitability of war would appear to be one such conflict, for disagreement over this issue has produced as contradictory a set of policy recommendations as any other doctrinal dispute.[39] Indeed, it would appear that the entire realist-traditionalist debate over the correlation of forces conforms to the contours of this disagreement. (This disagreement, of course, has been between those who believe war is inevitable and those who maintain that it need not be inevitable if the correlation of forces favors the Soviets and their allies.) One must ask, however, whether the dispute over the inevitability of war remains so central to the debates between realists and traditionalists that it is directly relevant to Kremlin policy making. The evidence in this study suggests that it is not. As we have seen, in certain cases the traditionalist analysis of the United States has proven so unrealistic in comparison with the realist analysis that it lacks the credibility to serve as a sound basis for policy. Where the realists recognize America's real strengths, such as its prodigious scientific and technological capacities, the traditionalists are led by their dogmatism to make statements that are mere wishful thinking: American capitalism is so decrepit that it fails to put the fruits of the scientific-technical revolution to optimum use. And where the realists discern growing American weakness in the various policy changes that acknowledge the new correlation of forces, the traditionalists continue to harp on the persistent threat of imperialist aggression. The realist analysis appears so credible, in fact, that many traditionalists have actually come to believe in the assessment that Stalin said was "not true" in his time—namely, that "powerful forces have come forward today in defense of peace and against world war" (thereby rendering obsolete the theory of the inevitability of war).[40] For example, as we have seen earlier, traditionalists like Khmara and Larionov have acknowledged the "invincibility" of the national liberation movement (as proved in Viet-

258

nam), the renunciation of automatic U.S. involvement in crisis situations, and the "reduced political and military possibilities" for the United States in the international arena due to the new correlation of forces.

In addition to reducing the primacy and relevance of the inevitability of war issue, the realist analysis of the new correlation of forces encourages the realists to pursue the very policies that they think responsible for changing the correlation of forces in the first place: increased military spending and the projection of Soviet power abroad. Their reading of the international situation encourages them to use detente as a means of advancing Soviet interests while lulling the United States into a false sense of security.* Finally, it allows them to support a set of domestic policies as repressive as the most paranoid and insecure traditionalist might advocate. This domestic stance costs the realists nothing, while proving their ideological fealty to any traditionalist doubter.

What we see, therefore, is the unifying dynamic of Soviet politics, reconciling disparate views in policies that conform to the basic tenets of the Marxist-Leninist ideology. We must emphasize that the views shared by the realists and traditionalists far outweigh their differences. Both believe that capitalism and imperialism are fundamentally evil. They have reached a consensus as to the nature of the economic means of American imperialism and its primary tactics, including exploitation, dependence relations, and blackmail. Both agree that the policies of force and the arms race are the basic inclinations of American military policy and that no matter how adverse the correlation of forces, American strategy seeks a way to retain force as an instrument of policy. There is little disagreement on the nature of American ideological strategy and none on the fundamental characteristics of American alliance policy. Indeed, as long as the NATO alliance exists, realists and traditionalists alike can only interpret it as an American-dominated community of anti-Soviet, imperialist interests. Both sides, in other words, espouse the same religion. The differences that remain concern the means rather than the ends of policy; they reveal themselves in varying

*As Brezhnev said at the 25th Party Congress, "We do not conceal the fact that we see detente as a way to create more favorable conditions for peaceful socialist and communist construction" (*Pravda,* 25 February 1976, p. 4).

assessments of American foreign and domestic capabilities and in the conflicting priorities that result from individual variations in the level of optimism and the appraisal of Soviet security. Even the few differences over apparently profound issues of dogma (such as the inevitability of war) do not preclude eventual cooperation in employing mutually acceptable and efficacious foreign policy means in the struggle against capitalism. Only in light of this unifying dynamic of common ideology and purpose can one fully understand how the Soviet realists may be quite amenable to a militaristic foreign policy; how the Soviet traditionalists will favor detente for the sake of imported technologies and the easing of those economic strains that weaken Soviet military potential; or, in other words, how the Soviet realists may be less "dovish" and the traditionalists less "hawkish" than the work of most analysts has led one to think.

Conclusion

I began this book by calling attention to two recent developments that have significant implications for contemporary international politics: the achievement by the Soviet Union of strategic parity with the United States and the tremendous growth of sophisticated Soviet analysis of American foreign policy and of international politics in general. Taken together, these developments raise the question of how the Soviets view the balance of power. The analysis of the new Soviet perceptions of U.S. foreign policy has not only answered this question but led us to new insights on a subject of considerable debate—the nature, ideas, and intentions of the Soviet leadership.

The plethora of recent Soviet analysis of the balance of power reveals a vigorous debate between two opposing schools of thought. On the one hand, the realist school, whose views dominate the new wave of sophisticated analysis, perceives a distinct shift in the "correlation of forces" between the two social systems. Realist commentators explain this change by pointing to the rise of Soviet military power and the growing weakness of the United States. The traditionalist school, on the other hand, is less sanguine about the shift in the correlation. While acknowledging a certain change in the balance of power, traditionalist analysts concentrate on themes that reveal an increased wariness of the United States and its "imperialist" policies. The caution implicit in their analyses suggests a disagreement with the conclusions reached by their realist comrades.

In studying the two schools' views of the domestic determinants of U.S. foreign policy, the subject, incidentally, upon which Morton Schwartz's study focuses, one's first impression may be considerably different. The disagreement between realists and traditionalists is· apparent enough, but the realists appear to be acknowledging American strengths while the traditionalists seem to emphasize weaknesses. For example, where the realists see American public opinion as having some genuine political influence, the traditionalists do not. The realist view implicitly acknowledges that the American government may have some of the popular support that derives from a public opinion that has some influence—a possibility that the traditionalists vehemently deny. Where the realists admit the considerable potential of the American economy and acknowledge its ability to recover from some of its recent dislocations, the traditionalists proclaim the "deepening of the crisis of capitalism" and insist that it is irreversible. Where the realists acknowledge U.S. ability to cultivate and harvest the fruits of the scientific-technical revolution, the traditionalists loudly protest that only a socialist system can achieve real progress in these fields. Indeed, such examples of Soviet analysis tempt one to conclude that the realists see the United States as just as strong as ever, while the traditionalists insist that the central capitalist power is inexorably disintegrating. But such a conclusion ignores several factors and thereby misreads some of these Soviet assessments.

It is important, first of all, to note one striking disagreement between Soviet realists and traditionalists as to the nature of the American ruling class. Whereas the traditionalists persist in their view that this class is a virtual monolith, uniformly malevolent in its militaristic and imperialistic policies, the realists discern a split between the American "realists" (those who recognize the new realities in the world, i.e., the new correlation of forces) and the "opponents of detente" (those members of the military-industrial complex with vested interests in continued international tension). In addition, the realists detect a related phenomenon in the "problem of political priorities"—the new "guns versus butter" debate that has further polarized the American ruling class. They interpret this debate not only as a sign of a new economic weakness, but also a symptom of the demoralization of a large segment of the ruling class. As such it is also a sign of ideological weakness, a sign that, in recognizing the failure of the capitalist path of development, parts of the ruling class have lost their confidence in the system.

Also ignored by the above conclusion is the Soviet view of American foreign policy itself. On this subject, the traditionalists persist in depicting the United States as a strong, crafty, and dangerous power, whereas the realists detect signs of American weakness in many U.S. policies.

Turning to the ideological means of American policy, the traditionalists see only a uniformly anticommunist and sinister attempt at "psychological warfare," whereas the realists interpret such American concepts as multipolarity and interdependence as signs of "realism." The realists argue that these concepts are a function of America's growing weakness and of its diminished role in the calculus of international relations.

As for the scientific-technical means of American policy, the traditionalists judge those Americans who advocate global "convergence" under the guidance of a technocratic elite to be just as dangerous as those who supported the concept of "technological warfare." The realists, contrarily, interpret the defeat of this latter school as a sign of the increased "realism" of American foreign policy—a sign, in other words, that parts of the American ruling class acknowledge the failure of the American path of development and recognize the need to accommodate such "new realities" as the growing power of the socialist system.

When analyzing American military means, Soviet traditionalists do acknowledge that a new correlation of forces and Soviet military assistance forced an American defeat in Vietnam, but they continue to stress that the United States is still wedded to policies of force and the arms race as the principal elements of its foreign policy. The realists, conversely, argue that the American ruling class, increasingly dominated by "realists," no longer sees militarism and the arms race as compatible with its class interests and recognizes the narrowing possibility that force can serve as a successful instrument of policy. Again, increased American "realism" is interpreted as evidence that the U.S. international position is weakening and that the ruling class increasingly realizes that fact.

The range of Soviet views on the broader diplomatic means of American policy reveals a similar pattern. Whereas the traditionalists see the policy of the status quo as proof of American imperialist aggression, the realists see it as a retreat from the expansionistic policy of force. Moreover, as they watch the United States switch from the direct methods of the policy of force to much more indirect methods, the realists again detect signs of an increase in American "realism"—a realization that neither the global nor the regional correlation of forces will permit the American bull to charge about the china shop.

As for American alliance policy, the traditionalists treat the continued existence of NATO as a vindication of their view that the United States remains aggressively anti-Soviet and imperialist. While not disputing the essentials of this assessment, the realists prefer to explore the more subtle components of U.S. alliance policy. As we have seen, they focus on the Nixon Doctrine's policy of "partnership" as another indicator of the decline in American strength: the United States is no longer either willing or able to shoulder the same responsibilities as in the past.

Soviet assessments of U.S. Third World policy reveal the same pattern. Soviet traditionalists judge America to be as imperialistic and exploitative as ever, but the realists focus on a turn from the use of direct and blatant tactics to a more subtle, covert, and indirect style of imperialism. These more indirect tactics are said to represent a decline of full American control over the processes and institutions used to pursue a full-fledged imperialist course. In addition, the realists note, American ruling circles gradually have come to recognize the failure of the "American path of development" in the Third World. The result, according to the realists, has been the reduction of American messianism and the onset of a demoralization—an ideological weakening—which is manifested in a diminished U.S. involvement in Third World affairs.

Our study of Soviet assessments of the full range of factors in American foreign policy thus shows how misleading it is to draw conclusions about Soviet perceptions from a study that is focused solely on their views of that policy's domestic determinants. In light of the broader, comprehensive set of Soviet views that we have considered, it is possible to conclude that although the realists do acknowledge various American strengths, it is they, not the traditionalists, who, on balance, make the case for the decline of American power.

The differences between traditionalists and realists and the credibility of their respective analyses prompt us to consider the nature of each group. The orthodox American interpretation of a Soviet "Left-Right" dichotomy would naturally lead one to identify traditionalists and realists in the same terms. As we have seen, however, a juxtaposition of recent Kremlin policies with the policy orientations of the realist and traditionalist schools reveals that the rift between them is not that great. The realists emerge as a group that favors detente, SALT, and East-West trade while exhibiting no real resistance to high military budgets or expanded foreign adventurism. In fact, their optimism, born of their conviction that the correlation of forces has changed and that the United States is retrenching as a result, appears to reinforce or even demand a more activist international policy. The credibility of its analysis would appear, furthermore, to be a function of Kremlin demands for precisely that kind of better intelligence that could be useful for the successful projection of Soviet power and influence abroad. The traditionalists, conversely, emerge as a group that is suspicious of detente, deterrence, and East-West trade. Wary of imperialist subversion, psychological warfare, and Soviet dependence on Western technology, the traditionalists ultimately depict a stronger, more threatening United States and a less auspicious correlation of forces. Traditionalist analysis reveals no loss of hostility towards the capitalist United States, but does suggest such caution as could prevent any reckless, offensive manifestation of that hostility. Impelled to some degree, no doubt, by bureaucratic imperatives (be they in the fields of ideological work, military preparedness, or the coordination of the international Communist movement), traditionalist commentators regularly sacrifice the credibility of their analyses to the requirements of propaganda. The different political functions of the realist and traditionalist analyses may explain, to some degree, the apparent sharpness of their differences.

There are two other factors that tend to diminish rather than accentuate the depth of the traditionalist-realist rift. One is the fact that disputes between Soviet factions almost never take the form of open debate in the Soviet press. The confrontations between opposed political opinions which one finds on an American newspaper's op-ed page are virtually nonexistent in the Soviet press. Similarly, Soviet scholars and journalists almost never refer directly to any of their colleagues when criticizing their positions, using instead the oblique reference to the errors of "some comrades." One can only conclude from this practice that the regime, which controls all the organs of information, demonstrates a continuing interest in maintaining a political environment that appears as free from controversy as possible. Since realists and traditionalists share responsibility for and play according to the rules of this control, the positions that they hold in common may have greater political significance than their differences.

The vast array of issues on which Soviet analysts agree is the second and far more important factor suggesting that the similarities between traditionalists and realists are more significant than their differences. To review, we have observed that realists and traditionalists agree: (1) on the nature of the fundamental reality of contemporary international relations—the struggle between the two social systems; (2) on almost all the elements essential to capitalism and imperialism; (3) on most of the elements that constitute the ideological means of American foreign policy; (4) on the nature of American foreign economic methods; (5) on American foreign policy's basic inclination to pursue the arms race and to use force as an instrument of policy; (6) on the anti-Soviet, imperialist nature of the NATO alliance; (7) on the nature of the ends and means of American alliance policy; (8) on the nature of American participation in and use of international organizations; (9) on the general ends and means of American policy toward the Third World; and even (10) on the notion that a favorable shift has occurred in the world correlation of forces. In short, both sides agree on the nature of the dialectical struggle and the basic ends and means of the forces of reaction. Both schools remain fundamentally Marxist-Leninist, and that fact, in the context of the struggle between the two social systems, overshadows all others. If one adds to this evidence those policy positions on which there is little or no evidence of clear disagreement (e.g., the proper level of military spending), the differences between realists and traditionalists no longer seem to constitute the factor of "critical importance" in any attempt to understand Soviet politics.

Despite the impressive degree of consensus, there remains one potentially crucial distinction between the two schools which demands consideration. The realists may be distinguished from the traditionalists precisely because their analysis appears less dogmatic, less colored by an ideology that insists that our era is characterized by the crisis of capitalism and its corollary, the violent, aggressive convulsions of imperialism. So great are their differences on particular issues—for example, capitalism's response to the scientific-technical revolution—that one can think that the realists have rejected orthodoxy and embraced pragmatism wholeheartedly. One is compelled to ask, therefore, if the realists are not in fact ideologues only in form and pragmatists in substance.

It is the thesis of this book that to treat ideology and pragmatism as mutually exclusive characteristics is to make an assumption that leads to a misinterpretation not only of the Soviet realists but of the Soviet system as a whole. One need only recall the Lenin-Bukharin dispute over the Treaty of Brest-Litovsk to see how groundless that assumption is. In this situation it was Lenin, the most orthodox Marxist-Leninist, who demonstrated the greater pragmatism in assessing the fledgling Soviet state's ability to prosecute revolution in Germany. Lenin simply followed his own basic principle, later stated succinctly in *"Left Wing" Communism,* that "tactics must be based on a sober and strictly objective estimation of all the class forces (in neighboring states, and in all states the world over) as well as of the experience of revolutionary movements." Having won the argument with Bukharin, Lenin demonstrated that his assessment was the most scientific and therefore the most correct ideologically. Bukharin (and even Trotsky) was subsequently accused of having been "non-Marxist" in his assessment: he had simply failed to apply the doctrine's principles properly. This example illustrates that in the Marxist-Leninist world view ideology and pragmatism, far from being mutually exclusive, are in fact complementary: ideology supplies purpose and direction to pragmatic tactics.

One can understand this relationship even more clearly if one examines the degree to which there exists a Soviet sense of mission and a concomitant sense of progress. If one defines a sense of mission as a purposefulness that extends beyond mere self-preservation, it seems that, given its long record of public statements and actions on issues beyond the perimeter of genuine defense interests, the USSR must have such a sense of mission. But it is not immediately clear whether it is a mission for state power, for communist power, or both.

A nation's sense of mission usually manifests itself at the time that the nation rises to international power and prestige. In the United States a feeling of "manifest destiny" emerged during the late nineteenth century as the expanding country sought new territory and even an overseas empire. The French proclaimed "la mission civilisatrice"; the British had their Empire; and the tsars had their concept of a Third Rome. The sense of mission has always been contingent upon the momentum and success of a nation's domestic and international policies. It develops when the leadership or enough of the population is convinced that its values are *good* and therefore deserve to be universalized. Clearly, the precise identification of these motivating values is essential to an understanding of any nation's sense of mission.

If the Soviet sense of mission is inspired by the desire to enhance the power of the Soviet state rather than by the impulse to spread communist "civilization," then one can argue that the Soviet leadership sees power as self-justifying, a "good" in and of itself. Indeed, a characteristic feature of the Soviet state and any other Communist regime is the maintenance of a monopoly of power by the Communist party whose members exclusively enjoy the perquisites of that power. The Soviets have found, however, that to maintain and extend this power they must prove that it is legitimate. Marxism-Leninism is regularly invoked to serve this purpose, justifying whatever configurations the regime may assume, from a "dictatorship of the proletariat" to a "state of the whole people." These justifications are always bolstered by the promise that the state will "wither away" once communism has triumphed throughout the world, that is, when the state is no longer needed for defense against imperialist aggression. This argument gives the Communist leadership a rationale for the continued, "legitimate" existence of the Soviet state.

In their attempt to legitimize the state's continued existence, then, the Soviets invoke a set of values upon which the "goodness" of communist power is predicated. One must remember, however, that these values are used to secure public approval for the continuation of the leadership's monopoly on power—the basic value or "good" that the party elite seeks to perpetuate and expand. Thus, even though they feel constrained to legitimize themselves by another set of values—those of Marxism-Leninism—it is conceivable that the Soviet leaders do not believe in these values and use them only as a cynical tool for self-preservation.

The question arises, however, as to what guides the Soviet leaders once their pursuit of power becomes a sense of mission and manifests itself on the international stage. They need some criterion in order to decide how to act in a particular situation, and that criterion cannot be mere cost-benefit analysis: to acquire power through the debilitation of any ally may result in the net accretion of power by an enemy. The Soviets must therefore have a criterion for distinguishing their allies from their enemies or, in other words, for identifying their legitimate friends. Given the value the Soviets place on proving their own legitimacy, it is not surprising that the test of which countries consider the Soviet regime legitimate is couched in the very terms according to which domestic legitimacy is established—the principles of Marxism-Leninism. Thus the Soviet mission, though seeking power for its own sake, is guided by the communist set of values, and the mere existence of this set of values becomes a value in itself—one that is crucial to the maintenance of Soviet power. Given this situation, it would not be surprising if the Soviets actually began to believe in these values, and perhaps they already do. We see, then, that an ideology used for purposes of rationalization must necessarily become a guide for action; in short, Soviet ideology and Soviet pragmatism are complementary rather than antagonistic.

Any consideration of the degree to which Soviet realists are committed to ideology must take into account the numerous other indexes of that commitment. Keeping in mind that the realists have a substantial, if not dominant say in Kremlin policy making, one should note that this same group actively demonstrates its fear of foreign ideology as a subversive threat by implementing travel restrictions, censorship of information, the jamming of radio broadcasts, and so on. The same group runs the country largely according to the collectivist principles mandated by Marxism-Leninism, duly criticizing and punishing any behavioral deviations. Finally, this group controls the immense Soviet propaganda apparatus, which has near total control over the domestic dissemination of information and ambitious designs for international influence. Soviet propaganda includes both an image of the world as the Kremlin would like it to be and images that, it is hoped, will lead others to act in a way that facilitates the realization of Soviet aims. Such propaganda thus represents the normative element of Soviet policy which is expressed by realists and traditionalists alike.

That this propaganda is normative and therefore a key index of ideological commitment may be confirmed not only by observation of its substance, but also by examining the words with which it works. As we have seen, a constant feature of the official Soviet lexicon is the use of words with double meanings—each has a face value appropriate for Western consumption and a special meaning for the Soviets themselves. Among such words are: "peaceful coexistence," "peace," "progress," "democracy," "realism," "security," "normalization," and so on—all of which have foreign policy significance. It may at first appear that these words conform to the practical imperatives of Soviet foreign policy, but to be entirely "practical," they would have to possess an "objective" meaning that they do not. Instead they have *normative* meanings that reflect the value system of Marxism-Leninism. This is the basis on which both realists and traditionalists distinguish between the forces of good and the forces of evil—their friends and their enemies in the international arena.

One final point should be made about the realists and their commitment to ideology. The realists are an integral part of a political system that coopts everyone except active dissidents into its ideological scheme. Though individuals may not be committed to this ideology, it is misleading to place one's emphasis on the degree of individual commitment. Communism exists as a *mass* phenomenon, a mass movement with a *social* rather than individualist character, even though the mass in question may comprise only a small minority of a population. In many ways communism resembles Thomas Kuhn's image of a coral reef, whose component thousands of tiny organisms, meaningless by themselves, find their strength and significance in unison. The very fact that a Communist "attaches" himself to others by participating in a Communist regime—for whatever reason or belief—is the essence of this social character of communism. This is not to say that whenever someone joins a ruling Communist party for reasons of opportunism or survival, he surrenders entirely his strength of individual spirit. It is clear that in Poland, for example, the social character of communism lacks the cohesion that makes strong collective beliefs and perceptions possible. Such a "loose" or "disjointed" quality is manifested everywhere in Polish society, particularly in the growing number of individual private enterprises and the free trade union movement. It is essential to note, however, that this lack of cohesion is accompanied by almost universal adherence to Catholicism, a religious phenomenon so strong that its outward expression serves as a political statement and challenge to the legitimacy of the regime. In the Soviet Union, however, with the exception of the vocal dissident movement, a collectivity of belief and perception effectively prevails. Even if individual scholars and journalists, for example, do not share these beliefs and perceptions, their individuality remains politically meaningless so long as it is not manifested outwardly. Indeed, such individuals support the existing reef because they cling, however half-heartedly, to the other organisms in their society. As a result, the only *operational* political beliefs and perceptions are those that are manifested openly—those being the beliefs and perceptions of the communist collective.

Thus, regardless of the particular nature of the Soviet sense of mission, and despite all individual beliefs and perceptions, the very existence of an avowed Communist regime involves the use of Marxist-Leninist ideology as a straitjacket for all political activity and expression. Ideology ceases to be merely a means; it begins to define the ends, thereby assuming an even greater signficance in the formulation and conduct of practical policy. In this way, ideology provides the criteria whereby priorities are set for the conduct of foreign policy.

As we have seen, ideology also serves as one of the key criteria in the measurement of the correlation of forces. The "forces" in question are measured according to their ideological position and its relationship to Marxism-Leninism as interpreted by the Soviets. This ideological measure gives the Soviets a basis on which to determine whether other "objective" forces pose a threat or not, allowing them to sort these forces into "fellow travelers," "useful idiots," true anticommunists, "opportunists," "revisionists," and so on.

From this perspective we can begin to see the link between Soviet ideology, the Soviet world view, and the perennial question of Soviet foreign policy—*"Chto delat'?"*—"What is to be done?" How, in other words, is Soviet foreign policy to proceed, given the ideological guide of Marxism-Leninism? The answer, as the historical record suggests, has often been the subject of fierce debate among the members of the Soviet ruling elite. The final policy choice is clearly subject to human judgment and error for Marxism-Leninism is not so "scientific" that it can measure social phenomena as accurately as the physical sciences measure physical phenomena. The "objective" forces, evidently, can be easily measured: the size and power of military forces, the strength of economies, and even the efficiency of political decision-making processes. It is conflicting judgments of ideological commitment, however, which constitute the basis of many of the policy debates among factions in the Kremlin. And it is this criterion which, *ceteris paribus,* will tip the balance to decide whether to take advantage of a situation in the context of the "struggle for opportunities," to maintain the status quo, or retreat.

One often hears the cliché that: "the only thing the Soviets understand is force." The statement is correct as far as it goes, but force is not the only thing the Soviets understand. They also understand who wields that force, and more specifically, what that person believes, how strongly he believes in it, and therefore, how much he values his beliefs. It is the value placed on one's convictions which constitutes the "force" behind the critical ideological element in any measurement of the correlation of forces; it represents the *will* to use force when necessary to defend one's values. As we have seen, the Soviet realists have demonstrated their understanding of this factor, applying their ideological yardstick effectively and realistically in assessing the strength of conviction of different groups of Americans.

Still, one may argue that, at least among some of the Soviet realists, the spirit underlying their support for "peaceful coexistence" is not fully Marxist-Leninist, for it is a spirit that can admit the possibility of American goodwill, that will ritually invoke Marxist-Leninist dogmas to avoid domestic upheaval but not to serve the purposes of global messianism; in other words, a spirit that is content to perpetuate the international status quo for the sake of peace. Furthermore, one may cite the realists' belief in nuclear deterrence as evidence that they do not really share the kind of Marxist-Leninist militancy that could provoke war. Such assumptions are very persuasive, for they derive, to a large extent, from the notion that there is a universal appreciation of an international code of behavior and of a desire to do things peacefully. This notion is closely related to the Western concept of Natural Law (which C. S. Lewis has called alternatively the Law of Human Nature, the Rule of

Decent Behavior, and Moral Law), that is, the "law" that makes humans distinguish between Right and Wrong and provides the basis on which they judge the comparative "goodness" of the moralities of different societies, cultures, and historical periods. This assumption causes many Americans to think that the Soviet leadership shares the concept of Decent Behavior, and that at least some of its members can therefore be persuaded to chart a path that leads to the political realization of this shared morality. It is important to note, however, that this view, and the concomitant interpretation of the significance of the Soviet realists' acceptance of deterrence, implicitly assumes that orthodox Marxism-Leninism always demands a dangerous form of messianic militancy, and that any Communist who behaves peaceably is somehow unorthodox. One need only glance at the history of Soviet foreign policy to see how mistaken this assumption is. For example, when Lenin wanted peace with Germany, or when he decided to import Western technology and management expertise, his policies could not have been more peaceable. Even when Soviet policy has exhibited an expansionist bent, it has invariably adopted a cautious, low-risk strategy designed to avoid provoking a counterattack that would endanger the Soviet state. The most orthodox Marxist-Leninists, then, have demonstrated and continue to demonstrate an abiding interest in achieving their goals as peacefully as possible: they do not want to fight for something if they can get it without fighting. But such peaceful inclinations by no means signify that they are unorthodox, that they could be content to accept the international status quo.

Similarly, it is incorrect to insist that Soviet participation in SALT negotiations represents a relaxation of ideological rigidity. Even the most orthodox communist stance has never precluded the use of negotiations as a tactic to attain "positive changes." The fact that the Soviets have made tactical compromises in the course of negotiations does not mean that they have ever compromised their morality, their goals, or even their general strategy. Indeed, such compromises are part of their general strategy, for they can mislead an adversary by hinting that the Soviets are willing to compromise their ideologically determined objectives.

In conclusion, there is simply no real evidence that Soviet ruling circles harbor a spirit so heretical as to facilitate genuine accommo-

273

dation with the capitalist West. Even if such a heresy does exist, it is still hidden, and thus can have no real political effect. The Soviet political system simply cannot tolerate any real moral relativism, yet the American hope that there is a hidden spirit of accommodation is predicated on the possibility that forces whose power depends upon moral absolutism will come to countenance such relativism. The necessary link between ideology and practical self-interest in Soviet politics renders such an outcome impossible. This link is the cement of the basic orthodoxy of the Soviet political mentality, both realist and traditionalist—an orthodoxy that no amount of wishful thinking can mitigate. A mentality like the Soviet perceives that it cannot (1) accomplish the goals dictated by its ideology or even (2) maintain its own self-interest (i.e., remain in power) if it permits any deviation in thinking or behavior. If the Soviets were concerned exclusively with the attainment of goals dictated by Marxism-Leninism, we would be dealing with messianic ideologues; if they sought only to maintain their own self-interest, we would confront collective insecurity—a lack of confidence in their legitimacy in the eyes of their own people. But since any concern with political legitimacy depends on the values by which legitimacy is assessed, the second concern must involve the first. In the Soviet case, then, political absolutism is necessarily linked to, and dependent on, absolutism in the realm of values. The system does not admit the possibility of moral or political pluralism. As a result, the hope (shared by many in the West) that there is a universal morality that can be realized politically is obviated by the fact that a different morality, Marxism-Leninism, operates in Soviet politics. This morality, which operates whether the Soviets believe in it or not, has entirely different criteria for discriminating betwen good and evil. It questions the legitimacy of the American "regime" just as Western morality questions the legitimacy of the Soviet regime. And just as Western morality can justify the use of force for certain purposes, so can communist morality. Thus, when the two moralities conflict at precisely the threshold where both sides can justify the use of force, violent confrontation may well occur. The apparently shared value of doing things peacefully is therefore not necessarily shared at all—not at the critical point where the opposed moralities conflict. This value can be made mutual only if those who are not absolutist exhibit tolerance of radically different value systems, or if those who would approach the threshold of conflict too aggressively prove willing to retreat.

Our analysis of Soviet commentary on U.S. foreign policy ultimately leads to the conclusion that there is a substantial harmony of interests between the realists and the traditionalists in the Soviet Union, that this harmony is based on the elemental common goals of self-preservation and legitimacy, and that these goals are achieved by means of a common adherence to the Marxist-Leninist ideology. As we have seen, significant differences do exist between these two groups, but they should not be permitted to obscure the more significant reality: the community of interests is the political fact of "critical importance" in understanding the nature of the Soviet system and its relations with other nations. Once this fact is clear, one can appreciate how well the Soviet foreign policy process takes into account the assessments, ambitions, and fears of both ends of the Soviet political spectrum, and how this policy is formed not so much by competition between two polarized factions as by consensus within a single ruling coalition.

Notes

Introduction

1. William Zimmerman, *Soviet Perspectives on International Relations* (Princeton: Princeton University Press, 1969), pp. 3 ff.

2. Ibid., p. 205.

3. Andrei Gromyko, "Programma mira v deistvii" [The peace program in action], *Kommunist,* September 1975, p. 5.

4. G. Arbatov, "Sobytie vazhnogo mezhdunarodnogo znacheniia" [An event of important international significance], *SShA: ekonomika, politika, ideologiia* [hereafter *SShA*], August 1972, p. 9.

5. Leonid Brezhnev, Report to the 25th CPSU Congress, *Pravda,* 25 February 1976, p. 4.

6. Stephen Gibert et al., *Soviet Images of America* (New York: Crane Russak, 1977).

7. Ibid., pp. 47, 48.

8. Ibid., p. 9.

9. Morton Schwartz, "Review of Gibert et al., *Soviet Images of America,*" *Slavic Review,* vol. 37 (September 1978): 503.

10. Morton Schwartz, *Soviet Perceptions of the United States* (A study prepared for the Office of External Research, Bureau of Intelligence and Research, U.S. Department of State, 1975), pp. 145-49. This study has been published in book form under the same title: (Berkeley: University of California Press, 1978).

11. Ibid, pp. 149-51.

12. For an interpretation of the two sides of this debate from a historical viewpoint, see Adam B. Ulam, *Expansion and Coexistence* 2d ed. (New York: Praeger, 1974), pp. 726 ff.

13. See Merle Fainsod, *Smolensk Under Soviet Rule* (Cambridge: Harvard University Press, 1958).

Chapter. 1.   *The Struggle between the Two Social Systems*

1. Two basic books on Marxism-Leninism are: O. V. Kuusinen, ed., *The Fundamentals of Marxism-Leninism* (Moscow: Foreign Languages Publishing House, 1963), and *ABC of Dialectical and Historical Materialism* (Moscow: Progress Publishers [hereafter, Progress], 1976). Among the best Western explanations of this theory is R. N. Carew Hunt, *The Theory and Practice of Communism* (New York: Macmillan, 1954).

2. Karl Marx, "Theses on Feuerbach," in Robert C. Tucker, ed. *The Marx-Engels Reader,* 1st ed. (New York: Norton, 1972), p. 108.

3. *ABC,* pp. 187, 188.

4. Ibid., p. 186.

5. Marx, "Theses on Feuerbach," in Tucker, *Marx-Engels Reader,* pp. 107, 109.

6. Hunt, *Theory and Practice of Communism,* pp. 33, 34.

7. *ABC,* p. 134.

8. Ibid., p. 150.

9. See Y. Krasin, *Lenin, Revolution and the World Today* (Moscow: Progress, 1971), pp. 190, 191.

10. G. Arbatov, *The War of Ideas in Contemporary International Relations* (Moscow: Progress, 1973), p. 33.

11. Ibid. p. 34.

12. Ibid. p. 9.

13. Ibid. p. 32.

14. For several perspectives on the role of the masses in world affairs see G. Morozov et al., eds., *Obshchestvennost' i problemy voiny i mira* [The public and problems of war and peace] (Moscow: Mezhdunarodnye otnosheniia izd., 1976).

15. Arbatov, *War of Ideas,* p. 27 ff.

16. Ibid., p. 52.

17. Ibid., p. 50.

18. Ibid., pp. 30, 32.

19. Ibid., p. 13.

20. Ibid., p. 19.

21. Robert Strausz-Hupé, *The Zone of Indifference* (New York: G. P. Putnam's Sons, 1952), p. 125.

22. See, in this connection, Eric Hoffer, *The True Believer* (New York: Harper & Row, 1951), for an excellent analysis of the psychology of mass movements.

23. Arbatov, *War of Ideas,* p. 13.

24. See G. Arbatov, "Sobytie vazhnogo mezhdunarodnogo znacheni-

Notes

ia" [An event of important international significance], *SShA,* August 1972, p. 7.

25. F. Konstantinov, "Mirnoe sosushchestvovanie i ideologicheskaia bor'ba" [Peaceful coexistence and the ideological struggle], *Izvestiia,* 29 September 1973, p. 5.

26. I. Sidelnikov, "Mirnoe sosushchestvovanie i bezopasnost' narodov" [Peaceful coexistence and the security of the peoples], *Krasnaia zvezda,* 14 August 1973, pp. 2, 3.

27. *Znamenosets,* 23 January 1974, pp. 26, 27 (translated in U.S. Foreign Broadcast Information Service *Daily Report: Soviet Union* [hereafter, FBIS], 20 March 1974, p. Al).

28. M. Mitin, "Uchenie, preobrazuiushchee mir" [The doctrine that is transforming the world], *Izvestiia,* 20 April 1974, pp. 4, 5.

29. V. Matveyev (Matveev), "Pobeda spravedlivogo dela V'etnama" [The triumph of the just cause of Vietnam], *Izvestiia,* 31 January 1973, p. 2.

30. G. Arbatov, "Tupiki politiki sily" [The dead-ends of the policy of force], *Problemy mira i sotsializma,* February 1974, p. 42.

31. Ibid.

32. Konstantinov, "Mirnoe sosushchestvovanie."

33. L. Leont'ev, "Amerikanskii imperializm v meniaiushchemsia mire" [American imperialism in a changing world], *SShA,* April 1971, p. 6.

34. Ibid., p. 7.

35. Arbatov, "Sobytie," p. 7.

36. Quoted by G. Arbatov, "Sovetsko-amerikanskie otnosheniia na novom etape" [Soviet-American relations at a new stage], *Pravda,* 22 July 1973, pp. 4, 5.

37. Arbatov, "Sobytie," p. 11.

38. M. Mitin, "Mezhdunarodnye otnosheniia i ideologicheskaia bor'-ba" [International relations and the ideological struggle], *Krasnaia zvezda,* 22 November 1973, p. 2.

39. Arbatov, "Sobytie," p. 11.

40. Mitin, "Mezhdunarodnye otnosheniia."

41. G. Arbatov, "Vneshniaia politika SShA i nauchno-tekhnicheskaia revoliutsiia" [U.S. foreign policy and the scientific-technical revolution], *SShA,* November 1973 (article no. 2), p. 10.

42. Ibid., pp. 10, 11.

43. Mitin, "Mezhdunarodnye otnosheniia."

44. G. Trofimenko, "SSSR-SShA: mirnoe sosushchestvovanie kak norma vzaimootnoshenii" [USSR-USA: peaceful coexistence as the norm of mutual relations], *SShA,* February 1974, p. 14.

45. V. Sobakin, "Kollektivnaia bezopasnost': istoricheskii opyt i

sovremennost' " [Collective security: historical experience and modern times], *Kommunist,* March 1974, p. 91.

46. S. Mokshin, "Vzaimodeistvie kul'tur i bor'ba idei" [The inter-action of cultures and the struggle of ideas], *Pravda,* 5 September 1973, pp. 4, 5.

47. G. Arbatov, interviewed by Giuseppe Boffa in *L'Unita,* 10 May 1974, p. 3, "How Is It Possible to Cooperate?" (translated in *FBIS,* 29 May 1974, p. B2), and Arbatov, "Vneshniaia politika SShA" (article no. 2), p. 10.

48. Arbatov interview in *L'Unita.*

49. Konstantinov, "Mirnoe sosushchestvovanie."

50. D. Gvishiani, "Nauchno-tekhnicheskaia revoliutsiia i sotsial'nyi progress" [The scientific-technical revolution and social progress], *Pravda,* 2 March 1974, pp. 3, 4.

51. Ibid.

52. Ibid.

53. D. Yermolenko (Ermolenko), "Nauchno-tekhnicheskaia revo-liutsiia i manevry burzhuaznoi ideologii" [The scientific-technical revo-lution and the maneuvers of bourgeois ideology], *Pravda,* 6 June 1973, p. 4.

54. Ibid.

55. Quoted by Arbatov, "Vneshniaia politika SShA" (article no. 2), p. 11.

56. Gvishiani, "Nauchno-tekhnicheskaia revoliutsiia."

57. Krasin, *Lenin, Revolution,* p. 191.

58. Ibid., p. 195.

59. Mitin, "Uchenie, preobrazuiushchee mir."

60. S. Alexandrov and V. Yegorov (Aleksandrov and Egorov), "Leninizm i mirovoi revoliutsionnyi protsess" [Leninism and the world revolutionary process], *Krasnaia zvezda,* 21 April 1974, p. 3.

61. Ibid., p. 2.

62. Ibid., p. 3.

63. Ibid., p. 2.

64. Krasin, *Lenin, Revolution,* p. 203.

65. Alexandrov and Yegorov, "Leninizm."

66. Ibid.

67. G. Shakhnazarov, "K probleme sootnosheniia sil v mire"[On the problem of the correlation of forces in the world], *Kommunist,* Febru-ary 1974, p. 86.

68. Anatoly Gromyko and A. Kokoshin, "Vneshnepoliticheskaia stra-tegiia SShA na 70-e gody" [U.S. foreign policy strategy in the 70s], *Mezhdunarodnaia zhizn,* September 1973, p. 87.

69. Ibid., p. 88.

70. Yermolenko, "Nauchno-tekhnicheskaia revoliutsiia."

71. Sobakin, "Kollektivnaia bezopasnost'," p. 89.

72. Arbatov, "Sobytie."

73. Arbatov, "Tupiki politiki sily," p. 42.

74. Mitin, "Mezhdunarodnye otnosheniia."

75. Comments by V. Lukin in " 'Doktrina Niksona': deklaratsii i real'nost' " [The "Nixon Doctrine": declarations and reality], *SShA,* February 1971, pp. 26, 27.

76. Comments by Iu. Davydov in ibid., p. 21.

77. Ibid.

78. Arbatov, "Vneshniaia politika SShA" (article no. 2), p. 4.

79. Arbatov, "Tupiki politiki sily," p. 42.

80. Matveyev, "Pobeda."

81. Arbatov, "Tupiki politiki sily," p. 45.

82. See William Zimmerman, *Soviet Perspectives on International Relations* (Princeton: Princeton University Press, 1969), chap. 5.

83. Ibid., pp. 172-174, 202. See also Herbert S. Dinerstein, *War and the Soviet Union* (New York: Praeger, 1959).

84. G. Arbatov, " 'Politicheskii god' i problema politicheskikh prioritetov" [The "political year" and the problem of political priorities], *SShA,* June 1972, p. 5.

85. A text of this document is in the appendix of Vladimir Petrov, *U.S.–Soviet Detente: Past and Future* (Washington, D.C.: American Enterprise Institute, 1975), pp. 57 ff.

86. Arbatov, "Sobytie."

87. Gromyko and Kokoshin, "Vneshnepoliticheskaia strategiia," p. 91.

88. Arbatov, *War of Ideas,* pp. 35, 36.

Chapter 2. *Domestic Determinants of U.S. Foreign Policy*

1. Anatoly Gromyko, "Dilemmy amerikanskoi diplomatii" [The dilemmas of American diplomacy], *SShA,* June 1970, p. 14.

2. Anatoly Gromyko, "Sovremennye tendentsii vneshnei politiki SShA" [Contemporary tendencies of U.S. foreign policy], *SShA,* April 1972, pp. 40, 41.

3. Anatoly Gromyko and A. Kokoshin, "Vneshnepoliticheskaia strategiia SShA na 70-e gody" [U.S. foreign policy strategy in the 70s], *Mezhdunarodnaia zhizn,* September 1973, p. 89.

4. Ibid.

5. N. Inozemtsev, *Contemporary Capitalism: New Developments and Contradictions* (Moscow: Progress, 1974), p. 77.

6. Ibid., p. 73.

7. V. Larionov, "Transformatsiia kontseptsii 'strategicheskoi dostatochnosti'" [The transformation of the concept of "strategic sufficiency], *SShA*, November 1971, p. 31.

8. M. Sturua, "Zloveshchii Kompleks" [The sinister complex], *Izvestiia*, 24 June 1969, p. 5.

9. Larionov, "Tranformatsiia kontseptsii," p. 31.

10. L. Semeiko, "Pruzhiny i rychagi voenno-promyshlennogo kompleksa" [The springs and levers of the military-industrial complex], *Krasnaia zvezda*, 24 June 1969, p. 3.

11. Ibid.

12. Gromyko and Kokoshin, "Vneshnepoliticheskaia strategiia," p. 89.

13. V. Kudriavtsev, "Mezhdunarodnoe obozrenia" [International review], *Izvestiia*, 1 March 1970, p. 2.

14. T. Kolesnichenko, "Pered golosovaniem" [Before the voting], *Pravda*, 3 November 1972, p. 5.

15. E. Shershnev, "Sovetsko-amerikanskaia torgovlia: problemy i vozmozhnosti" [Soviet-American trade: problems and possibilities], *SShA*, April 1972, p. 4.

16. V. Matveyev, "Perspektivy sovetsko-amerikanskikh otnoshenii" [Prospects of Soviet-American relations], *SShA*, May 1972, pp. 5, 6.

17. Comments by Iu. Shvedkov in " 'Doktrina Niksona': deklaratsii i real'nost' " [The 'Nixon Doctrine': declarations and reality], *SShA*, February 1971, p. 45.

18. Comments by Arbatov in ibid., p. 46.

19. G. Trofimenko "Politicheskii realizm i strategiia 'realisticheskogo sderzhivaniia' " [Political realism and the strategy of "realistic deterrence"], *SShA*, December 1971, p. 7.

20. G. Trofimenko, "Ot politiki konfrontatsii k politike sosushchestvovaniia" [From a policy of confrontation to a policy of coexistence], *Mezhdunarodnaia zhizn*, September 1975, p. 43.

21. A. Krivopalov, "Poteri Pentagona" [The losses of the Pentagon], *Izvestiia*, 22 November 1975, p. 3.

22. S. Kondrashov, "Pered vyborami" [Before the elections], *Izvestiia*, 26 October 1972, p. 4.

23. See G. Arbatov, *The War of Ideas in Contemporary International Relations* (Moscow: Progress, 1973).

24. G. Arbatov, " 'Politicheskii god' i problema politicheskikh prioritetov" [The "political year" and the problem of political priorities], *SShA*, June 1972, p. 3.

25. Ibid.

26. Ibid.

27. Gromyko, "Sovremennye tendentsii," p. 40.

28. T. Kolesnichenko and V. Nekrasov, "SShA: ekonomika i vybory" [The USA: the economy and the elections], *Pravda*, 2 March 1972, p. 4.

29. Arbatov, " 'Politicheskii god,' " p. 3.

30. G. Gevorgian, "The Lackeys of Capital," *Trud*, 27 June 1969, p. 3, translated in *FBIS*, 8 July 1969, pp. A43, A44.

31. Iu. Zhukov, "Novyi amerikanskii militarizm" [The new American militarism], *Pravda*, 13 July 1969, p. 4.

32. V. Sisnev, "The Battle for the Votes, *Trud*, 21 October 1976, p. 5, translated in *FBIS*, 27 October 1976, p. B9.

33. Ibid.

34. Ibid., p. B7.

35. Arbatov, " 'Politicheskii god,' " p. 3.

36. Ibid., p. 4.

37. A. Krivopalov, "Sluzhit' tseliam mira" [To serve the goals of peace], *Izvestiia*, 19 September 1976, p. 1.

38. Ibid.

39. Ibid.

40. Iu. Shvedkov, "The Nixon Doctrine and the Domestic Political Situation in the USA," in Yu. (Iu.) Davydov, V. Zhurkin, and V. Rudnev, eds., *The Nixon Doctrine* (Arlington, Va.: Joint Publications Research Service [hereafter JPRS], 1973), p. 30.

41. Inozemtsev, *Contemporary Capitalism*, p. 88.

42. See, for example, N. Inozemtsev, "Sovremennye SShA i sovetskaia amerikanistika" [The contemporary USA and Soviet studies of America], *SShA*, January 1970, p. 12.

43. Iu. Shvedkov, ed., *SShA: vneshnepoliticheskii mekhanizm* [The USA: the foreign policy mechanism] (Moscow: Nauka, 1972). See, for example, pp. 22, 23.

44. Inozemtsev, *Contemporary Capitalism*, p. 88.

45. B. Ponomarev et al., "Uchenie i delo V. I. Lenina—bessmertny" [The doctrine and the cause of V. I. Lenin are immortal], *Izvestiia*, 19 January 1974, p. 2.

46. See, for example, Inozemtsev, *Contemporary Capitalism*, pp. 147 ff.

47. T. Timofeyev (Timofeev), "O nekotorykh tendentsiiakh rabochego dvizheniia na sovremennom etape obshchego krizisa kapitalizma" [On some tendencies of the workers movement at the current stage of the general crisis of capitalism], *Rabochii klass i sovremennyi mir*, September–October 1975, p. 34.

48. Afanasyev et al., *The Political Economy of Capitalism* (Moscow: Progress, 1974), p. 55.

49. Karl Marx, *Wage Labour and Capital*, in Robert C. Tucker, ed., *The Marx-Engels Reader*, 1st ed. (New York: Norton, 1972), p. 178.

50. Ibid., pp. 189-90.

51. Karl Marx and Friedrich Engels, *Manifesto of the Communist Party*, in ibid., p. 340.

52. See, for example, Inozemtsev, *Contemporary Capitalism*, pp. 83, 84.

53. See, for example, O. S. Bogdanov, *Valiutnaia sistema sovremennogo kapitalizma—osnovnye tendentsii i protivorechiia* [The monetary system of contemporary capitalism—basic tendencies and contradictions] (Moscow: Mysl', 1976).

54. See A. Yefremov (Efremov), "Obshchestvo lishennoe budushchego" [The society devoid of a future], *Pravda*, 15 July 1976, p. 4.

55. N. Inozemtsev, "O kharaktere protivorechii v nashu epokhu" [On the character of contradictions in our epoch], *Problemy mira i sotsializma*, September 1973, p. 36.

56. Inozemtsev, *Contemporary Capitalism*, p. 137.

57. Ibid., p. 39.

58. Afanasyev et al., *Political Economy of Capitalism*, pp. 288, 289.

59. Ibid., p. 222.

60. Inozemtsev, *Contemporary Capitalism*, p. 40.

61. Ibid.

62. F. Konstantinov, "Mirnoe sosushchestvovanie i ideologicheskaia bor'ba" [Peaceful coexistence and the ideological struggle], *Izvestiia*, 29 September 1973, p. 5.

63. Inozemtsev, *Contemporary Capitalism*, p. 146.

64. Ibid., pp. 46, 47.

65. D. Yermolenko, "Nauchno-tekhnicheskaia revoliutsiia i manevry burzhuaznoi ideologii" [The scientific-technical revolution and the maneuvers of bourgeois ideology], *Pravda*, 6 June 1973, p. 4.

66. Inozemtsev, *Contemporary Capitalism*, p. 59.

67. G. Arbatov, "Vneshniaia politika SShA i nauchno-tekhnicheskaia revoliutsiia" [U.S. foreign policy and the scientific-technical revolution], *SShA*, November 1973 (article no. 2), p. 12.

68. Inozemtsev, *Contemporary Capitalism*, p. 40.

69. See Inozemtsev, "O kharaktere," p. 38.

70. Inozemtsev, *Contemporary Capitalism*, p. 55.

71. Quoted by A. Migolat'ev in "Sovremennyi militarizm i ego advokaty" [Contemporary militarism and its advocates], *Krasnaia zvezda*, 18 September 1970, p. 2.

Notes

72. Ibid.

73. Comments by Iu. Bobrakov in "Militarizm i ekonomika" [Militarism and economics], *SShA*, December 1971, p. 29.

74. Marx and Engels, *Works,* vol. 20, p. 175, as quoted by G. Arbatov in "Vneshniaia politika SShA i nauchno-tekhnicheskaia revoliutsiia" [U.S. foreign policy and the scientific-technical revolution], *SShA,* October 1973 (article no. 1), p. 10.

75. Ibid.

76. Ibid.

77. Comments by Iu. Katasonov in "Militarizm i ekonomika," p. 27.

78. Inozemtsev, *Contemporary Capitalism,* p. 86.

79. Comments by Katasonov in "Militarizm i ekonomika," p. 27.

80. Arbatov, " 'Politicheskii god,' " p. 12.

81. Ibid.

82. Ibid., p. 13.

83. See William Zimmerman, *Soviet Perspectives on International Relations* (Princeton: Princeton University Press, 1969), pp. 195, 222-225; and Zbigniew Brzezinski, *Ideology and Power in Soviet Politics* (New York: Praeger, 1962), p. 105.

84. Zimmerman, *Soviet Perspectives,* pp. 222-225.

85. Ibid., p. 236.

86. Ibid., p. 241.

87. Ibid., pp. 194-96.

88. Inozemtsev, *Contemporary Capitalism,* p. 87.

89. Afanasyev et al., *Political Economy of Capitalism,* p. 208.

90. Inozemtsev, *Contemporary Capitalism,* p. 88.

91. Ibid.

92. Ibid., p. 87.

93. Ibid., p. 88.

94. Ibid.

95. Ibid., p. 90.

96. A. Grigoriants, "Taktika monopolii" [The tactics of the monopolies], *Izvestiia,* 15 January 1974, p. 3.

97. Ibid.

98. T. Kolesnichenko, "Mezhdunarodnaia nedelia" [The international week], *Pravda,* 17 March 1974, p. 4.

99. N. Kurdiumov, "SShA: simptomy moral'nogo krizisa" [The USA: symptoms of a moral crisis], *Pravda,* 19 October 1976, p. 4.

100. Ibid.

101. Yefremov, "Obshchestvo lishennoe budushchego."

102. B. Ponomarev, "Speech on Lenin Anniversary," *FBIS,* 23 April 1974, p. R22.

103. G. Arbatov, interviewed by Giuseppe Boffa in *L'Unita,* 10

May 1974, p. 3, translated in *FBIS,* "How Is It Possible to Cooperate?" 29 May 1974, p. B2.

104. A. Bovin, "Sumerki kapitalizma" [The twilight of capitalism], *Krasnaia zvezda,* 29 October 1974, p. 3.

105. Comments made by Inozemtsev while visiting the West, and quoted in David Lascelles, "Soviet Expert Predicts Economic Growth in West," *Financial Times,* 3 November 1976, p. 4.

106. Ibid.

107. Zimmerman, *Soviet Perspectives,* pp. 220, 228, 229.

108. Inozemtsev, *Contemporary Capitalism,* p. 90.

Chapter 3. *General Ends and Means of U.S. Foreign Policy*

1. Anatoly Gromyko, "Sovremennye tendentsii vneshnei politiki SShA" [Contemporary tendencies of U.S. foreign policy], *SShA,* April 1972, p. 40.

2. Ibid., p. 41.

3. G. Arbatov, " 'Politicheskii god' i problema politicheskikh prioritetov" [The 'political year' and the problem of political priorities], *SShA,* June 1972, p. 14.

4. G. Arbatov, "Amerikanskii imperializm i novye real'nosti mira" [American imperialism and the new realities of the world], *Pravda,* 4 May 1971, p. 4.

5. Arbatov, " 'Politicheskii god,' " p. 15.

6. Arbatov, "Amerikanskii imperializm."

7. Arbatov, " 'Politicheskii god,' " p. 14.

8. B. Shabad, "American Doctrines of Power Politics," in *Problems of War and Peace* (Moscow: Progress, 1972), p. 193.

9. Ibid., p. 196.

10. Ibid., p. 193.

11. Ibid., p. 198.

12. V. Krivokhizha, "Poniatie 'natsional'nyi interes' v amerikanskikh vneshnepoliticheskikh issledovaniiakh" [The concept of the "national interest" in American foreign policy research], *SShA,* November 1974, p. 121.

13. Ibid., p. 122.

14. Ibid., p. 121.

15. Robert Osgood et al., *America and the World* (Baltimore: The Johns Hopkins University Press, 1970), p. 1.

16. Shabad, "American Doctrines of Power Politics," p. 205.

17. B. Shabad, "Ideologiia militarizma i agressii" [The ideology of militarism and aggression], *Kommunist,* October 1969, p. 111.

18. Ibid.

19. Shabad, "American Doctrines of Power Politics," p. 205.

20. Ibid., pp. 195, 196.

21. Shabad, "Ideologiia militarizma i agressii," p. 111.

22. Ibid., p. 113.

23. Ibid., pp. 195, 196.

24. A. Migolat'ev, "Sovremennyi militarizm i ego advokaty" [Contemporary militarism and its advocates], *Krasnaia zvezda,* 18 September 1970, p. 2.

25. Shabad, "Ideologiia militarizma i agressii," p. 111.

26. Ibid., p. 113.

27. Ibid., p. 114.

28. Ibid.

29. Migolat'ev, "Sovremennyi militarizm."

30. Ibid.

31. G. Trofimenko, "Uroki V'etnama" [The lessons of Vietnam], *SShA* June 1975, p. 77.

32. Ibid. pp. 77-78.

33. V. Matveyev, "Perspektivy sovetsko-amerikanskikh otnoshenii" [Prospects of Soviet-American relations], *SShA,* May 1972, p. 5.

34. Arbatov, " 'Politicheskii god,' " p. 14.

35. Gromyko, "Sovremennye tendentsii," p. 42.

36. A. Baryshev, "Novye doktriny—starye tseli amerikanskoi politiki" [The new doctrines are the old aims of American policy], *Mezhdunarodnaia zhizn,* December 1969, p. 19.

37. Anatoly Gromyko, "Amerikanskii 'tiazheloves' na evropeiskoi arene" [The American "heavyweight" in the European arena], *Mezhdunarodnaia zhizn,* January 1971, p. 29.

38. Ibid., p. 30.

39. L. Leont'ev, "Amerikanskii imperializm v meniaiushchemsia mire" [American imperialism in a changing world], *SShA,* April 1971, p. 9.

40. G. Trofimenko, "Politicheskii realizm i strategiia 'realisticheskogo sderzhivaniia' " [Political realism and the strategy of "realistic deterrence"], *SShA,* December 1971, pp. 5, 6.

41. Gromyko, "Sovremennye tendentsii," p. 43.

42. Arbatov, " 'Politicheskii god,' " pp. 5, 6.

43. A. Sergiev, "Burzhuaznye teorii 'vzaimozavisimosti' na sluzhbe neokolonializma" [Bourgeois theories of "interdependence" in the service of neocolonialism], *Mezhdunarodnaia zhizn,* October 1976, pp. 115, 116.

44. See also A. Kokoshin, " 'Vzaimozavisimost': real'nosti, kontseptsii i politika" ["Interdependence": realities, concepts, and policy], *SShA,* January 1977.

45. Iu. Nalin, "Povorot k razriadke i zaboty ideologicheskikh diversiantov" [The turn toward detente and the concerns of the ideological saboteurs], *Za rubezhom*, 20 September 1974, p. 11.

46. "Mezhdunarodnye otnosheniia i ideologicheskaia bor'ba" [International relations and the ideological struggle], *Kommunist*, September 1973, p. 14.

47. Ibid., p. 16.

48. Ibid., p. 13.

49. Ibid., p. 15.

50. O. Reinhold and F. Ryzhenko, eds., *Contemporary Anti-communism: Policy and Ideology* (Moscow: Progress, 1976), pp. 98, 99. Although the collected authors of this volume are listed at the beginning, the specific author of each chapter is not identified.

51. Ibid., pp. 102, 103.

52. Ibid., p. 45.

53. Ibid., pp. 54, 56.

54. Ibid., p. 58.

55. Ibid.

56. Ibid., p. 46.

57. Ibid.

58. Ibid., p. 48.

59. Ibid., p. 46.

60. Ibid., p. 50.

61. Ibid.

62. Ibid., pp. 50, 51.

63. Leon Gouré et al., *Convergence and Capitalism: The Soviet View* (Center for Advanced International Studies, University of Miami, 1973).

64. D. Yermolenko, "Nauchno-tekhnicheskaia revoliutsiia i manevry burzhuaznoi ideologii" [The scientific-technical revolution and the maneuvers of bourgeois ideology], *Pravda*, 6 June 1973, p. 4.

65. Reinhold and Ryzhenko, *Contemporary Anti-communism*, p. 67.

66. "Mezhdunarodnye otnosheniia," *Kommunist*, pp. 11, 12.

67. Ibid., p. 11.

68. Ibid., p. 12.

69. Ibid.

70. V. Kudinov and V. Pletnikov, "Razriadka napriazhennosti i manevry antikommunizma" [The relaxation of tension and the maneuvers of anticommunism], *Pravda*, 9 August 1974, p. 3.

71. Reinhold and Ryzhenko, *Contemporary Anti-communism*, p. 52.

72. Yermolenko, "Nauchno-tekhnicheskaia revoliutsiia."

73. Ibid.

74. Reinhold and Ryzhenko, *Contemporary Anti-communism*, p. 58.

75. Ibid., p. 98.

76. M. Mitin, "Mezhdunarodnye otnosheniia i ideologicheskaia bor'-ba" [International relations and the ideological struggle], *Krasnaia zvezda*, 22 November 1973, p. 2.

77. Reinhold and Ryzhenko, *Contemporary Anti-communism*, p. 112.

78. Ibid., p. 112-13.

79. Ibid., pp. 114, 116.

80. Ibid.

81. Ibid., pp. 113, 114.

82. Gromyko, "Amerikanskii 'tiazheloves,'" p. 30.

83. Reinhold and Ryzhenko, *Contemporary Anti-communism*, p. 117.

84. Ibid.

85. V. Shelyag, "Dva mirovozzreniia—dva vzgliada na voinu" [Two world views—two views on war], *Krasnaia zvezda*, 7 February 1974, p. 2.

86. Reinhold and Ryzhenko, *Contemporary Anti-communism*, p. 69.

87. G. Arbatov, "Manevry protivnikov razriadki" [Maneuvers of the opponents of detente], *Izvestiia*, 4 September 1975, p. 3.

88. Kudinov and Pletnikov, "Razriadka napriazhennosti."

89. Reinhold and Ryzhenko, *Contemporary Anti-communism*, p. 29; and Mitin, "Mezhdunarodnye otnosheniia."

90. Mitin, "Mezhdunarodnye otnosheniia."

91. Ia. Zasurskii, "Mutnye vody 'svobodnogo potoka'" [The troubled waters of "free flow"], *Literaturnaia gazeta*, 5 December 1973, p. 15.

92. "Mezhdunarodnye otnosheniia," *Kommunist*, p. 10.

93. Zasurskii, "Mutnye vody."

94. V. Korobeinikov, "Chto skryvaetsia za kontseptsiei 'svobody informatsii'" [What is concealed behind the concept of "freedom of information"], *Mezhdunarodnaia zhizn*, January 1976, pp. 100, 101.

95. V. Gushchin, "Po tu storonu 'svobodnogo obmena'" [On the other side of "free exchange"], *Sovetskaia kultura*, 20 April 1976, p. 7.

96. V. Kortunov, "Torzhestvo marksistsko-leninskikh idei i manevry antikommunizma" [The triumph of Marxist-Leninist ideas and the maneuvers of anticommunism], *Kommunist*, May 1970, p. 119.

97. Korobeinikov, "Chto skryvaetsia," p. 98.

98. Ibid.

99. V. Korionov, "Razriadka napriazhennosti i ee protivniki" [The

relaxation of tension and its opponents], *Novoe vremia,* 23 November 1973, p. 19.

100. Reinhold and Ryzhenko, *Contemporary Anti-communism,* p. 27.

101. Ibid., p. 29.

102. Ibid., p. 111.

103. Kortunov, "Torzhestvo," p. 120.

104. Reinhold and Ryzhenko, *Contemporary Anti-communism, p.* 29.

105. Kortunov, "Torzhestvo," p. 120.

106. Kudinov and Pletnikov, "Razriadka napriazhennosti."

107. Mitin, "Mezhdunarodnye otnosheniia."

108. Kudinov and Pletnikov, "Razriadka napriazhennosti."

109. Reinhold and Ryzhenko, *Contemporary Anti-communism,* p. 75.

110. Kortunov, "Torzhestvo," p. 123.

111. Reinhold and Ryzhenko, *Contemporary Anti-communism,* p. 75.

112. Yermolenko, "Nauchno-tekhnicheskaia revoliutsiia."

113. Mitin, "Mezhdunarodnye otnosheniia."

114. "Mezhdunarodyne otnosheniia," *Kommunist,* p. 9.

115. Korionov, "Razriadka napriazhennosti," p. 19.

116. V. Zagladin, ed., *The Revolutionary Movement of Our Time and Nationalism* (Moscow: Progress, 1975), p. 7. Although the collected authors of this volume are listed at the beginning, the specific author of each chapter is not identified.

117. Reinhold and Ryzhenko, *Contemporary Anti-communism,* p. 107.

118. Zagladin, *Nationalism,* p. 16.

119. Ibid., pp. 16-17.

120. Ibid., p. 17.

121. Reinhold and Ryzhenko, *Contemporary Anti-communism,* p. 72.

122. Zagladin, *Nationalism,* p. 7.

123. Kortunov, "Torzhestvo," p. 123.

124. Kudinov and Pletnikov, "Razriadka napriazhennosti."

125. Ibid.

126. Reinhold and Ryzhenko, *Contemporary Anti-communism,* p. 28.

127. Ibid.

128. "Mezhdunarodnye otnosheniia," *Kommunist,* pp. 19, 21.

Notes

129. Kortunov, "Torzhestvo," p. 123.
130. Reinhold and Ryzhenko, *Contemporary Anti-communism*, p. 35.
131. Kortunov, "Torzhestvo," p. 123.
132. Kudinov and Pletnikov, "Razriadka napriazhennosti."
133. Kortunov, "Torzhestvo." p. 121.
134. Ibid.
135. Ibid.
136. Baryshev, "Novye doktriny," p. 21.
137. Ibid., pp. 21, 22.
138. Nalin, "Povorot k razriadke."
139. Reinhold and Ryzhenko, *Contemporary Anti-communism*, p. 77.
140. Ibid., p. 78.
141. Ibid.
142. Ibid., p. 83.
143. Ibid., p. 85.
144. Kortunov, "Torzhestvo," p. 122.
145. Reinhold and Ryzhenko, *Contemporary Anti-communism*, p. 86.
146. "Mezhdunarodnye otnosheniia," *Kommunist,* p. 14.
147. Kortunov, "Torzhestvo," p. 122.
148. Ibid., pp. 122-23.
149. Yermolenko, "Nauchno-tekhnicheskaia revoliutsiia."
150. N. Bogomolova, *The 'Human Relations' Doctrine: Ideological Weapon of the Monopolies* (Moscow: Progress, 1973), pp. 7, 8.
151. Ibid., p. 7.
152. Reinhold and Ryzhenko, *Contemporary Anti-communism*, p. 15.
153. Ibid., p. 93.
154. Ibid., p. 137.
155. Ibid., pp. 15-16.
156. V. Lukin, "Amerikano-kitaiskie otnosheniia: kontseptsii i deistvitel'nost'" [American-Chinese relations: concepts and reality], *SShA* February 1973, p. 17.
157. Comments by V. Lukin in " 'Doktrina Niksona': deklaratsii i real'nost'" [The "Nixon Doctrine": declarations and reality], *SShA*, February 1971, p. 27.
158. Ibid.
159. L. Afanasyev et al., *The Political Economy of Capitalism* (Moscow: Progress, 1974), p. 230.

160. Ibid., pp. 230, 236.
161. Ibid., p. 230.
162. Ibid., p. 235.
163. Ibid., p. 232.
164. Ibid., p. 234.
165. Ibid., p. 235.
166. Ibid., p. 230.
167. Ibid., p. 231.
168. Ibid., p. 237.
169. I. Mosin, "Novye plany 'pomoshchi' inostrannym gosudarstvam" [New plans of "aid" to foreign states], *SShA*, July 1970, p. 68.
170. Afanasyev et al., *Political Economy of Capitalism*, p. 235.
171. Ibid., p. 236.
172. N. Inozemtsev, *Contemporary Capitalism: New Developments and Contradictions* (Moscow: Progress, 1974), p. 135.
173. Comments by M. Zakhmatov in "Militarizm i ekonomika" [Militarism and economics], *SShA*, December 1971, p. 34.
174. Ibid., p. 33.
175. Ibid.
176. Mosin, "Novye plany," p. 68.
177. N. Turkatenko, "V ushcherb natsional'nym interesam" [To the detriment of national interests], *Pravda*, 28 February 1974, p. 4.
178. Ibid.
179. R. Puchkov, "Ekonomicheskii shantazh" [Economic blackmail], *Pravda*, 13 September 1975, p. 5.
180. V. Kudriavtsev, "Taktika shantazha" [The tactics of blackmail], *Izvestiia*, 2 March 1972, p. 4.
181. Inozemtsev, *Contemporary Capitalism*, p. 40.
182. Afanasyev et al., *Political Economy of Capitalism*, p. 222.
183. Trofimenko, "Politicheskii realizm," p. 8.
184. V. Zhurkin, "SShA i mezhdunarodno-politicheskie krizisy" [The USA and international political crises], *SShA*, December 1970, p. 17.
185. Ibid., pp. 18-20.
186. Ibid., p. 21.
187. Anatoly Gromyko, "Washington's 'New Technological Policy,' " in Yu. (Iu.) Davydov, V. Zhurkin, and V. Rudnev, eds., *The Nixon Doctrine* (Arlington, Va.: JPRS, 1973), p. 111.
188. Ibid., p. 112.
189. Ibid., p. 114.
190. Ibid., p. 113.
191. Ibid., p. 106.

Notes

192. G. Arbatov, "Vneshniaia politika SShA i nauchno-tekhnicheskaia revoliutsiia" [U.S. foreign policy and the scientific-technical revolution], *SShA,* October 1973 (article no. 1), pp. 8, 9.

193. G. Arbatov, "Vneshniaia politika SShA i nauchno-tekhnicheskaia revoliutsiia" [U.S. foreign policy and the scientific-technical revolution], *SShA,* November 1973 (article no. 2), p. 3.

194. Ibid., p. 5,

195. Ibid.

196. Ibid., p. 6.

197. Gromyko, "Washington's 'New Technological Policy,' " p. 117.

198. Arbatov, "Vneshniaia politika SShA" (article no. 2), p. 8.

199. Ibid.

200. Comments by G. Khozin in " 'Doktrina Niksona,' " p. 39.

201. Gromyko, "Washington's 'New Technological Policy,' " p. 117.

202. Ibid., p. 120.

203. Comments by Khozin in " 'Doktrina Niksona,' " p. 39.

204. Gromyko, "Washington's 'New Technological Policy,' " p. 105.

205. Arbatov, "Vneshiaia politika SShA" (article no. 2), p. 6.

206. Comments by Khozin in " 'Doktrina Niksona,' " p. 39.

207. Gromyko, "Washington's 'New Technological Policy,' " p. 121.

208. Ibid., p. 116.

209. Arbatov, "Vneshniaia politika SShA" (article no. 1), p. 7.

210. Arbatov, "Vneshniaia politika SShA" (article no. 2), p. 15.

211. K. Vorob'ev, "Armiia i politika" [The army and politics], *Krasnaia zvezda,* 17 September 1976, p. 2.

212. V. Berezin, "Orudie agressii" [A tool of aggression], *Krasnaia zvezda,* 2 July 1976, p. 3.

213. Vorob'ev, "Armiia i politika."

214. Migolat'ev, "Sovremennyi militarizm."

215. Ibid.

216. See "Militarizm i ekonomika," note 173 above.

217. Comments by Iu. Katasonov in ibid., p. 26.

218. Ibid.

219. Ibid.

220. Comments by G. Mukhanova in ibid., pp. 37, 38.

221. V. Kuznetsov, "Vsesilie razuma i bessilie sily" [The omnipotence of reason and the impotence of force], *Novoe vremia,* 25 June 1976, p. 4.

222. See V. Vakhrushev, *Neocolonialism: Methods and Maneuvers* (Moscow: Progress, 1973), p. 199 ff.; and N. Khmara, "Interventsionizm—politika pozora i provalov" [Interventionism—a policy of infamy and failures], *Kommunist vooruzhennykh sil,* May 1975, pp. 16, 17.

On crisis policy, see Zhurkin, "SShA i mezhdunarodno-politicheskie krizisy."

223. V. Mochalov, "Strategiia illiuzii" [A strategy of illusions], *Krasnaia zvezda*, 16 September 1969, p. 3.

224. R. Simonian, "Opasnye platsdarmy" [Dangerous bases], *Krasnaia zvezda*, 2 March 1974, p. 3.

225. Iu. Gavrilov, "Pentagon i bazy" [The Pentagon and bases], *Krasnaia zvezda*, 10 October 1975, p. 3.

226. Simonian, "Opasnye platsdarmy."

227. V. Mayevskii (Maevskii), "Glubkaia diversiia" ["Complete sabotage"], *Pravda*, 19 September 1975, p. 5.

228. Ibid.

229. Iu. Kharlanov, "Nagnetaiut napriazhennost' " [They pump up tension], *Pravda*, 5 September 1976, p. 5.

230. A. Bovin, "Mir i sotsial'nyi progress" [Peace and social progress], *Izvestiia*, 11 September 1973, p. 4.

231. Gromyko, "Amerikansii 'tiazheloves,' " p. 33.

232. G. Trofimenko, "Nekotorye aspekty voenno-politicheskoi strategii SShA" [Some aspects of U.S. military-political strategy], *SShA*, October 1970, p. 17.

233. Kuznetsov, "Vsesilie razuma," p. 4.

234. Ibid.

235. See examples of this debate in William Kintner and Harriet Scott, *The Nuclear Revolution in Soviet Military Affairs* (Norman: University of Oklahoma Press, 1968).

236. Trofimenko, "Uroki V'etnama," p. 76.

237. Ibid., pp. 76, 77.

238. Khmara, "Interventsionizm," p. 16.

239. Ibid.

240. Trofimenko, "Politicheskii realizm," p. 9.

241. Comments by G. Arbatov in " 'Doktrina Niksona,' " p. 19.

242. Trofimenko, "Politicheskii realizm," p. 9.

243. Ibid., pp. 9, 10.

244. Ibid., p. 10.

245. R. Simonian, "Kontseptsiia 'strategicheskoi dostatochnosti' " [The concept of "strategic sufficiency"], *Krasnaia zvezda*, 24 August 1976, p. 3.

246. V. Larionov, "Transformatsiia kontseptsii 'strategicheskoi dostatochnosti' " [The transformation of the concept of "strategic sufficiency"], *SShA*, November 1971, p. 28.

247. Ibid.

248. Ibid., pp. 31, 32.

Notes

249. Ibid., p. 31.
250. Simonian, "Kontseptsiia 'strategicheskoi dostatochnosti.' "
251. Larionov, "Tranformatsiia kontseptsii," p. 31.
252. Ibid.
253. Simonian, "Kontseptsiia 'strategicheskoi dostatochnosti.' "
254. Larionov, "Transformatsiia kontseptsii," p. 31.
255. Trofimenko, "Nekotorye aspekty," p. 16.
256. Trofimenko, "Politicheskii realizm," p. 15.
257. Ibid., pp. 14, 15.
258. Trofimenko, "Nekotorye aspekty," p. 15.
259. Trofimenko, "Politicheskii realizm," p. 8.
260. Ibid., p. 13.
261. Ibid., p. 14.
262. Trofimenko, "Nekotorye aspekty," p. 16.
263. Ibid., pp. 17, 18.
264. R. Simonian, "Kontseptsiia 'vybora tselei' " [The concept of "selective targeting"], Krasnaia zvezda, 28 September 1976, p. 3.
265. Ibid.
266. Ibid.
267. L. Semeiko, "Formy novye, sut' prezhniaia" [New forms, previous essence], Krasnaia zvezda, 8 April 1975, p. 3.
268. Ibid.
269. A Karenin, "Razriadka i novye varianty starykh doktrin" [Detente and new variants of old doctrines], Mezhdunarodnaia zhizn, May 1975, p. 109.
270. Semeiko, "Formy novye."
271. Karenin, "Razriadka i novye," p. 109.
272. Ibid.
273. Simonian, "Kontseptsiia 'vybora tselei.' "
274. Trofimenko, "Politicheskii realizm," p. 3.
275. Ibid.
276. Ibid., p. 10.
277. G. Sviatov, "Konseptsiia 'polutora voin' " [The concept of "one and one-half wars"], Krasnaia zvezda, 15 October 1976, p. 3.
278. Trofimenko, "Politicheskii realizm," pp. 10, 11.
279. Ibid., p. 11.
280. Ibid., p. 12.
281. Comments by V. Larionov in " 'Doktrina Niksona,' " p. 29.
282. Comments by G. Trofimenko in ibid., p. 31.
283. Ibid., p. 32.
284. Zhurkin, "SShA i mezhdunarodno-politicheskie krizisy," p. 14.

285. Comments by V. Zhurkin in " 'Doktrina Niksona,' " pp. 39, 40.

286. Zhurkin, "SShA i mezhdunarodno-politicheskie krizisy," p. 15.

287. Comments by Zhurkin in " 'Doktrina Niksona,' " pp. 39, 40.

288. Zhurkin, "SShA i mezhdunarodno-politicheskie krizisy," pp. 17 ff.

289. Comments by Zhurkin in " 'Doktrina Niksona,' " p. 40.

290. Ibid.

291. Trofimenko, "Nekotorye aspekty," p. 19.

292. Ibid., pp. 19, 20.

293. Comments by Trofimenko in " 'Doktrina Niksona,' " p. 30.

294. Larionov, "Transformatsiia kontseptsii," p. 33.

295. Ibid., pp. 33, 34.

296. Comments by Zhurkin in " 'Doktrina Niksona,' " pp. 40, 41.

297. Larionov, "Transformatsiia kontseptsii," p. 33.

298. Comments by Trofimenko in " 'Doktrina Niksona,' " p. 31.

299. Comments by Larionov in ibid., p. 28.

300. Ibid.

301. Sviatov, "Kontseptsiia 'polutora voin.' "

302. R. Simonian, "Voiny glazami Pentagona" [Wars from the perspective of the Pentagon], Krasnaia zvezda, 27 May 1976, p. 3.

303. Ibid.

304. Iu. Gavrilov and V. Berezin, "Opasnaia politika, zloveshchii biznes" [Dangerous policy, sinister business], Krasnaia zvezda, 14 March 1976, p. 3.

305. Iu. Gavrilov and V. Vinogradov, "Zloveshchii biznes" [Sinister business], Krasnaia zvezda, 7 September 1975, p. 3.

306. V. Berezin and O. Nikiforov, "Komu pomogaet Pentagon" [Whom is the Pentagon helping], Krasnaia zvezda, 16 November 1975, p. 3.

307. Trofimenko, "Politicheskii realizm," p. 12.

308. Comments by Trofimenko in " 'Doktrina Niksona,' " p. 32.

309. Trofimenko, "Politicheskii realizm," p. 13.

310. Ibid., p. 15.

311. Comments by Arbatov in " 'Doktrina Niksona,' " p. 42.

312. Ibid.

313. Sviatov, "Kontseptsiia 'polutora voin.' "

314. Karenin, "Razriadka i novye varianty," p. 107.

315. V. Soldatov, " 'Kontseptsiia sily'—antipod razriadki" [The "concept of force"—the opposite of detente], Sovetskaia Rossiia, 20 June 1975, p. 3.

316. Comments by Zhurkin in " 'Doktrina Niksona,' " p. 41.

317. Ibid.

318. Trofimenko, "Politicheskii realizm," p. 4.

319. Larionov, "Transformatsiia kontseptsii," p. 34.

320. Comments by Gromyko in " 'Doktrina Niksona,' " p. 35.

321. G. Arbatov, *The War of Ideas in Contemporary International Relations* (Moscow: Progress, 1973) pp. 225, 238.

322. See Lukin, "Amerikano-kitaiskie otnosheniia," for a Soviet view of the contemporary application of this policy vis-à-vis China.

323. Leont'ev, "Amerikanskii imperializm," p. 9.

324. "Rastet i shiritsia natsional'no-osvoboditel'noe dvizhenie" [The national liberation movement is growing and expanding], *Sovetskaia Rossiia,* 31 October 1969, p. 1.

325. V. Saprykov, "Opiraias' na shtyk i dollar" [Relying upon the bayonet and the dollar], *Krasnaia zvezda,* 22 September 1970, p. 3.

326. V. Sobakin, "Kollektivnaia bezopasnost': istoricheskii opyt i sovremennost' " [Collective security: historical experience and modern times], *Kommunist,* March 1974, p. 87.

327. D. Volskii, "Vashington i aziatskii regionalizm" [Washington and Asian regionalism], *SShA,* January 1970, p. 65.

328. Ibid., p. 66.

329. D. Kraminov, "Doktriny novye, plany starye" [New doctrines, old plans], *Izvestiia,* 9 August 1969, p. 3.

330. Ibid.

331. Ibid.

332. V Kudriavtsev, "Litsemerie 'mirotvortsev' " [The hypocrisy of the "peacemakers"], *Izvestiia,* 18 December 1971, p. 3.

333. S. Beglov, "SShA-Zapadnaia Evropa: nekotorye aspekty vzaimootnoshenii" [USA–Western Europe: some aspects of mutual relations], *SShA,* June 1970, p. 8.

334. See, for example, M. Kudrin, "Ob odnoi fal'shivoi kontseptsii Maoistov" [On a false concept of the Maoists], *Mezhdunarodnaia zhizn,* April 1974, p. 101.

335. Beglov, "SShA-Zapadnaia Evropa," p. 9.

336. A. Topornin, "Doktrina 'balansa sil' i Vashington" [The "balance of power" doctrine and Washington], *SShA,* November 1970, p. 9.

337. Karenin, "Razriadka i novye varianty," pp. 106, 107.

338. Topornin, "Doktrina 'balansa sil,' " p. 9.

339. Karenin, "Razriadka i novye varianty," p. 107.

340. Comments by Lukin in " 'Doktrina Niksona,' " p. 26.

341. Topornin, "Doktrina 'balansa sil,' " p. 10.

342. Ibid.
343. Ibid., p. 17.
344. Ibid, pp. 15–17.
345. Ibid., p. 18.
346. Lukin, "Amerikano-kitaiskie otnosheniia," p. 15.
347. Ibid., p. 21.
348. Karenin, "Razriadka i novye varianty," p. 105; and Topornin, "Doktrina 'balansa sil,' " p. 16.
349. Karenin, ibid.
350. Topornin, "Doktrina 'balansa sil,' " p. 17.
351. Ibid., p. 18.
352. Ibid., p. 19.
353. Ibid., p. 8.
354. E. Zhukov, "Natsional'no-osvoboditel'noe dvizhenie narodov A-zii i Afriki" [The national liberation movement of the peoples of Asia and Africa], *Kommunist,* March 1969, p. 34.
355. Ibid.
356. V. Kudriavtsev, "Berech' i krepit' edinstvo" [To guard and to strengthen unity], *Izvestiia,* 27 July 1976, p. 4.
357. L. Levchenko, " 'Differentiated' U.S. Policy in Latin America Analyzed," radio commentary, *FBIS,* 18 November 1971, p. G5.
358. Ibid.
359. V. Levin, "Kurs na raskol" [A policy of splitting], *Pravda,* 12 December 1971, p. 5.
360. G. Arbatov, "O sovetsko-amerikanskikh otnosheniiakh" [On Soviet-American relations], *Kommunist,* February 1973, p. 103.
361. Ibid.
362 Sobakin, "Kollektivnaia bezopasnost,' " p. 89.
363. Z. Mirskii, "Dialektika razriadki" [The dialectics of detente], *Novoe vremia,* 5 September 1975, p. 4; and E. Grigorev, "Mezhduna-rodnaia nedelia" [The international week], *Pravda,* 10 August 1975, p. 4.
364. G. Shakhnazarov, "Mirnoe sosushchestvovanie i sotsial'nyi pro-gress" [Peaceful coexistence and social progress], *Pravda,* 27 December 1975, p. 4.
365. Iu. Oleshchuk, "O teorii 'ogranichennoi razriadki' " [On the theory of "limited detente"], *SShA,* April 1975, p. 3.
366. Comments by Arbatov in " 'Doktrina Niksona,' " p. 25.
367. Ibid.
368. Shakhnazarov, "Mirnoe sosushchestvovanie."
369. Oleshchuk, "O teorii," p. 4.

370. A. Arbatov and G. Arbatov, "Idei Dzh. Shlesindzhera po forme i soderzhaniiu" [The ideas of J. Schlesinger in form and content], *Novoe vremia*, 25 July 1975, p. 18.

371. Ibid.

372. Ibid.

373. Comments by Arbatov in " 'Doktrina Niksona,' " p. 25.

374. Shakhnazarov, "Mirnoe sosushchestvovanie."

375. Oleshchuk, "O teorii," p. 9.

376. Ibid., p. 10.

377. Yu. (Iu.) Davydov, "The 'Nixon Doctrine'—the Crisis of Globalism," in Davydov et al., *Nixon Doctrine*, p. 17.

378. Ibid.

379. Ibid.

380. Comments by Arbatov in " 'Doktrina Niksona,' " p. 26.

Chapter 4. U.S. Relations with Its Allies

1. E. Novosel'tsev, "The USA and Western Europe—'Mature Partnership,' " in Yu. (Iu.) Davydov, V. Zhurkin, and V. Rudnev, eds., *The Nixon Doctrine* (Arlington, Va.: JPRS, 1973), p. 146.

2. Anatoly Gromyko, "Amerikanskii 'tiazheloves' na evropeiskoi arene" [The American "heavyweight" in the European arena], *Mezhdunarodnaia zhizn*, January 1971, p. 26.

3. Ibid.

4. Novosel'tsev, "The USA and Western Europe," p. 149.

5. Yu. (Iu.) Davydov, "The 'Nixon Doctrine'—the Crisis of Globalism," in Davydov et al., *Nixon Doctrine*, p. 18.

6. Novosel'tsev, "The USA and Western Europe," p. 148.

7. Gromyko, "Amerikanskii 'tiazheloves,' " p. 27.

8. Ibid.

9. Ibid.

10. Iu. Davydov, "SShA-Zapadnaia Evropa: predely kompromissa" [USA-Western Europe: the limits of compromise], *SShA*, June 1975, p. 36; and Novosel'tsev, "The USA and Western Europe," p. 157.

11. Novosel'tsev, ibid., pp. 156, 157.

12. S. Beglov, "SShA-Zapadnaia Evropa: nekotorye aspekty vzaimootnoshenii" [USA-Western Europe: some aspects of mutual relations], *SShA*, June 1970, p. 6.

13. Davydov, "The 'Nixon Doctrine,' " p. 14.

14. Ibid., p. 19.

15. Novosel'tsev, "The USA and Western Europe," p. 149.

16. Ibid., p. 151.

17. Davydov, "The 'Nixon Doctrine,' " p. 22.

18. Ibid.

19. Novosel'tsev, "The USA and Western Europe," p. 148.

20. Ibid., p. 151.

21. Iu. Davydov, " 'God Evropa'—god protivorechii" [The 'year of Europe'—a year of contradictions], *SShA,* March 1974, p. 77.

22. Novosel'tsev, "The USA and Western Europe," p. 148.

23. Davydov, "The 'Nixon Doctrine,' " p. 15.

24. Ibid., p. 23.

25. Novosel'tsev, "The USA and Western Europe," p. 151.

26. O. Reinhold and F. Ryzhenko, eds., *Contemporary Anti-communism: Policy and Ideology* (Moscow: Progress, 1976), p. 22.

27. Ibid.

28. Ibid., pp. 15, 18, 19.

29. N. Inozemtsev, *Contemporary Capitalism: New Developments and Contradictions* (Moscow: Progress, 1974), p. 94.

30. Ibid.

31. L. Afanasyev et al., *The Political Economy of Capitalism* (Moscow: Progress, 1974), p. 259.

32. Ibid.

33. Ibid.

34. Reinhold and Ryzhenko, *Contemporary Anti-communism,* p. 18.

35. Ibid.

36. Inozemtsev, *Contemporary Capitalism,* p. 95.

37. Ibid., p. 115.

38. Ibid., p. 95.

39. Davydov, "SShA-Zapadnaia Evropa," p. 36.

40. Ibid.

41. E. Shershnev, "Sovetsko-amerikanskaia torgovlia: problemy i vozmozhnosti" [Soviet-American trade: problems and possibilities], *SShA,* April 1972, p. 7.

42. M. Zakhmatov, "The Principle of 'Partnership' and Foreign Economic Instruments," in Davydov et al., *Nixon Doctrine,* p. 98.

43. Ibid.

44. Iu. Nikolayev (Nikolaev), "Fiasko . . . " [Fiasco . . .], *Izvestiia,* 18 August 1971, p. 2.

45. Novosel'tsev, "The USA and Western Europe," p. 159.

46. Ibid., p. 160.

47. Inozemtsev, *Contemporary Capitalism,* p. 136.

48. Ibid., p. 132.

49. Afanasyev et al., *Political Economy of Capitalism,* p. 264.

50. Inozemtsev, *Contemporary Capitalism,* p. 134.

51. Reinhold and Ryzhenko, *Contemporary Anti-communism*, p. 41.

52. Ibid.

53. Inozemtsev, *Contemporary Capitalism*, p. 136.

54. Afanasyev et al., *Political Economy of Capitalism*, p. 260.

55. Ibid., p. 159.

56. Davydov, "SShA-Zapadnaia Evropa," p. 36.

57. Novosel'tsev, "The USA and Western Europe," p. 160.

58. Ibid.

59. Ibid., pp. 160, 161.

60. Afanasyev, et al., *Political Economy of Capitalism*, p. 223.

61. Anatoly Gromyko, "Washington's 'New Technological Policy,' " in Davydov et al., *Nixon Doctrine*, p. 120.

62. Ibid.

63. Ibid., p. 118.

64. Ibid.

65. Novosel'tsev, "The USA and Western Europe," p. 161.

66. Inozemtsev, *Contemporary Capitalism*, p. 40.

67. Davydov, "SShA-Zapadnaia Evropa," p. 36.

68. Davydov, " 'God Evropa,' " p. 76.

69. Gromyko, "Amerikanskii 'tiazheloves,' " p. 25.

70. Ibid., p. 27.

71. V. Kremenyuk, "The Near East—Partnership in Action," in Davydov et al., *Nixon Doctrine*, p. 163.

72. Ibid., p. 166.

73. Ibid.

74. Ibid., p. 167.

75. Comments by G. Arbatov in " 'Doktrina Niksona': deklaratsii i real'nost' " [The "Nixon Doctrine": declarations and reality], *SShA*, February 1971, p. 44.

76. Davydov, " 'God Evropa,' " pp. 76, 77.

77. Ibid., p. 76.

78. Ibid., p. 77.

79. Novosel'tsev, "The USA and Western Europe," p. 159.

80. Ibid.

81. Ibid.

Chapter 5. *U.S. Relations with the Third World*

1. L. Klochkovsky, *Economic Neocolonialism* (Moscow: Progress, 1975), p. 8.

2. N. Khmara, "Interventsionizm—politika pozora i provalov" (In-

terventionism—A policy of infamy and failures"), *Kommunist vooruzhennykh sil,* May 1975, p. 16.

3. V. Zagladin, ed., *The Revolutionary Movement of Our Time and Nationalism* (Moscow: Progress, 1975), p. 59. Although the collected authors of this volume are listed at the beginning, the specific author of each chapter is not identified.

4. Ibid.

5. Ibid.

6. Ibid.

7. Ibid.

8. Ibid., p. 62.

9. Ibid., p. 61.

10. Ibid., p. 11.

11. Ibid., p. 25 ff.

12. Ibid., p. 7.

13. Ibid., p. 16.

14. Ibid., p. 15.

15. Klochkovsky, *Economic Neocolonialism,* p. 15; and L. Afanasyev et al., *The Political Economy of Capitalism* (Moscow: Progress, 1974), p. 280.

16. I. Mosin, "Novye plany 'pomoshchi' inostrannym gosudarstvam" [New plans of "aid" to foreign states], *SShA,* July 1970, p. 68.

17. Ibid., p. 67; and M. Zakhmatov, "The Principle of 'Partnership' and Foreign Economic Instruments," in Yu. (Iu.) Davydov, V. Zhurkin, and V. Rudnev, eds., *The Nixon Doctrine* (Arlington, Va.: JPRS, 1973), p. 91.

18. Mosin, "Novye plany," p. 67.

19. Ibid.

20. Zakhmatov, "The Principle of 'Partnership,' " p. 92.

21. V. Vahrushev, *Neocolonialism: Methods and Maneuvers* (Moscow: Progress, 1973), p. 78 ff.

22. Ibid.

23. Zakhmatov, "The Principle of 'Partnership,' " p. 94.

24. Vakhrushev, *Neocolonialism,* pp. 78 ff.

25. Zakhmatov, "The Principle of 'Partnership,' " p. 94.

26. Ibid., p. 95.

27. Ibid.

28. Ibid., p. 94.

29. Ibid., pp. 95, 96.

30. Ibid., p. 100.

31. Ibid., p. 99.

32. Ibid.

33. Vakhrushev, *Neocolonialism*, p. 145-146.
34. Ibid., p. 147.
35. Ibid., p. 149.
36. Ibid., pp. 149, 150.
37. Ibid., p. 166.
38. Ibid., pp. 154, 155.
39. Ibid., p. 162.
40. Ibid., pp. 164, 165.
41. Ibid., p. 163.
42. Ibid., pp. 179, 180.
43. Ibid., p. 151.
44. Ibid., p. 156.
45. Ibid., p. 180.
46. Ibid., p. 183.
47. Ibid., p. 186.
48. Ibid., p. 191.
49. Ibid., p. 207.
50. Ibid., p. 208.
51. Ibid., p. 207.
52. Ibid., p. 221.
53. Ibid., pp. 228 ff.
54. Ibid., pp. 229, 233.
55. Ibid., p. 235.
56. Ibid., p. 236.
57. Ibid., p. 210.
58. Ibid., p. 236.
59. Ibid., p. 237.
60. Ibid., p. 238.
61. Klochkovsky, *Economic Neocolonialism*, pp. 14, 16.
62. Ibid., p. 16.
63. Ibid., p. 12.
64. Vakhrushev, *Neocolonialism*, p. 54.
65. Ibid., p. 55.
66. Ibid., p. 53.
67. Ibid., p. 56.
68. Klochkovsky, *Economic Neocolonialism*, p. 19.
69. Afanasyev et al., *Political Economy of Capitalism*, p. 239.
70. Anatoly Gromyko, "Washington's 'New Technological Policy,'" in Davydov et al., *Nixon Doctrine*, p. 108.
71. Klochkovsky, *Economic Neocolonialism*, p. 19.
72. N. Inozemtsev, *Contemporary Capitalism: New Developments and Contradictions* (Moscow: Progress, 1974), p. 127.

73. Klochkovsky, *Economic Neocolonialism,* p. 20.
74. Ibid., p. 18; and Vakhrushev, *Neocolonialism,* p. 90.
75. Inozemtsev, *Contemporary Capitalism,* p. 127.
76. Vakhrushev, *Neocolonialism,* p. 100.
77. Ibid., p. 96.
78. Ibid., pp. 96, 98.
79. Klochkovsky, *Economic Neocolonialism,* p. 17.
80. Ibid.
81. Vakhrushev, *Neocolonialism,* p. 105; and Afanasyev et al., *Political Economy of Capitalism,* p. 251.
82. Afanasyev et al., ibid.
83. Ibid., p. 279.
84. Ibid.
85. Zakhmatov, "The Principle of 'Partnership,' " p. 92.
86. Khmara, "Interventsionizm," p. 18.
87. G. Arbatov, "Vneshniaia politika SShA i nauchno-tekhnicheskaia revoliutsiia" (U.S. foreign policy and the scientific-technical revolution), *SShA,* November 1973, (article no. 2), p. 6.
88. Ibid., p. 7.
89. Ibid.
90. Klochkovsky, *Economic Neocolonialism,* p. 21.
91. Afanasyev et al., *Political Economy of Capitalism,* p. 223.
92. Arbatov, "Vneshniaia politika SShA" (article no. 2), p. 9.
93. Ibid.
94. Ibid.
95. Ibid.
96. O. Reinhold and F. Ryzhenko, eds., *Contemporary Anti-communism: Policy and Ideology* (Moscow: Progress, 1976), p. 157. Although the collected authors of this volume are listed at the beginning, the specific author of each chapter is not identified.
97. R. Simonian, "Opasnye platsdarmy" [Dangerous bases], *Krasnaia zvezda,* 2 March 1974, p. 3.
98. Khmara, "Interventsionizm," pp. 16, 17.

Chapter 6. *U.S. Relations with Socialist Countries: Some Remaining Issues*

1. G. Arbatov, "Vneshniaia politika SShA i nauchno-tekhnicheskaia revoliutsiia" [U.S. foreign policy and the scientific-technical revolution], *SShA,* November 1973 (article no. 2), p. 13.
2. Ibid., p. 15.
3. Alexander Solzhenitsyn, *Warning to the West,* trans Harris L.

Coulter and Nataly Martin (New York: Farrar, Straus, & Giroux, 1977), p. 12.

4. A. Yefremov, "Ot konfrontatsii k vzaimoponimaniiu" [From confrontation to mutual understanding], *Za rubezhom,* 22 February 1974, p. 8.

5. S. Frederick Starr, "The Russian View of America," *Wilson Quarterly,* vol. 1 (Winter 1977), p. 112.

6. "Mezhdunarodnye otnosheniia i ideologicheskaia bor'ba" [International relations and the ideological struggle], *Kommunist,* September 1973, p. 10.

7. Otto Reingol'd, "Nauchno-tekhnicheskaia revoliutsiia i bor'ba dvukh sistem" [The scientific-technical revolution and the struggle of the two systems], *Mirovaia ekonomika i mezhdunarodnye otnosheniia,* April 1969, p. 114.

8. Iu. Zhukov, "Okhotniki za golovami" [The head hunters], *Pravda,* 4 June 1974, p. 4.

9. Ibid.

10. Arbatov, "Vneshniaia politika SShA" (article no. 2), p. 14.

11. See, for example, Anatoly Gromyko, "Washington's 'New Technological Policy,'" in Yu. (Iu.) Davydov, V. Zhurkin, and V. Rudnev, eds., *The Nixon Doctrine* (Arlington, Va.: JPRS, 1973), p. 121.

12. Arbatov, "Vneshniaia politika SShA" (article no. 2), p. 14.

13. V. Sobakin, "Kollektivnaia bezopasnost': istoricheskii opyt i sovremennost'" Collective security: historical experience and modern times], *Kommunist,* March 1974, p. 94.

14. G. Arbatov, "Sobytie vazhnogo mezhdunarodnogo znacheniia" [An event of important international significance], *SShA,* August 1972, p. 10.

15. Ibid., pp. 10, 11.

Chapter 7. *Traditionalists and Realists*

1. Morton Schwartz, *Soviet Perceptions of the United States* (A study prepared for the Office of External Research, Bureau of Intelligence and Research, U.S. Department of State, 1975), p. 149. This study has been published in book form under the same title (Berkeley: University of California Press, 1978).

2. Ibid., p. 150.

3. Vernon Aspaturian, "The Soviet Military-Industrial Complex— Does It Exist?" *Journal of International Affairs* vol. 26, no. 1 (1972), p. 3.

4. Robert Donaldson, "Global Power Relationships in the Seventies: The View from the Kremlin," in Paul Cocks et al., eds., *The Dynamics of Soviet Politics* (Cambridge: Harvard University Press, 1976), pp. 317-319.

5. Klaus Mehnert, Congressional testimony in *Detente* (Hearings before the Subcommittee on Europe, Committee on Foreign Affairs, House of Representatives, May-June 1974), p. 280. See also Adam B. Ulam's comments on this subject in "Detente under Soviet Eyes," *Foreign Policy*, no. 24 (Fall 1976), pp. 158, 159.

6. Roman Kolkowicz, *The Red Hawks on the Rationality of Nuclear War* (Santa Monica: Rand Corp. RM-4899, 1966); and "The Military," in H. Gordon Skilling and Franklyn Griffiths, eds., *Interest Groups in Soviet Politics* (Princeton: Princeton University Press, 1971), p. 141.

7. William Zimmerman, *Soviet Perspectives on International Relations* (Princeton: Princeton University Press, 1969), p. 238.

8. Vladimir Petrov, *U.S.-Soviet Detente: Past and Future* (Washington, D.C.: American Enterprise Institute, 1975), p. 9.

9. Marshall Shulman, "Toward a Western Philosophy of Coexistence," *Foreign Affairs*, vol. 52 (October 1973), p. 40.

10. Ibid., p. 47.

11. Ibid.

12. Alexander Dallin, "Soviet Foreign Policy and Domestic Politics: A Framework for Analysis," in Erik Hoffmann and Frederic Fleron, eds., *The Conduct of Soviet Foreign Policy* (Chicago: Aldine Atherton, 1971), p. 44.

13. From ibid., p. 45.

14. Ibid., p. 46.

15. A. Grechko, "Na strazhe mira i sotsializma" [Guarding peace and socialism], *Pravda*, 23 February 1974, p. 2.

16. Ye. (E.) Rybkin, "On the Nature of Nuclear Rocket War," *Kommunist vooruzhennykh sil*, September 1965, translated in William Kintner and Harriet Scott, eds., *The Nuclear Revolution in Soviet Military Affairs* (Norman: University of Oklahoma Press, 1968), p. 114.

17. William Odom, "A Dissenting View on the Group Approach to Soviet Politics," *World Politics*, vol. 28 (July 1976), p. 545.

18. William Odom, "Who Controls Whom in Moscow," *Foreign Policy*, no. 19 (Summer 1975), p. 110.

19. Ibid.

20. Ibid.

21. Ibid., pp. 116, 122.

22. K. P. Ivanov, *Leninskoye osnovy vneshnei politiki SSSR* (Moscow: 1969), p. 50, quoted by Aspaturian, "The Soviet Military-Industrial," p. 4.

23. P. V. Sokolov, ed., *Voenno-ekonomicheskie voprosy v kurse politekonomii* (Moscow: 1968), p. 254, quoted by Aspaturian in ibid., p. 5.

24. A. Lagovskii, "The State's Economy and Its Military Might," *Krasnaia zvezda*, 25 September 1969, quoted by Aspaturian in ibid., p. 4.

25. Ibid.

26. A. Kosygin, Report to the 24th CPSU Congress, *Pravda*, 17 April 1971, p. 3.

27. Ibid.

28. Aspaturian, "The Soviet Military-Industrial Complex," p. 5.

29. Bruce Parrott, "Technological Progress and Soviet Politics," *Survey*, vol. 23 (Spring 1977–1978), pp. 41, 43.

30. See Harold Brown, *Department of Defense Annual Report FY 1980* (Washington, D.C.: U.S. Government Printing Office, 1979) pp. 32, 33; and John Collins, *American and Soviet Military Trends since the Cuban Missile Crisis* (Washington, D.C.: Center for Strategic and International Studies, Georgetown University, 1978).

31. Dallin, "Soviet Foreign Policy," p. 46.

32. Ibid.

33. Schwartz, *Soviet Perceptions*, p. 150.

34. Ibid., p. 151.

35. See Robert Moss, "Who's Meddling in Iran?" *New Republic*, 2 December 1978, for an example of the least visible of these Soviet activities.

36. Schwartz, *Soviet Perceptions*, pp. 149, 150.

37. See Rowland Evans and Robert Novak, "The SS-19 Loophole," *Washington Post*, 27 July 1979; and "SALT, Soviet Style," *Washington Post*, 10 August 1979. See also the treaty text: *New York Times*, 19 June 1979.

38. Shulman, "Toward a Western Philosophy," p. 56.

39. See Robert C. Tucker, "The Dialectics of Coexistence, in *The Soviet Political Mind*, 1st ed. (New York: Praeger, 1963).

40. Josef Stalin, *Economic Problems of Socialism in the USSR* (New York: International Publishers, 1952), p. 30.

Index

AFL-CIO, 71
African Development Bank
  (AFDB), 220-221
Alexandrov, S., 50
Allende, Salvador, 142
Alliance for Progress, 186
Allies. *See* U.S. allies; Europe
  (Western)
Anarchism, 129
Angola
  national liberation movement in,
    38, 184-185, 193
  Soviet actions in, 251, 255
Anti-Ballistic Missile (ABM), 75
Anticommunism, 113-122, 124-131,
  135-137
Arbatov, Georgi, 17, 33-37, 42-45,
  48, 57-60, 70-72, 84, 87-89, 96,
  101-102, 109, 112, 122, 138,
  148, 163, 174, 177, 187, 191,
  193, 208-209, 228-229, 233,
  235-237, 245
Arms race. *See* U.S. foreign policy
Arms sales by U.S., 64, 173
Asia
  regional cooperation, 179-180
  and U.S. influence, 180
Asian and Pacific Council
  (ASPAC), 179-180
Aspaturian, Vernon, 240, 248-249
Association of Southeast Asian
  Nations (ASEAN), 179

Balance of power
  defined, 51, 181-182
  dual meaning of term, 181-182
  in favor of socialism, 40
  as means of U.S. diplomacy,
    181-185
  Soviet views of, 18, 26, 43, 56,
    261
  Soviet vocabulary for, 16-17
  and triangular diplomacy, 136
  to U.S. advantage, 56
  See also Correlation of forces
Baryshev, A., 130-131
"Basic Principles of (Mutual)
  Relations between the Union of
  Soviet Socialist Republics and
  the United States of America,"
  58, 186, 244
Beglov, S. I., 181, 196
Belorussian Communist party, 48
Berezin, V., 151
Bobrakov, Iu., 86
Bogdanov, O. S., 283n
Bogomolova, N., 134
Bolsheviks, 243-244
Bovin, A., 96, 156
Brest-Litovsk, Treaty of (1918),
  243-244, 267
Bretton Woods monetary system,
  203
  breakdown of, 79, 88
Brezhnev, Leonid I., 16-17, 41, 48,

Brezhnev, Leonid I. (cont.)
  130, 187, 246-247, 250, 258,
    259n
Brown, Harold, 306n
Brzezinski, Zbigniew, 110, 124, 136,
    284n
Building bridges, strategy of, 124-
  125, 137-138, 191, 235-236
Bukharin, Nikolai I., 243, 267
Bureaucratic responsibilities
  differences of opinion and, 19-20
  Soviet policy statements as func-
    tion of, 245-246, 250-251, 265

Capitalism
  contradictions of, 47-49, 55, 57,
    77. 80-84, 92-94, 97, 133-134,
    143-145, 150, 182, 236
  crisis of, 53, 55-57, 62, 65, 73, 75,
    77-98, 203-204, 216, 223, 237,
    253, 262, 266
  and East-West trade, 236
  and the energy crisis, 93-94
  and militarism, 39-40, 61, 85-
    87, 153
  and "neofascism," 95-106
  versus socialism, 33-34, 45-49, 59,
    82, 118, 204, 207
  Soviet views of, 17, 44, 61, 77,
    81, 266
  strengths of, 79-80
  the U.S. and, 54-57, 59
  and Western countries, 50
  "whitewashing" of, 131-135
Catholicism, 271
Central Intelligence Agency (CIA),
    73, 95, 124, 228
Chile, 131, 142, 228-229
Class consciousness, 31-32, 100, 103,
    126, 134, 151, 181-182, 192,
    199, 201, 213
Clausewitz, Karl von, 38
Cold war, 36, 105, 151, 232, 241
  and economic struggle, 45
  imperialism and, 42, 180
  as means of political and psycho-
    logical pressure, 156
  as policy, 175
  prerequisites for ending, 43
Collective colonialism, 137
Collective security, 137, 187, 233

communist, 204
  connotation of, 188
  and correlation of forces, 53-54
  differing conceptions of, 44
  European, 207
  and military blocs, 179, 185
Collins, John, 306n
Columbia (University) Research
    Institute on Communist Affairs,
    136
Communism, 23-24, 47, 115, 233,
    237, 248, 268
  character of, 268, 270-271
  Eastern versus Western, 129
  Western centers for the study of,
    136-137, 200
  Western struggle against, 34
Communist movement, 128-129
  as vanguard of world revolution,
    51
Communist Party of the Soviet
    Union (CPSU), 20, 41, 76, 100,
    114, 125, 246-247
  purpose of, 121
  and role in Soviet society, 120,
    268
  24th Congress of (1971), 118,
    121
  25th Congress of (1976), 95,
    249-250, 259n
  as vanguard of proletariat, 31
Containment, strategy of, 137
Contradictions. See Soviet analysts
Convergence theory, 117-120, 125,
    137, 146-147, 263
Correlation of forces (Sootnoshenie
    sil), 19, 111, 174, 176-178, 186-
    187, 193, 196-197, 204, 211,
    215, 227, 229-233, 235, 242,
    245, 263
  and American military thought,
    146
  and balance of power, 16-17, 51
  measurement of, 52-58, 97, 102,
    234
  shift in favor of socialism, 53, 89,
    101, 137-138, 145, 157, 194-
    195, 236, 265-266
  between socialism and imperial-
    ism, 158, 182
  and Soviet "Right" versus "Left,"

Correlation of forces (cont.)
  252-254, 259
  between U.S. and USSR, 134,
    148, 162, 165, 172, 261
  See also Balance of power
Cuban Missile Crisis, 16, 176
Cyprus, 155-156

Dallin, Alexander, 241-242, 252
Davydov, Iu., 56, 192, 198-199,
  207, 209-210
Democracy, 33, 49-50
Detente, 26, 36, 42, 59, 68, 101,
  181, 186, 195, 198, 237, 256-
  257, 260
  bourgeois attack against, 122
  limited detente, 189
  as means of U.S. foreign policy,
    175, 189, 245
  Nixon Doctrine and, 186
  proponents and opponents of, 19,
    89, 189-191, 193, 232-233, 240-
    247, 250-251, 262, 265
  U.S. allies and, 196, 199
Dialectical materialism, 27-31, 48,
  60, 266
  See also Marxism-Leninism
Dinerstein, Herbert S., 280n
Distribution of power, 16
  See also Balance of power
Dominican Republic, 37
Donaldson, Robert, 240
Dulles, John Foster, 178

East-West trade, 233-237
Economic struggle, 32, 37, 44-45, 48
Emigration, 45
Engels, Friedrich, 48, 78-79, 87
  Communist Manifesto, 78
Equilibrium (*ravnovesie sil*), 16
  See also "Symmetry of power"
European Economic Community
  (EEC), 90, 112, 201, 203, 209
Europe (Eastern), 110, 127, 138
Europe (Western), 56, 77, 110
  Communists and, 129
  integration of, 201-202
  military strength of, 195, 209
  security of, 37, 146, 193, 196,
    198, 207, 210
  U.S. balance-of-power policy and,
    183-184
  U.S. military forces in, 173, 207,
    210
  U.S. partnership with, 197-198
  See also European Economic
    Community; U.S. allies
Evans, Rowland, 206n

Factions and groups in Soviet
    politics
  differing assessments of, 19-20,
    250
  opponents and advocates of de-
    tente, 19, 89, 189-191, 193, 232-
    233, 240-247, 250-251, 262
  Soviet "hawks" and "doves," 19,
    239, 254, 256-257
  "neo-Stalinists" and revisionists,
    18, 80, 177, 239, 241, 243-244
  Soviet "radicals" and "moder-
    ates," 18-19, 253-256
  Soviet "Right" and "Left," 19,
    239, 241-245, 248-257
  See also Soviet leadership; Tradi-
    tionalists and realists
Fainsod, Merle, 276n
Federal Bureau of Investigation
    (FBI), 95
Fleron, Frederic, 305n
Force, policy of. *See* U.S. foreign
    policy
French Revolution (1789), 31
Fulbright, J. W., 71

Gavrilov, Iu., 155
Gibert, Stephen, 17-18
Goure, Leon, 287n
Grechko, Andrei, 245
Greece, 155
Griffiths, Franklyn, 305n
Grigoriants, A., 94
Gromyko, Anatoly A., 52-53, 70,
  101, 109-110, 112, 146-150,
  177, 195-196, 205-207, 225
Gromyko, Andrei A., 17, 55, 64
Grudinin, I. A., 158
Gvishiani, D., 45-46

Helsinki accords (1975), 37, 186-
  188, 193

Hitler, Adolph, 80, 96
Hoffer, Eric, 277n
Hoffmann, Erik, 305n
Human rights campaign, U.S., 122, 191
Hunt, R. N. Carew, 28

Ideas
    American, 137-138
    dissemination of, 32
    as ideological means of U.S. foreign policy, 135
    war of, 36, 43, 102-104
Ideological struggle, 106, 126, 257
    connotation of, 188
    forms of, 42-44
    intensification of, 48
    and peaceful coexistence, 190, 257
    and Third World, 37
    as U.S. foreign policy weapon, 103-104, 113
Ideology
    bourgeois, 103, 119
    communist, 20
    and foreign policy, 34-37, 100, 271
    and measurement of correlation of forces, 54-55, 271-272
    power of, 36
    and psychological warfare, 113
    strategy of American, 124
Imperialism
    capital investment and, 202
    and economic blackmail, 107, 142-143, 154, 229, 259
    economic means of, 138-142, 227-228, 259
    ideology of, 117-118
    international organizations and, 217-224
    justification of, by U.S., 109
    limitations of, 112
    militarism and, 86, 91
    and national liberation struggles, 50, 53, 110, 184
    nature of, 101-102, 130, 245, 266
    normative connotation of term, 188
    science and technology and, 228-229
    as source of contradictions and

    tensions, 32, 54-56, 85, 88, 99, 182
    Soviet interests and, 37-41, 90, 121, 137
    strategy and tactics of, 135, 184, 201
    the U.S. and, 37, 56, 70, 75, 88, 99, 104, 109, 112-113, 147
    and U.S. balance-of-power policy, 184-185
    and weakening economic and political basis of capitalism, 48-49, 58, 61, 204
Income distribution in U.S., Soviet view of, 85-93
India
    U.S. imperialism and, 180-181
    U.S. loan commitments to, 143
Indochina
    national liberation movement in, 39, 193, 254
Indonesia
    U.S. imperialism and, 180
Industrial revolution, 47
Inozemtsev, N., 74, 81-83, 85, 92, 96, 201, 204
Inter-American Development Bank (IDB), 220
Interdependence, 112-113, 263
Interest groups in Soviet politics
    approaches to study of, 19
    as theory of Soviet politics, 246
    See also Factions and groups in Soviet politics
International Development Association (IDA), 219
International Finance Corporation (IFC), 219
International Monetary Fund (IMF) 217, 220-225
International relations
    American convergence theory and, 118
    bourgeois theory and, 121-134
    contradiction in, 60
    restructuring of, 187
    and role of ideology and propaganda, 35-37
    science and technology and, 147
    and socialism, 31, 34
    Soviet view of, 31-32, 37, 106, 266

International relations (cont.)
stages in Soviet analysis of, 16-17
between U.S. and USSR. *See*
Struggle between two systems
International Telephone and Telegraph (ITT), 142
Israel
and Arab states, 185
and imperialism, 173
U.S. relations with, 208
U.S. support of, 94, 142, 209, 244
Ivanov, K. P., 248

Jackson-Vanik Amendment, 45
Japan, 112, 146, 183, 203

Karenin, A., 167-168, 175, 184
Katasonov, Iu., 153-154
Kennecott Copper, 142
Kennedy, John F., 90, 160, 169
and principle of "measured out use of force," 164-165, 167
Keynes, J. M., 77
KGB, 234
Kharlanov, Iu., 156
Khmara, N., 159, 258
Khozin, G. 149
Khrushchev, Nikita S., 16, 60, 89-91, 97, 251-252
Kintner, William, 293n
Kissinger, Henry, 181, 187, 246n
Klochkovsky, L., 225
Kokoshin, A., 52-53, 64
Kolesnichenko, T., 71, 94
Kolkowicz, Roman, 240
Konstantinov, F., 82-83
Korionov, V., 126
Korobeinikov, V., 123
Kortunov, V., 132
Kosygin, Alexei N., 249-250
Kraminov, D., 180
Krasin, Y., 49
Kremenyuk, V., 208
Krivokhizha, V. I., 105
Krivopalov, A., 67
Kudinov, V., 122, 125, 130
Kudriavtsev, V., 181, 184-185
Kuhn, Thomas, 270
Kurdiumov, N., 94-95
Kuusinen, O. V., 277n

Kuznetsov, V., 157

Lagovskii, A., 248, 250
Laird, Melvin, 164, 168, 171
Larionov, V., 161-162, 170, 172, 177 258
Latin America, 56
Soviet actions in, 251
U.S. policy toward, 185-186
See also Chile
Legitimacy, 268-269, 274
Leninism. *See* Marxism-Leninism
Lenin, V. I., 48-49, 75, 81, 85, 140, 221, 243-244, 267, 273
Leont'ev L. A., 40, 111
Levin, V., 185
Lewis, C. S., 272
Liberman, E. G., 247
Linkage, U.S. policy of, 189
Lukin, V. P., 56, 136-137, 183

McNamara, Robert, 160-161
Maoism, 119, 185, 252
Marxism-Leninism
ambiguities of, 47, 75
and American economic schools of thought, 116-117, 119-120, 135
and capitalism, 61, 76, 132
as doctrine and guiding ideology, 21-23, 27, 42-43, 59, 61, 82, 120, 126, 177, 259, 266, 271, 275
as form of analysis, 155
ideological basis of, 27-30
and legitimacy of state and power, 268-269
Leninism as Russian doctrine, 120
and peace, 273
and peaceful coexistence, 159
and the proletariat, 47, 129
rigidity of, 76, 273
scientific techniques of, 80, 103-104, 271-272
theory versus practice in, 48-49, 69, 90, 127, 267, 269, 272-275
as value system, 270
Marx, Karl, 28, 30, 48-49, 75, 77-79, 96-97
Communist Manifesto, 78
Das Kapital, 77

Index

Marx, Karl (cont.)
  "Theses on Feuerbach," 28
Matveyev, V., 39
Mayevskii, V., 155
Meany, George, 71
Media
  American, 72-74, 103
  and foreign policy, 35-37
  role in socialist revolution, 32-34
  Soviet control of, 20-24, 35-36, 42, 252, 266, 269
  Western, 35-36, 123-124, 126
Mehnert, Klaus, 240
Menshevism, 129
Middle East
  Arab-Israeli Wars (1973), 193, 198, 209, 244 (1967), 208
  conflict, 94
  oil, 142
  U.S. policy and Arab states, 185, 208
Migolat'ev, A., 85, 107
Militarism
  American, 86, 159, 251
  and the arms race, 153, 263
  economic effects of, 87-88
  as function of scientific-technical revolution, 85, 91
  and imperialism, 39-40
  and interests of monopolies, 141, 152-153
  the media and, 123
  as source of contradictions, 89, 95
  and the working class, 85-86
Military conflict, 38-40, 107
  Soviet use of, 255
Military force
  as basis of U.S. foreign policy, 151, 156-157
  theories justifying, 106-109
  and U.S. national interest, 105-106
  U.S. use of, 50, 90, 170, 172, 174-175
  See also U.S. foreign policy
Military-industrial complex, 40, 62-64, 75, 162, 191, 262
  army as instrument of monopolies, 151
  and militarism, 86-87, 91, 141
  in USSR, 240, 243

Mirskii, Z., 187
Mitin, M., 42-43, 49-51, 120, 122, 125
Mokshin, S., 44
Monroe Doctrine, 182
Morozov, G., 277n
Moscow summit meeting (1972), 58
Mosin, I., 141-142
Moss, Robert, 306n
Mukhanova, G., 154

Nalin, Iu., 131
National liberation movement(s), 179, 183, 193-194, 201, 206-208, 227, 258
  in Angola, 184-185, 193
  balance of power and, 182
  and bourgeois concept of nationalism, 126-128, 212-213
  domino theory and, 108-109
  as element of correlation of forces, 53, 57-58, 134, 157, 229-230, 254
  in Indochina, 39, 193
  and just wars, 38
  U.S. foreign aid and, 215
  world socialist revolution and, 50-51, 53, 111, 153, 240
National Security Council
  and Washington Special Actions Group, 145
Nationalism, 126-128, 212-214
Negotiation, 186, 189, 191-192
Nekrasov, V., 71
Nixon Doctrine, 56, 67, 137, 147-148, 159, 169, 183-184, 186, 193, 195, 198-199, 210, 264
Nixon-Ford era, 25-26
Nixon, Richard M., 180, 187, 246n
  presidential administration of, 71, 88, 145, 161, 164
Nonaligned countries, 37. See also Third World
North Atlantic Treaty Organization (NATO), 113, 131, 155-156, 165, 173, 175, 184, 195-196, 198-201, 207, 210-211, 259, 264, 266
Novak, Robert, 306n

Novosel'tsev, E., 197-198, 203, 205, 210
Nuclear weapons, strategy, war, 156-169, 171-173, 233, 245-246, 256
  and conventional warfare, 169, 174
  and flexible response, 159-160, 166-168, 171
  and "Red Hawks," 240
  and Soviet realists, 272-273
  and Strategy of Realistic Deterrence, 159-164, 168-169
  Third World conflicts and, 156, 180

Odom, William, 246-248
Oleshchuk, Iu., 188-191
Organization for Economic Cooperation and Development (OECD), 195
Osgood, Robert E., 105

Pakistan
  U.S. imperialism and, 180-181
Palestinian resistance movement, 185
Parrott, Bruce, 250
Partnership. See U.S. foreign policy
Peace
  differing conceptions of, 39-40
  as form of war, 156
  Marxism-Leninism and, 273
  and peaceful coexistence, 54, 272
  Soviet policy of, 121
  Soviet prescriptions for, 39
Peaceful coexistence, 210, 232-233, 237
  bourgeois concept of, 122, 179
  and convergence theory, 118
  and correlation of forces, 54
  Europe and, 207
  and ideological struggle, 190, 257
  and limited detente, 189
  and policy of the status quo, 111, 113, 187
  principle of, 58-59, 159, 186
  and selective coexistence, 124
  Soviet foreign policy and, 59, 208, 244, 247, 250
  Soviet view of, 41, 43-45, 151
  supporters and opponents of, 241, 272

People's Republic of China (PRC), 181, 185
  leadership of, 129, 136
  U.S. balance-of-power policy and, 183
  See also Sino-Soviet relations
Petrov, Vladimir, 241
Pletnikov, V., 122, 125, 130
Poland, 270
Ponomarev, Boris N., 76, 95-96, 246
Portugal
  ITT and, 142-143
Pragmatism. See Marxism-Leninism: theory versus practice in
Preponderance of power, 16, 55
  See also Balance of power
Propaganda
  assessments of U.S. and, 18
  bourgeois, 121, 123-125, 127, 129
  and foreign policy, 34-35
  the media and, 32-33
  military expenditures and, 154
  NATO and, 200
  as normative element of Soviet policy, 269-270
  persuasiveness of, 22-23, 269
  religion and, 35
  systematization of, 24, 35-36
  techniques of Soviet, 44, 108n
Psychological warfare, 42-43, 113, 156, 263, 265
  Soviet use of term, 190
Public opinion, 64-72, 100, 262
Puchkov, R., 142

Radio Free Europe, 42, 124
Radio Liberty, 42, 124
Realism, U.S. policy of. See U.S. foreign policy
Realists
  Soviet realists. See Traditionalists and realists
  U.S. realists. See U.S. foreign policy
  See also Schools of thought
Reston, James, 246n
Revolution
  and nationalism, 128, 214
  prospects for, 16-17, 31, 48-50, 90
  success of, 16, 97, 243
Roosevelt, Franklin D., 187

Index

Roosevelt, Franklin D. (cont.)
  and New Deal, 96
Ruling class. *See* U.S. leadership
Rybkin, Ye., 158, 246

Sakharov, Andrei D., 129
SALT negotiations and agreements,
  39, 41, 58, 163, 186, 191, 241,
  244-245, 250, 256-257, 265, 273
Saprykov, V., 179
Schlesinger, James, 190
  and "Schlesinger Doctrine," 165
Schools of thought in U.S., Soviet
  views of, 41
  economic theory, 116-117
  global convergence, advocates of,
    146-147, 263
  moderate conservatives versus
    liberals, 127
  neoconservatism, 106
  nonmilitary confrontation, advo-
    cates of, 146
  political realism, 104-105, 111-
    112, 137, 151, 157, 262-264
  "technological warfare" or "posi-
    tion of strength," theoreticians
    of, 146, 148, 162-163, 263
  See also U.S. leadership
Schorr, Daniel, 73
Schwartz, Morton, 17-18, 57, 239,
  253, 255-256
Scientific-technical revolution, 32,
  45-48, 53, 235, 253, 262
  and American convergence theory,
    117, 119
  and capitalism, 82-85, 91-93, 143-
    144, 258, 266-267
  and CPSU, 120
  as lever of U.S. foreign policy,
    146, 148, 150, 200
Scott, Harriet F., 293n
Sergiev, A., 112-113
Shabad, B. A., 104-106
Shakhnazarov, G., 51-53
Shershnev, E., 65, 202
Shulman, Marshall, 241, 251-252,
  257
Shvedkov, Iu., 66, 73
Simonian, R., 155, 160-162, 165-168,
  173
Sino-Soviet relations, 37, 136, 183
Sisnev, V., 72

Skilling, H. Gordon, 305n
Smolensk archive of CPSU documents, 23
Sobakin, V., 44, 54, 237
Socialism
  inevitable victory of, 48, 59
  revolutionary success of. *See*
    Revolution
  rise and growth of, 31-34, 40, 46,
    49, 55-56, 192
  scientific-technical struggle against,
    154
  strengths of, 116
Sokolov, P. V., 248
Soldatov, V., 175
Solzhenitsyn, Alexander, 131, 233-
  234
Soviet analysts
  and American ideas, 102-104, 135
  and analysis of contradictions, 32,
    44, 75, 83, 89, 97, 137, 143,
    151, 164, 174-175, 182, 185,
    194-195, 197-199, 203-204, 206,
    209-210, 237
  categories of argument, 104-113
  coincidence of views with Ameri-
    cans, 168, 234
  consistency of, 137
  divergent views among, 20, 41, 46,
    100. *See also* Traditionalists and
    realists
  and doctrinal innovations, 16
  and falsifications, 120-121, 127-
    128
  increasing sophistication of, 18,
    61, 65-69, 79, 101, 158, 261
  use of and view of distortions,
    105-106, 113-115, 222
Soviet foreign policy
  determinants of, 15, 37-38
  and East-West trade, 234-237,
    243-244, 250
  formulation of, 18
  ideology versus pragmatism in.
    See Marxism-Leninism: theory
    versus practice
  the masses and, 32-34
  See also Soviet leadership; Soviet
    analysts
Soviet intentions, 22-23, 261, 267-
  275
Soviet leadership, 16, 36, 96, 247

Soviet leadership (cont.)
  factions within, 18-20, 249, 272.
    See also Factions and groups;
    Traditionalists and realists
  ideological insecurity of, 104, 138
  intentions of. *See* Soviet intentions
  and the military, 240-251
  policies of, 251n, 252
Soviet optimism, 16, 59-60, 97, 108,
    177, 245, 253-254, 260, 265
Soviet perceptions
  determinants of, 25, 74-75, 96-97,
    99-100
  double-entry bookkeeping, 23
  methods of, 21-24, 27-30, 76,
    103
  of U.S. strengths and weaknesses,
    15, 17-19, 56, 65, 97-98, 111,
    253-254, 262-263
    See also U.S. foreign policy; Soviet
    analysts; Traditionalists and
    realists
Soviet political system
  and coercion, 20
  and cooptation, 270
  ideological foundations of, 23,
    267-275
  and the military, 240-251
  orthodox American interpretation
    of, 243-244, 254, 257, 264
  and primacy of consensus, 258
  totalitarian versus interest group
    models, 19-20, 246
    See also Marxism-Leninism
Soviet statements
  as function of bureaucratic duties,
    245-246, 250-251, 265
  problems of interpreting, 16-17,
    20-24
    See also Propaganda
Stalin, Joseph V., 158, 258
Starr, S. Frederick, 304n
State, in capitalist societies, 91-93,
    97
Strategic parity, 15, 17, 26, 55, 57,
    62, 254-255, 261
Strategy. *See* U.S. foreign policy
Strausz-Hupe, Robert, 35
Struggle between two systems
  and allied organizations, 195
  basis of, 232
  as class struggle, 31-32, 37, 41, 60

defined, 24, 31, 49, 266
  as economic struggle, 32, 37, 44-
    45, 48
  as ideological struggle, 37, 42-44,
    48
  ideology and, 27-37
  irreconcilability of, 96, 274-275
  measurement of, 51-59
  militarism and, 153
  as political struggle, 37-42
  as scientific-technical struggle, 37,
    45-48, 233
  and the Third World, 214
Sturua, M., 63
Suslov, Mikhail A., 252
Sviatov, G., 169, 175
"Symmetry of power," 110

Talenskii, N., 158
Terminology. *See* Vocabulary of
    Soviet analysis
Third World
  exploitation of, 31, 212
  and international trade, 226-227
  and manipulation of nationalism,
    213-214
  and neocolonialism, 186, 212, 214,
    217-221, 224-227, 231
  regional development banks, 220
  Soviet actions in, 255
  the U.S. and, 57, 112, 180, 264,
    266
  and U.S. foreign aid, 202, 215-
    220, 226-227
  and war of ideas, 37
Tito, Josip Broz, 252
Topornin, A., 182-184
Totalitarianism, 19-20, 22-23, 246
  as U.S. policy concept, 114
Trade. *See* East-West trade; U.S.
    foreign policy
Traditionalists and realists, 19-20
  on American ideas, 103, 137-138
  on balance of power, 183, 261
  on correlation of forces, 97-98,
    186, 235, 252-254, 259
  on crisis of capitalism, 77-82
  on detente, 186-187, 189, 191-
    193, 240-247, 265
  on deterrence, 159-164, 168-169,
    272-273
  differences among, 135, 239, 255-

Traditionalists and realists (cont.)
262, 264, 267-268
on East-West trade, 234-237, 244,
264
on freedom of the press, 73-74
on Helsinki accords, 186-187
on international cooperation, 233
on international organizations,
217
on means of U.S. foreign policy,
262-264
on militarism, 85-89
on military issues, 151-153, 157-
168, 174-177, 230, 254-257,
265-266
on policy of status quo, 178-179,
186
on role of state in bourgeois
society, 91-93
on SALT, 265
on scientific-technical revolution,
82-84, 143-145, 147-148, 150,
262
shared views of, 256, 259, 266,
269-270, 275
on U.S. alliance policy, 197-
199, 210-211, 259, 264, 266
on U.S. economic system, 93-97,
262
on U.S. elections, 70-72
on U.S. foreign aid, 216-217
on U.S. public opinion, 65-69, 262
on U.S. ruling class, 62-65, 74, 89-
91, 101-102, 135n, 262-263
on U.S. scholarship, 75
on U.S. strengths and weaknesses,
262
on U.S.–Third World relations,
231, 264
on U.S. threat, 251
Western names for, 239-241
See also Soviet analysts; Soviet
leadership; Factions and groups
in Soviet politics
Triangular diplomacy, 136-137
Trofimenko, G. A., 40n, 43, 67,
108-109, 111-112, 138, 144,
156, 158, 160, 162-165, 167-
171, 173-174, 176
Trotsky, Lev (Trotskyism), 129, 267
Tucker, Robert C., 277n, 306n

Turkatenko, N., 142
"Two Camps," doctrine of, 31

Ulam, Adam B., 276n, 305n
United Nations, 36, 180-181, 219
United Nations Conference on Trade
and Development (UNCTAD),
226
United Nations Educational, Scientific and Cultural Organization
(UNESCO), 219
U.S. allies, 56, 112, 164, 169-170,
172-174, 183, 194-195
American nuclear umbrella and,
207
contradictions between U.S. and,
203
and economic integration, 201-
203, 205
and imperialism, 194
independent policies of, 196, 206,
210
and politico-military and economic
blocs, 195, 199, 201
and science and technology, 204-
206
U.S. dominance over, 195-211
and U.S. foreign assistance, 202-
203
See also North Atlantic Treaty
Organization
U.S. foreign policy
alliance policy. See U.S. allies;
Traditionalists and realists
ambitions of, 100-101
anticommunism of, 113-122, 124-
131, 135-137
and arms race, 89, 109, 153-156,
162-163, 168, 175-176, 259,
263, 266
and balance of power, 182-185.
See also correlation of forces
and concealment of aims, 130-135,
191
and controlled tension, 156, 180
crisis policy of, 170-171, 176
and detente. See Detente
determinants of, 24-25, 53, 61-
80, 86-87, 99-100, 135, 261,
266
and divide and rule, 184-185, 202,

U.S. foreign policy (cont.)
214
and domino theory, 108
and exploitation of ideological
diversity, 128-130
and export of capital, 139-142,
224-225
and export of know-how, 225
and free flow of ideas and information, 122-124, 235
general means of, 25, 103-107
and global responsibility, 172-173
goals of, 25, 99-102, 130
and human rights campaign, 122,
191
ideological implications of, 110,
120
inferiority complex of, 174
and interdependence, 112-113, 263
and interventionism, 230-231
and isolationism, 182, 240
and limited detente, 189-190
and limited strategic war, 165-167
and linkage, 189
maneuvers, concessions, and compromises of, 177-178
and measured use of force, 163-
165, 167, 174
and multipolarity, 111-112, 137-
138, 163
and nationalism, 126-128
and negotiation, 186, 189, 191-
192
"New Technological Policy" of,
147-150, 205, 228
and partnership, 196-199, 202-203,
206, 208-211, 216, 230-231, 264
and peaceful penetration, doctrine of, 125-126
and policy of force, 104-109,
141, 144-145, 147, 152-154,
156-158, 175-178, 192, 195,
227, 230-231, 259, 263, 266
and policy of realism, 111-113,
168, 173-174, 188, 231, 262-
263
and policy of the status quo, 109-
111, 178-181, 186, 192, 231,
263
and position of strength, 146, 148,
152, 162-163, 184, 195

priorities and methods of, 56, 91
psychological aspects of, 171-172
scientific methods of, 144-145,
263
and selective targeting, 166
and Soviet threat, concept of, 91,
109, 175, 195, 207, 210
and strategic sufficiency, 160-163
and strategy of building bridges,
124-125, 137-138, 191, 235-
236
and Strategy of Realistic Deterrence, 159-164, 168-169
and threat of force, 155-157
and U.S. allies. See U.S. allies
toward USSR and socialist countries, 234-237
See also U.S. leadership; Soviet
analysts
U.S. leadership, 62-75, 101
and crisis of capitalism, 80-81
and decision making, 170
ideological strength of, 91-92, 98,
103, 264
and ideology versus interest, 135
and military expenditure, 88-89
and national interest, 105
splits within, 89-91, 98, 262. See
also Schools of thought in U.S.,
Soviet views of
two camps of, 236
U.S. foreign policy and, 138, 176
U.S. political system, 180
and class consciousness, 103
and elections, 94-95
and public opinion, 64-72, 100,
262
See also Capitalism
U.S.–Soviet agreements, 26, 58, 186,
189, 237, 244
See also SALT negotiations and
agreements
U.S.–Soviet rivalry. See Struggle
between two systems

Vakhrushev, V., 218-224, 226, 231
Values
of capitalism, 130
as determinants of Western and
U.S. policies, 34, 89, 100
and leadership, 258, 268

Index

Values (cont.)
  and legitimacy, 268-269, 274
  as morality, 274-275
Vietnam
  imperialism and, 37-39
  national liberation struggle of,
    157-159, 193, 230, 258
  Soviet action in, 251
  U.S. actions in, 67-68, 71, 73, 75,
    87-88, 241
  U.S. failure in, 26, 95, 109, 158,
    168-171, 180, 208, 263
  and U.S. military-industrial com-
    plex, 62-63
Vocabulary of Soviet analysis
  for balance of power, 16-17, 181-
    182
  and changing Soviet perceptions,
    16-17, 24, 56
  definitions of particular terms:
    "hegemonism," 179; "indepen-
    dence," 209; "national" versus
    "nationalist," 214; "relaxation
    of tension," 232; "peaceful co-
    existence," 232
  double meanings in, 47n, 180,
    181-182, 188-191, 236, 270
  pejorative terms, 234
  and SALT, 163
  terms avoided: "defensive," 178;
    "superpower," 181; "legiti-
    macy," 188
  U.S. use of, 187
Volskii, D., 179
Vorob'ev, K., 151-152

War
  American theories of, 107-108
  causes of, 38, 181
  inevitability of, 16, 107, 244-245,
    258-260
  as instrument of policy, 90, 155-
    156, 160, 163-165, 173
  just versus unjust, 38, 121
  Marxism-Leninism and, 38
  as a political means, 174
  prospects of, 37
  and "Schlesinger Doctrine," 165
  See also Nuclear weapons, strat-
    egy, war
War of ideas, 36, 43, 102-104

  See also Ideas; Ideological struggle
Watergate, 95
World Bank, 217-221, 225

Yegorov, V., 50
Yermolenko, D., 47, 53, 83-84, 119,
  133

Zagladin, V., 127
Zakhmatov, M., 141, 202, 216, 231
Zasurskii, Ia., 123
Zhdanov, Andrei A., 31, 252
Zhukov, E., 184
Zhukov, Iu., 235
Zhurkin, V., 144-145, 170-171, 175-
  176
Zimmerman, William, 16-17, 90,
  240-241
Zinoviev, Grigori E., 252
Zionism and Zionist organizations,
  136, 208

Library of Congress Cataloging in Publication Data

Lenczowski, John.
    Soviet perceptions of U.S. foreign policy.

    Includes index.
    1. United States—Foreign relations—1945-   —Public opinion. 2. Public opinion—Soviet Union. I. Title. II. Title: Soviet perceptions of US foreign policy. III. Title: Soviet perceptions of United States foreign policy.
E840.L42   327.73   81-70713
ISBN 0-8014-1451-2   AACR2